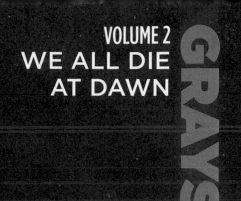

VOLUME 2
WE ALL DIE
AT DAWN

GRAYSON

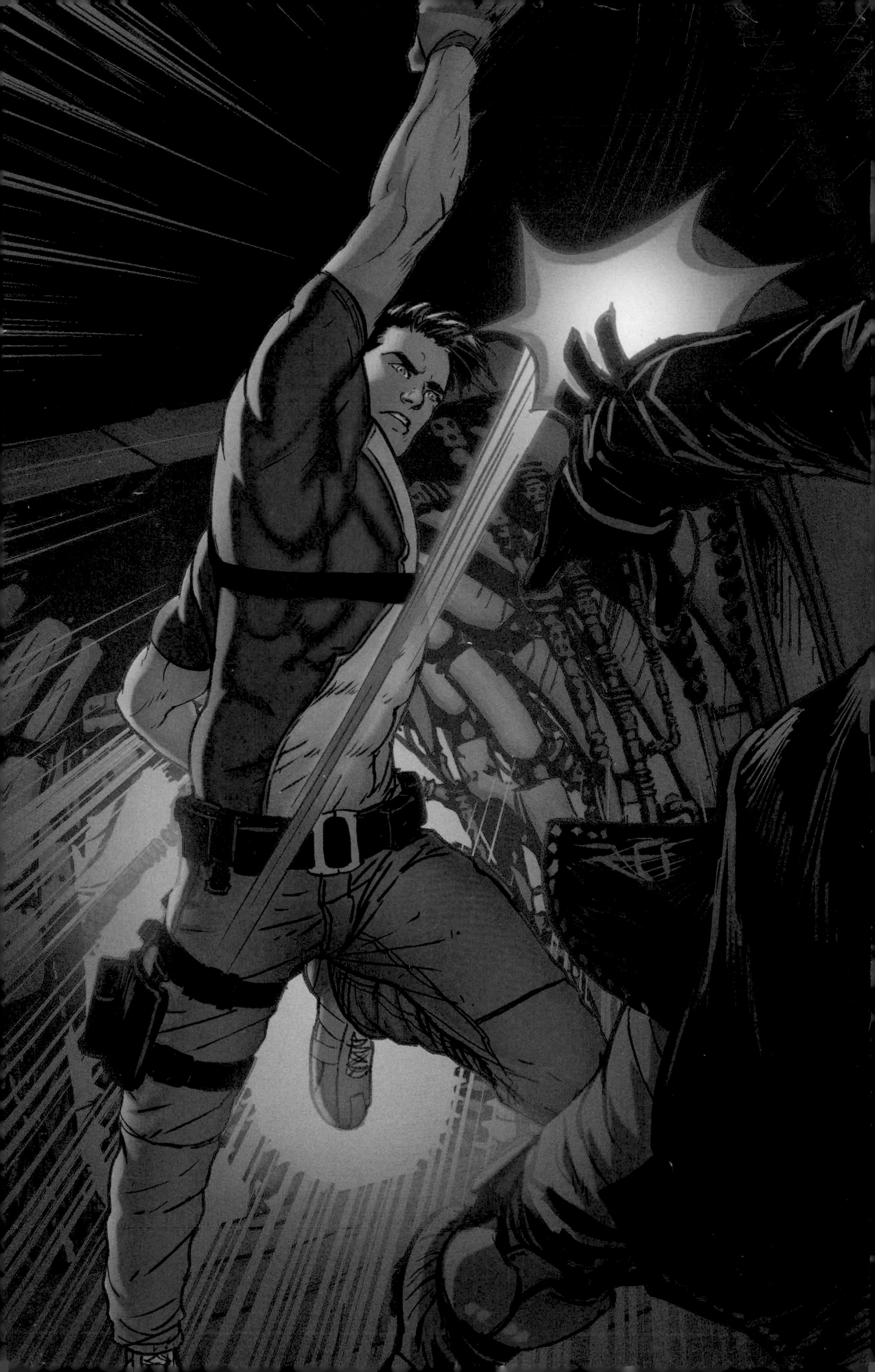

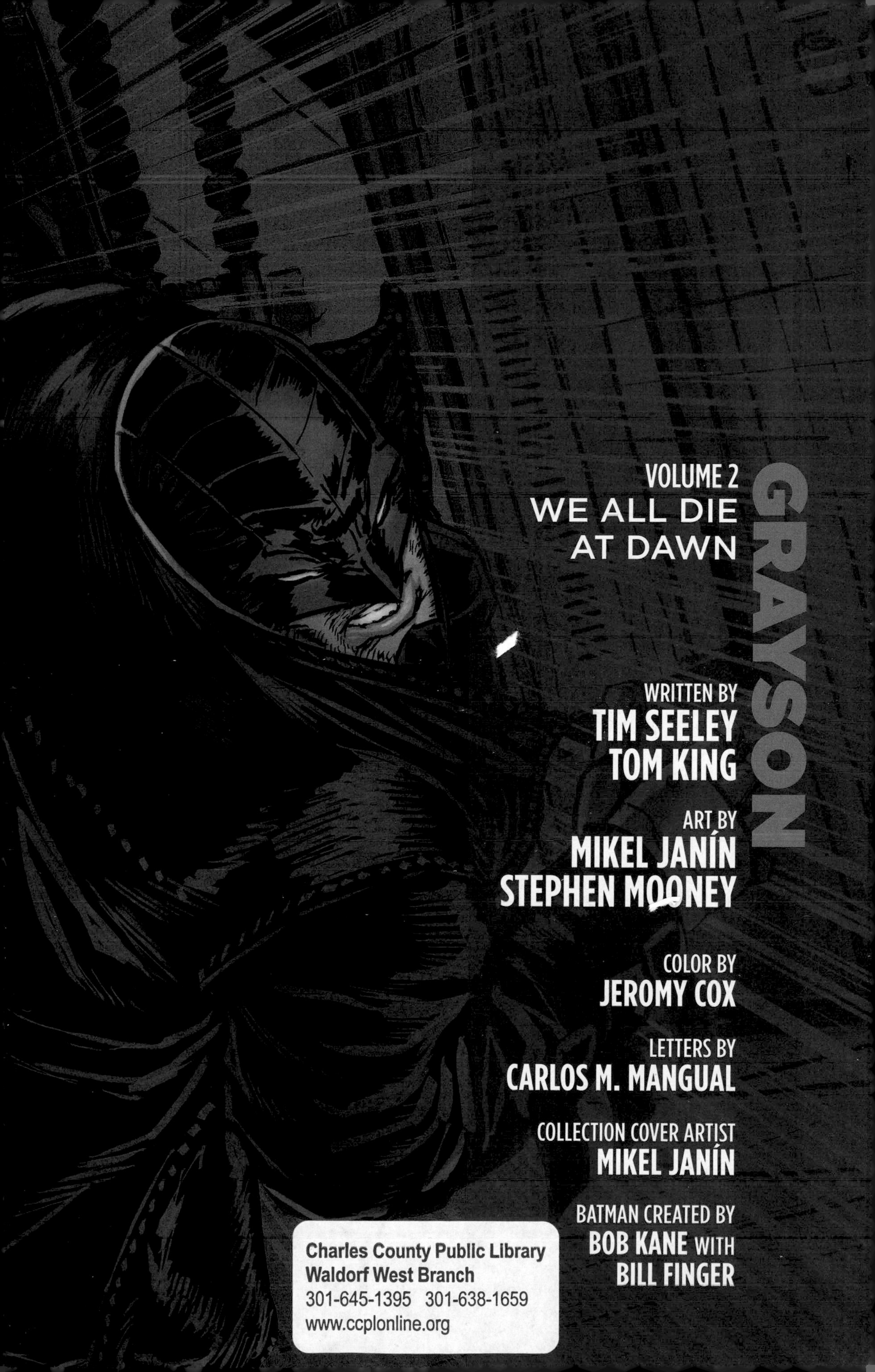

GRAYSON

VOLUME 2
WE ALL DIE AT DAWN

WRITTEN BY
TIM SEELEY
TOM KING

ART BY
MIKEL JANÍN
STEPHEN MOONEY

COLOR BY
JEROMY COX

LETTERS BY
CARLOS M. MANGUAL

COLLECTION COVER ARTIST
MIKEL JANÍN

BATMAN CREATED BY
BOB KANE WITH
BILL FINGER

MARK DOYLE Editor – Original Series
MATT HUMPHREYS Associate Editor – Original Series
JEB WOODARD Group Editor – Collected Editions
STEVE COOK Design Director – Books
DAMIAN RYLAND Publication Design

BOB HARRAS Senior VP – Editor-in-Chief, DC Comics

DIANE NELSON President
DAN DiDIO and JIM LEE Co-Publishers
GEOFF JOHNS Chief Creative Officer
AMIT DESAI Senior VP – Marketing & Global Franchise Management
NAIRI GARDINER Senior VP – Finance
SAM ADES VP – Digital Marketing
BOBBIE CHASE VP – Talent Development
MARK CHIARELLO Senior VP – Art, Design & Collected Editions
JOHN CUNNINGHAM VP – Content Strategy
ANNE DePIES VP – Strategy Planning & Reporting
DON FALLETTI VP – Manufacturing Operations
LAWRENCE GANEM VP – Editorial Administration & Talent Relations
ALISON GILL Senior VP – Manufacturing & Operations
HANK KANALZ Senior VP – Editorial Strategy & Administration
JAY KOGAN VP – Legal Affairs
DEREK MADDALENA Senior VP – Sales & Business Development
JACK MAHAN VP – Business Affairs
DAN MIRON VP – Sales Planning & Trade Development
NICK NAPOLITANO VP – Manufacturing Administration
CAROL ROEDER VP – Marketing
EDDIE SCANNELL VP – Mass Account & Digital Sales
COURTNEY SIMMONS Senior VP – Publicity & Communications
JIM (SKI) SOKOLOWSKI VP – Comic Book Specialty & Newsstand Sales
SANDY YI Senior VP – Global Franchise Management

GRAYSON VOLUME 2: WE ALL DIE AT DAWN

DC Comics, 2900 West Alameda Avenue, Burbank, CA 91505
Printed by RR Donnelley, Owensville, MO, USA. 12/18/15.
ISBN: 978-1-4012-5760-6
First Printing.

Library of Congress Cataloging-in-Publication Data

King, Tom, 1978- author.
Grayson. Volume 2 / Tom King, Tim Seeley, writers ; Mikel Janín, artist.
pages cm. — (The New 52!)
ISBN 978-1-4012-5760-6 (paperback)
1. Graphic novels. I. Seeley, Tim, author. II. Janín, Mikel, illustrator. III. Title.
PN6728.G723K56 2016
741.5'973—dc23
2015033154

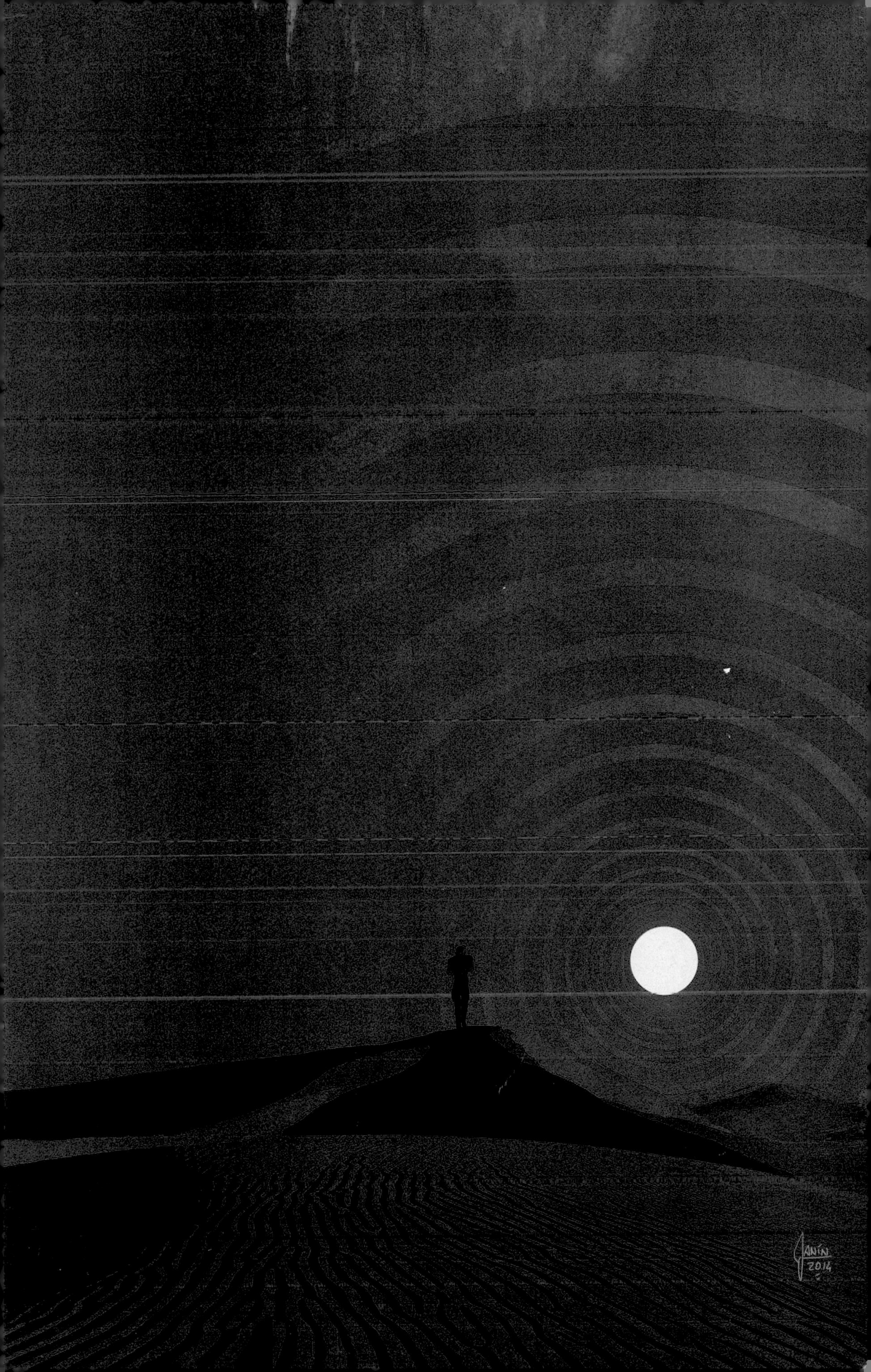

JANÍN
2014

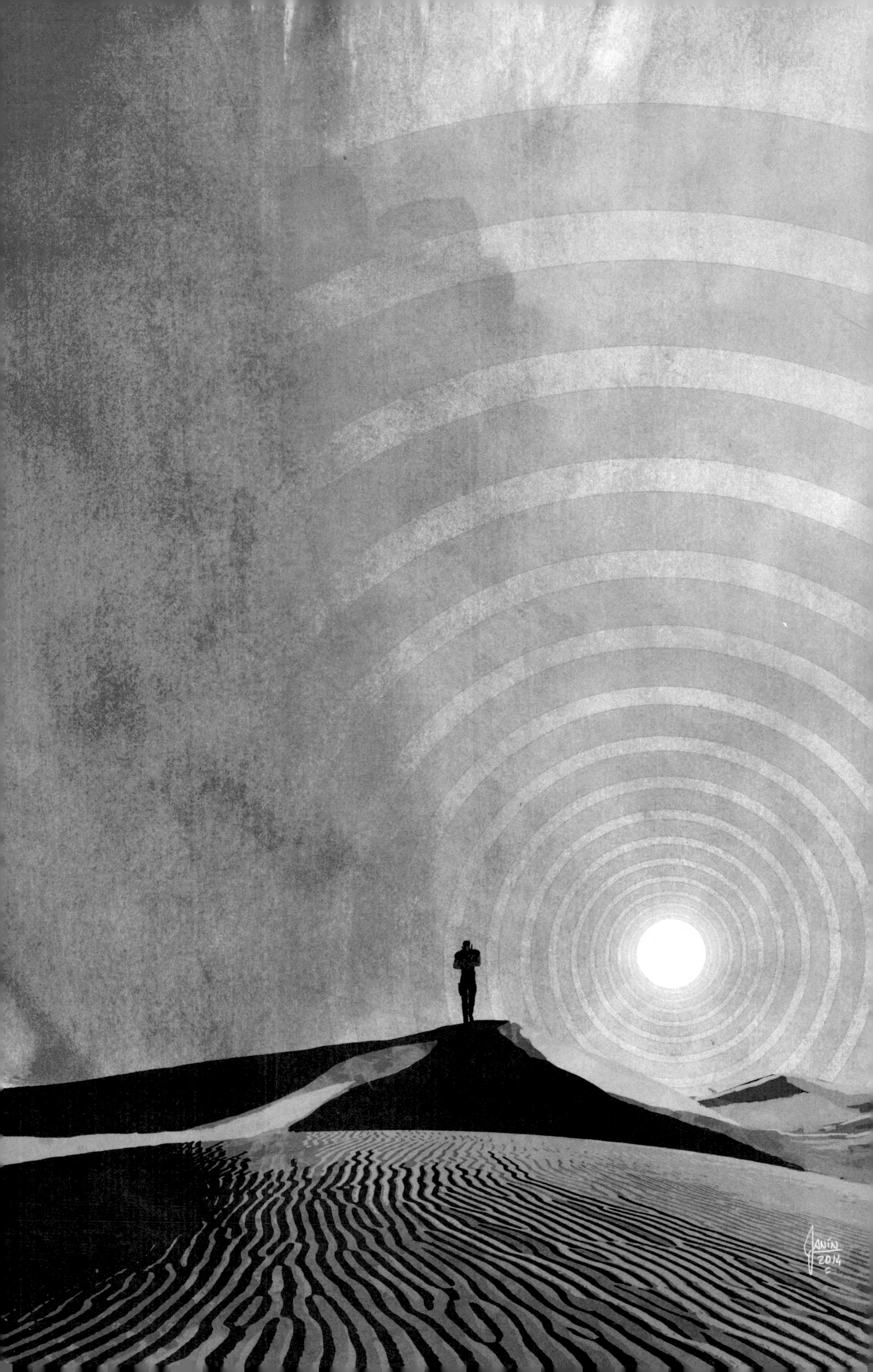
JANÍN
2014

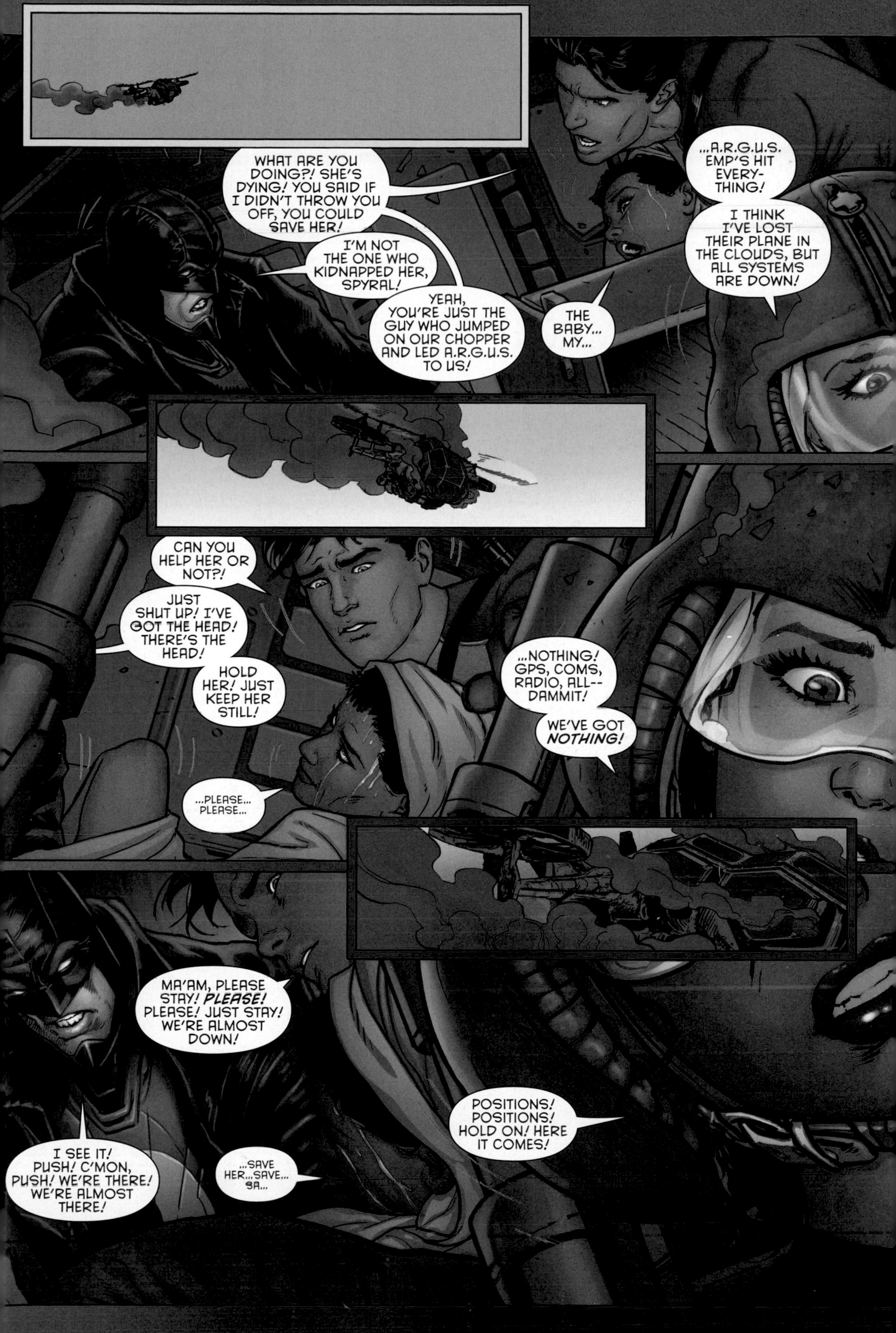
WHAT ARE YOU DOING?! SHE'S DYING! YOU SAID IF I DIDN'T THROW YOU OFF, YOU COULD SAVE HER!
I'M NOT THE ONE WHO KIDNAPPED HER, SPYRAL!
YEAH, YOU'RE JUST THE GUY WHO JUMPED ON OUR CHOPPER AND LED A.R.G.U.S. TO US!
THE BABY... MY...
...A.R.G.U.S. EMP'S HIT EVERY-THING!
I THINK I'VE LOST THEIR PLANE IN THE CLOUDS, BUT ALL SYSTEMS ARE DOWN!
CAN YOU HELP HER OR NOT?!
JUST SHUT UP! I'VE GOT THE HEAD! THERE'S THE HEAD!
HOLD HER! JUST KEEP HER STILL!
...PLEASE... PLEASE...
...NOTHING! GPS, COMS, RADIO, ALL-- DAMMIT!
WE'VE GOT *NOTHING!*
MA'AM, PLEASE STAY! *PLEASE!* PLEASE! JUST STAY! WE'RE ALMOST DOWN!
POSITIONS! POSITIONS! HOLD ON! HERE IT COMES!
I SEE IT! PUSH! C'MON, PUSH! WE'RE THERE! WE'RE ALMOST THERE!
...SAVE HER...SAVE... SA...

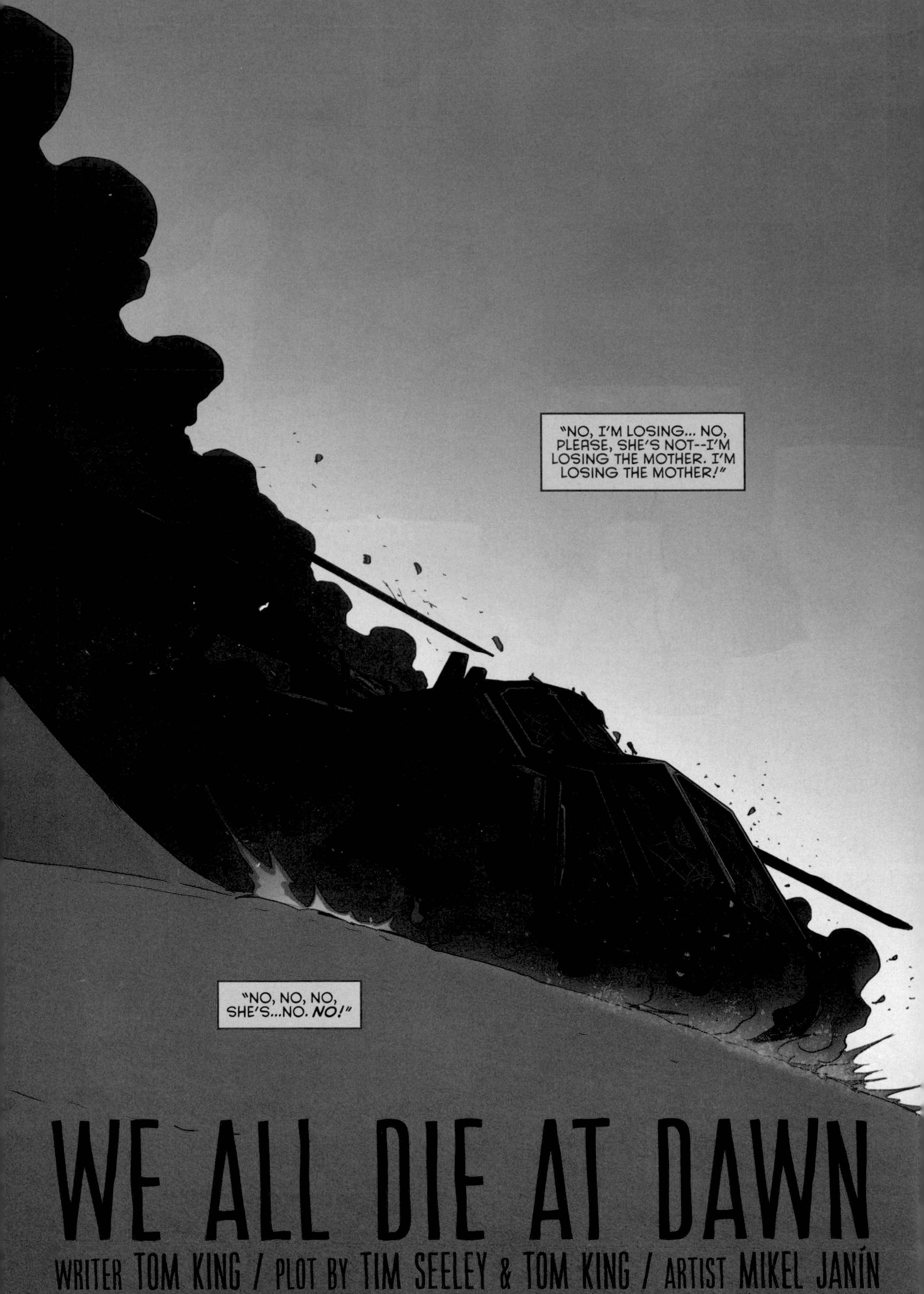
"NO, I'M LOSING... NO, PLEASE, SHE'S NOT--I'M LOSING THE MOTHER. I'M LOSING THE MOTHER!"
"NO, NO, NO, SHE'S...NO. *NO!*"

WE ALL DIE AT DAWN

WRITER TOM KING / PLOT BY TIM SEELEY & TOM KING / ARTIST MIKEL JANÍN
COLORIST JEROMY COX / LETTERER CARLOS M. MANGUAL / COVER MIKEL JANÍN

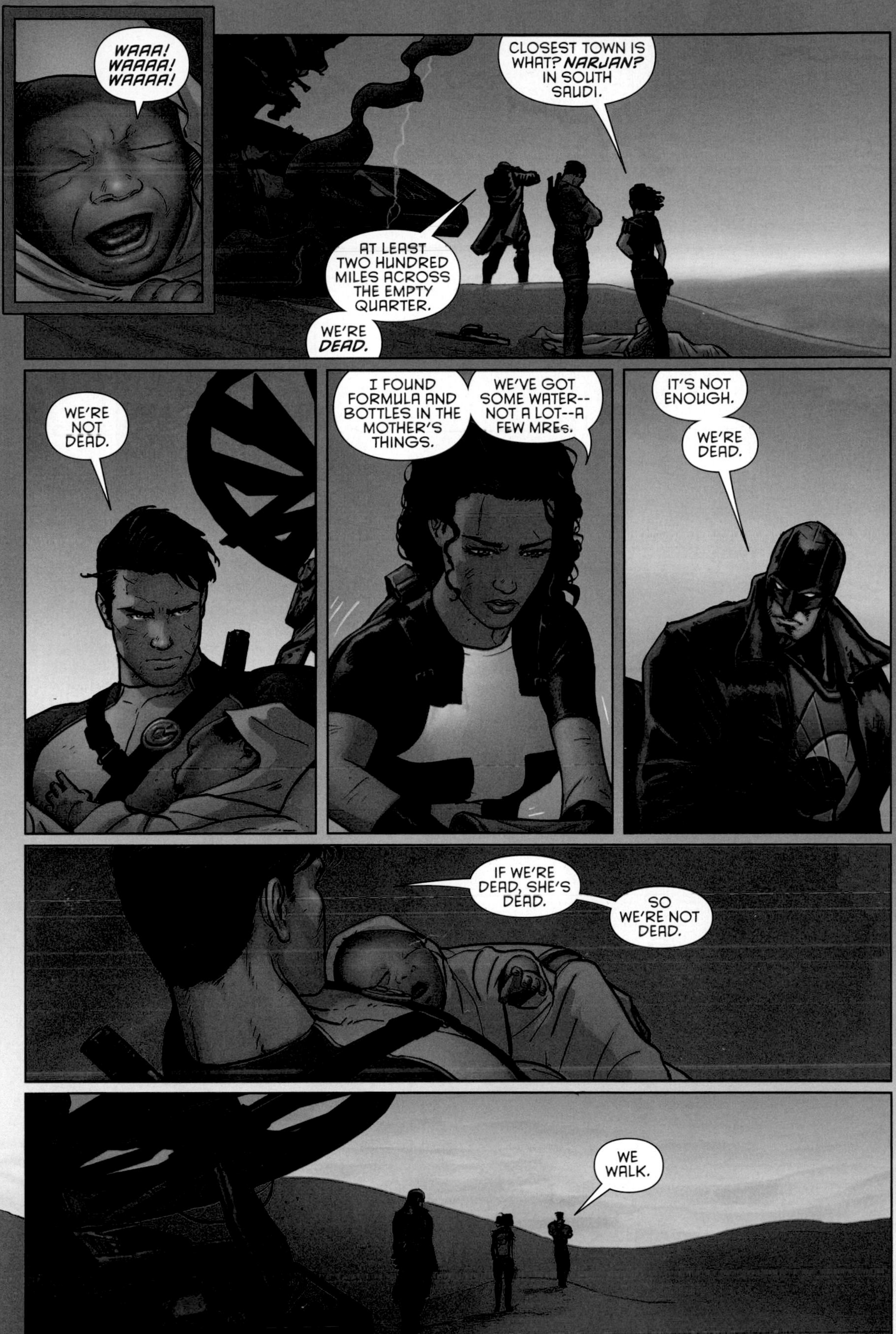
WAAA! WAAAA! WAAAA!
CLOSEST TOWN IS WHAT? *NARJAN?* IN SOUTH SAUDI.
AT LEAST TWO HUNDRED MILES ACROSS THE EMPTY QUARTER.
WE'RE *DEAD.*
WE'RE NOT DEAD.
I FOUND FORMULA AND BOTTLES IN THE MOTHER'S THINGS.
WE'VE GOT SOME WATER-- NOT A LOT--A FEW MREs.
IT'S NOT ENOUGH.
WE'RE DEAD.
IF WE'RE DEAD, SHE'S DEAD.
SO WE'RE NOT DEAD.
WE WALK.

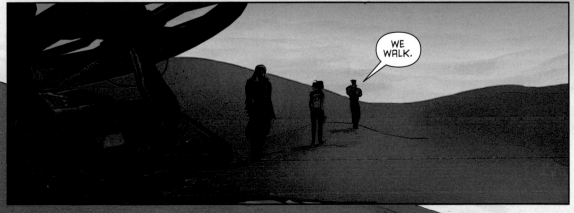

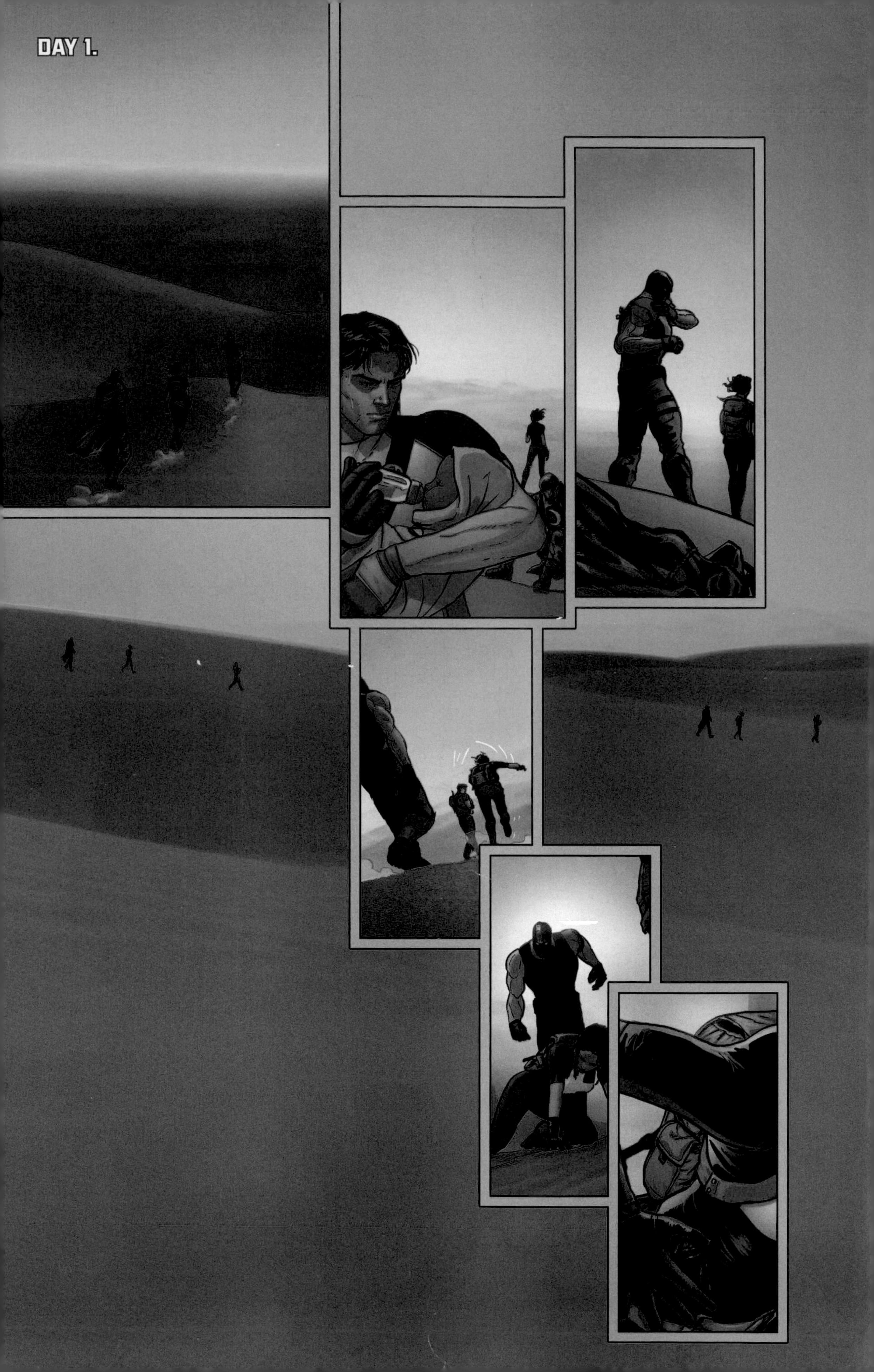
DAY 1.

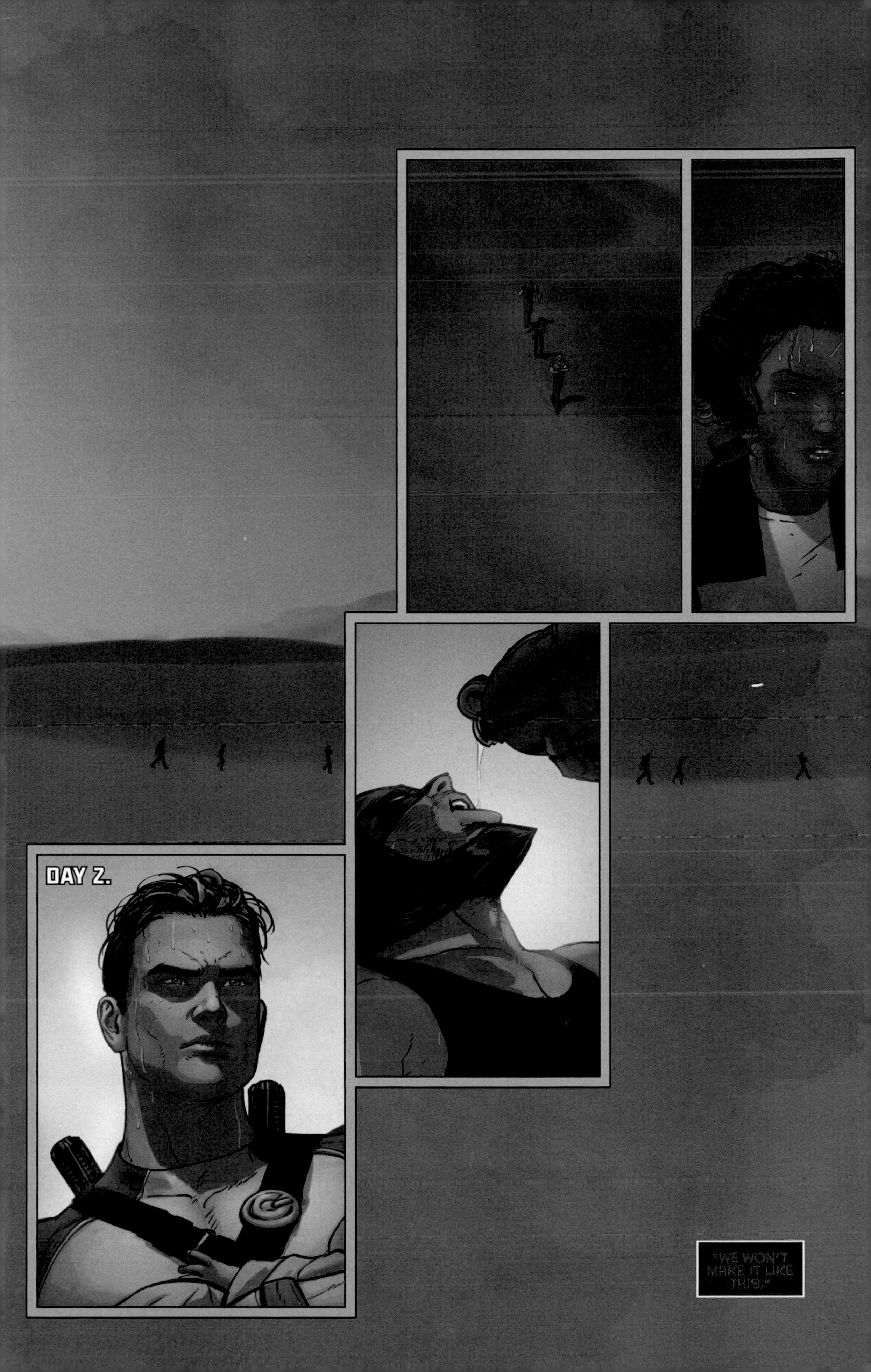
DAY 2.
"WE WON'T MAKE IT LIKE THIS."

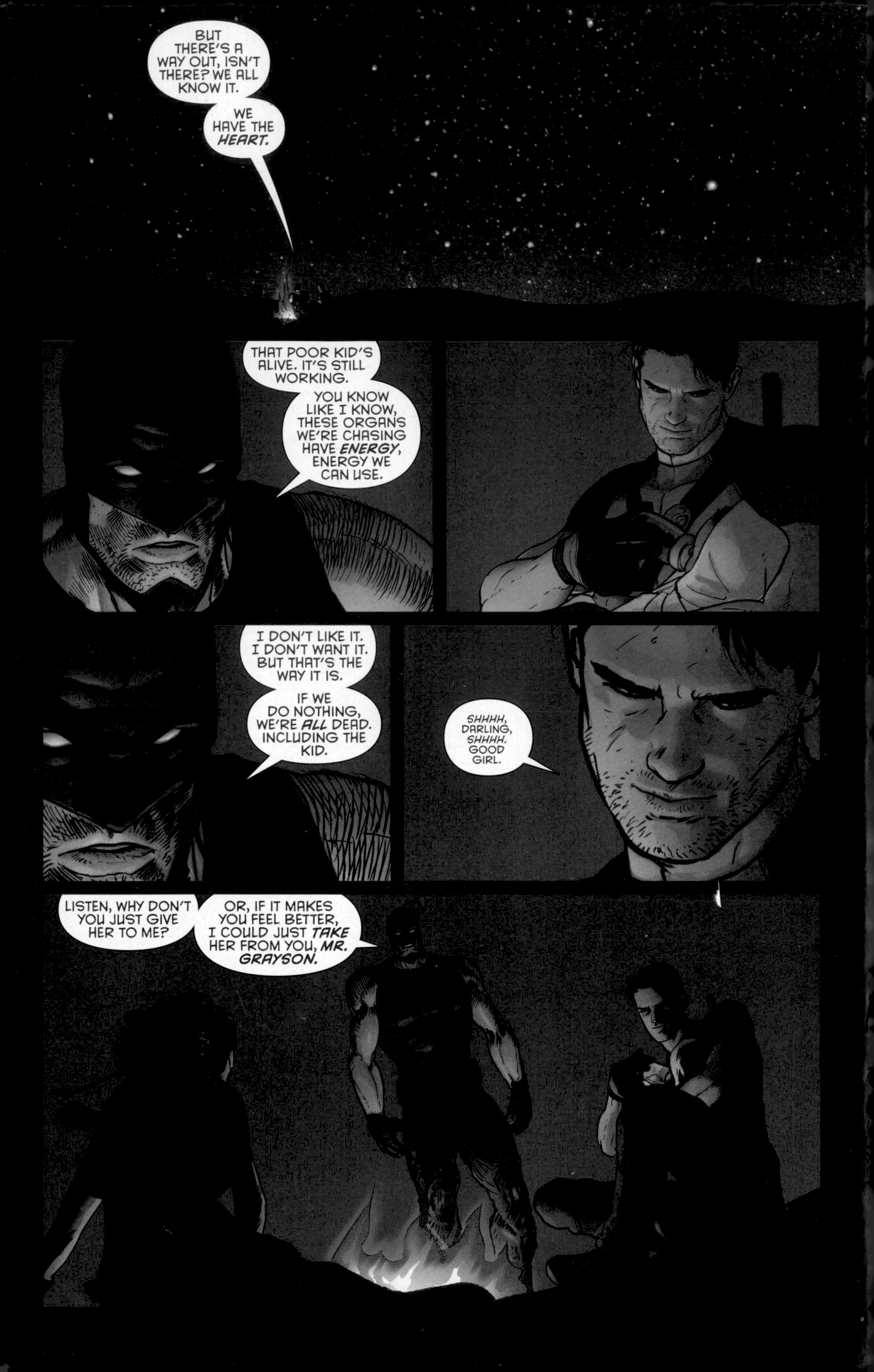
BUT THERE'S A WAY OUT, ISN'T THERE? WE ALL KNOW IT.
WE HAVE THE HEART.
THAT POOR KID'S ALIVE. IT'S STILL WORKING.
YOU KNOW LIKE I KNOW, THESE ORGANS WE'RE CHASING HAVE ENERGY, ENERGY WE CAN USE.
I DON'T LIKE IT. I DON'T WANT IT. BUT THAT'S THE WAY IT IS.
IF WE DO NOTHING, WE'RE ALL DEAD. INCLUDING THE KID.
SHHHH, DARLING, SHHHH. GOOD GIRL.
LISTEN, WHY DON'T YOU JUST GIVE HER TO ME?
OR, IF IT MAKES YOU FEEL BETTER, I COULD JUST TAKE HER FROM YOU, MR. GRAYSON.

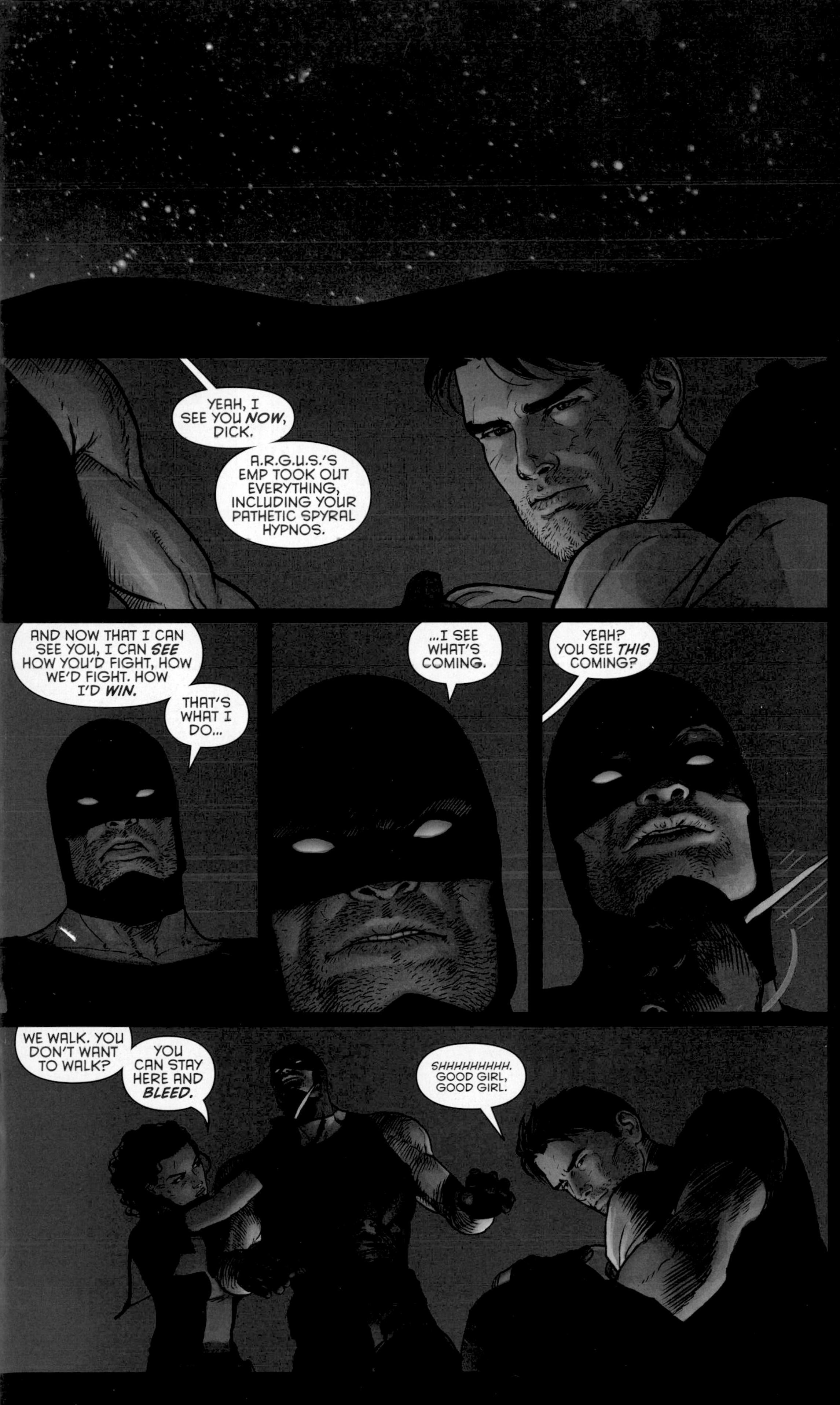
YEAH, I SEE YOU NOW, DICK.
A.R.G.U.S.'S EMP TOOK OUT EVERYTHING, INCLUDING YOUR PATHETIC SPYRAL HYPNOS.
AND NOW THAT I CAN SEE YOU, I CAN SEE HOW YOU'D FIGHT, HOW WE'D FIGHT. HOW I'D WIN.
THAT'S WHAT I DO...
...I SEE WHAT'S COMING.
YEAH? YOU SEE THIS COMING?
WE WALK. YOU DON'T WANT TO WALK?
YOU CAN STAY HERE AND BLEED.
SHHHHHHHHH. GOOD GIRL, GOOD GIRL.

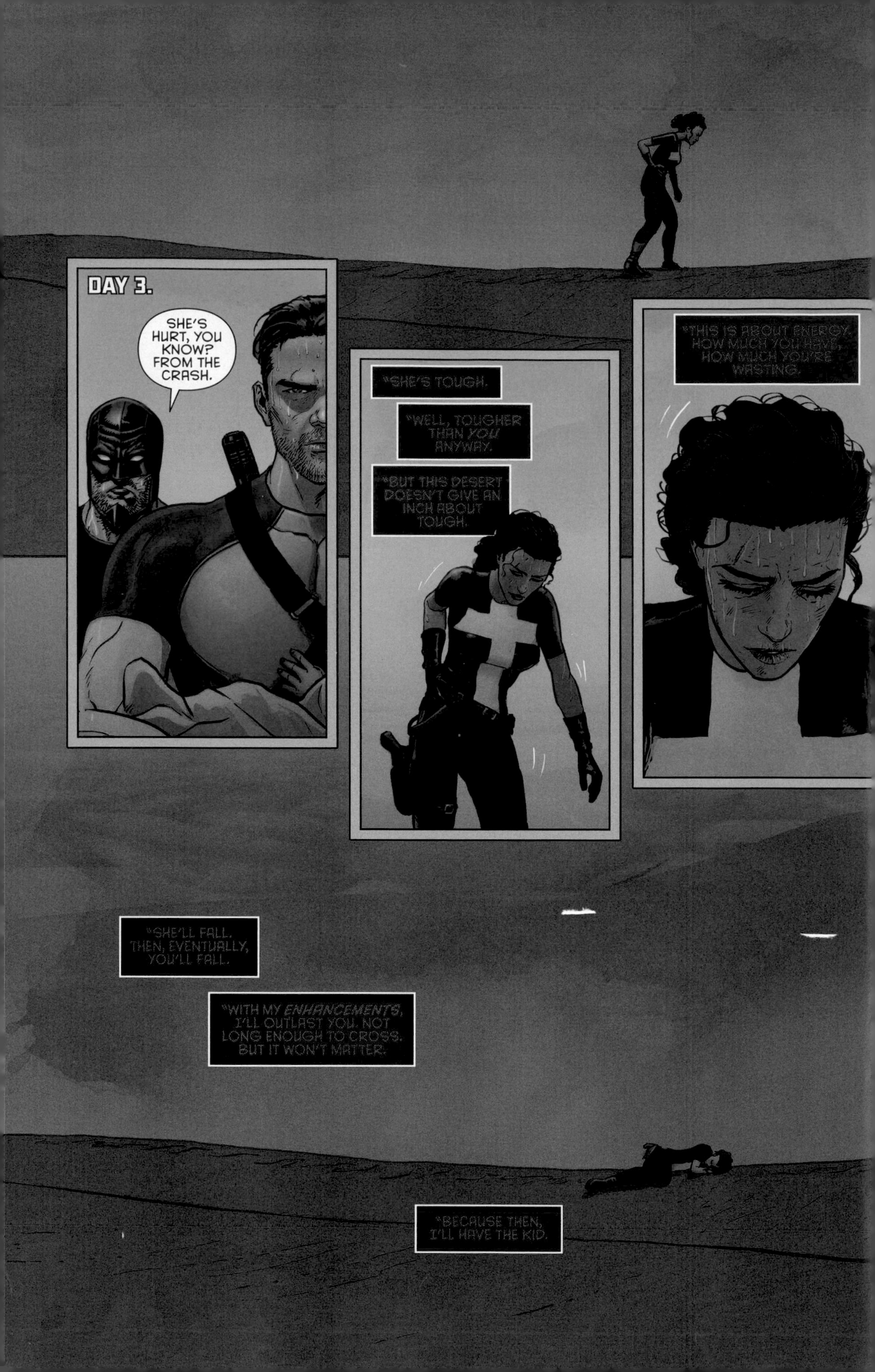

DAY 3.
SHE'S HURT, YOU KNOW? FROM THE CRASH.
"SHE'S TOUGH.
"WELL, TOUGHER THAN YOU ANYWAY.
"BUT THIS DESERT DOESN'T GIVE AN INCH ABOUT TOUGH.
"THIS IS ABOUT ENERGY. HOW MUCH YOU HAVE, HOW MUCH YOU'RE WASTING.
"SHE'LL FALL. THEN, EVENTUALLY, YOU'LL FALL.
"WITH MY ENHANCEMENTS, I'LL OUTLAST YOU. NOT LONG ENOUGH TO CROSS. BUT IT WON'T MATTER.
"BECAUSE THEN, I'LL HAVE THE KID.

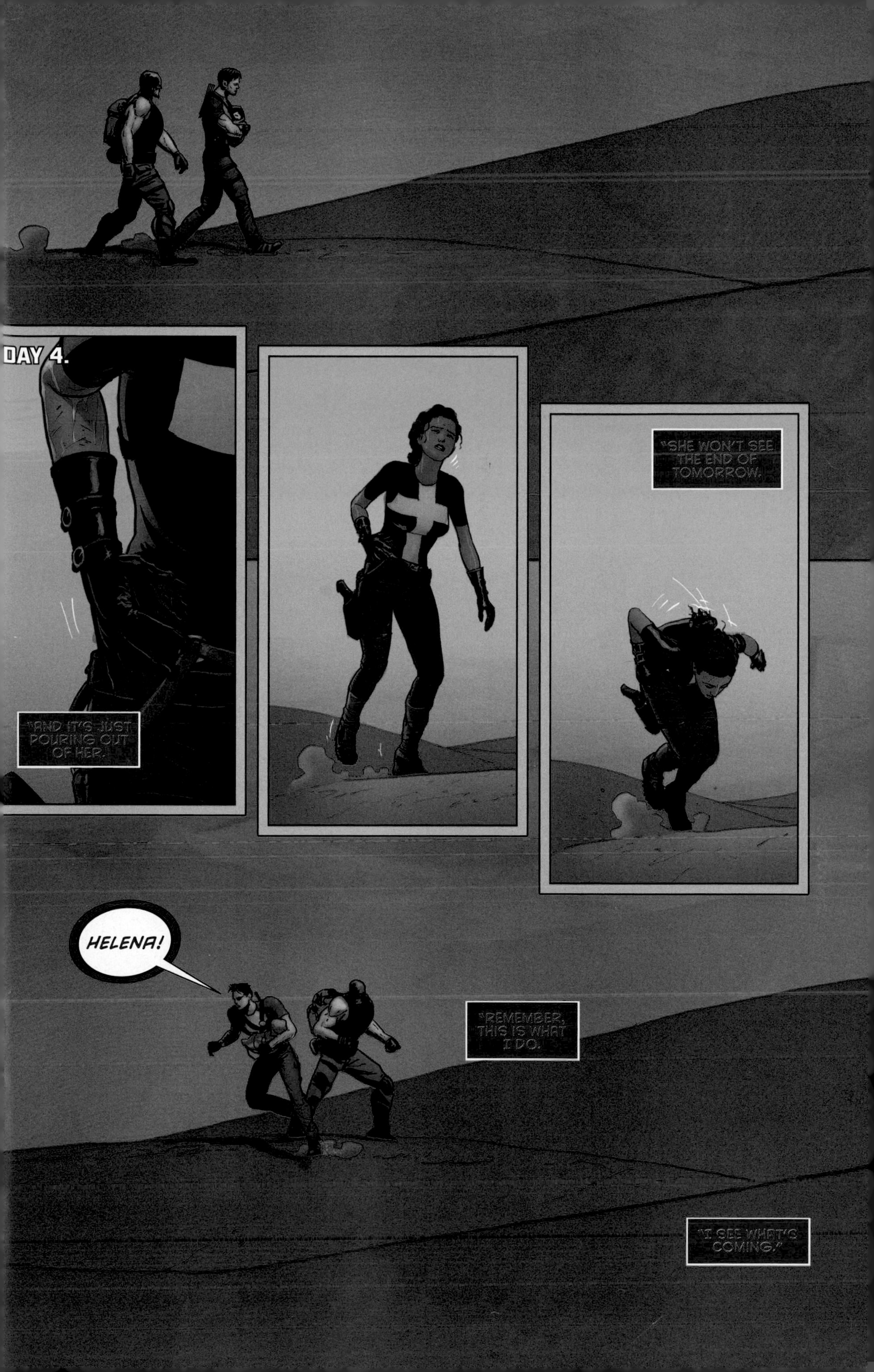
DAY 4.
"AND IT'S JUST POURING OUT OF HER.
"SHE WON'T SEE THE END OF TOMORROW.
HELENA!
"REMEMBER, THIS IS WHAT I DO.
"I SEE WHAT'S COMING."

WE HAVE WATER-- I'LL GET YOU MORE WATER.

HANG ON, OKAY? OKAY?

NO.

YOU JUST NEED SOME MORE WATER.

NO!

THE WATER'S FOR THE BABY.

WE WENT AFTER HER, WE PUT HER HERE.

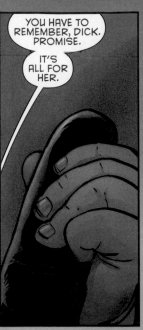

YOU HAVE TO REMEMBER, DICK. PROMISE.

IT'S ALL FOR HER.

WE BUILD HER A TENT. WE LEAVE SUPPLIES. WE MARK WHERE WE ARE.

WE COME BACK FOR HER.

WE WALK.

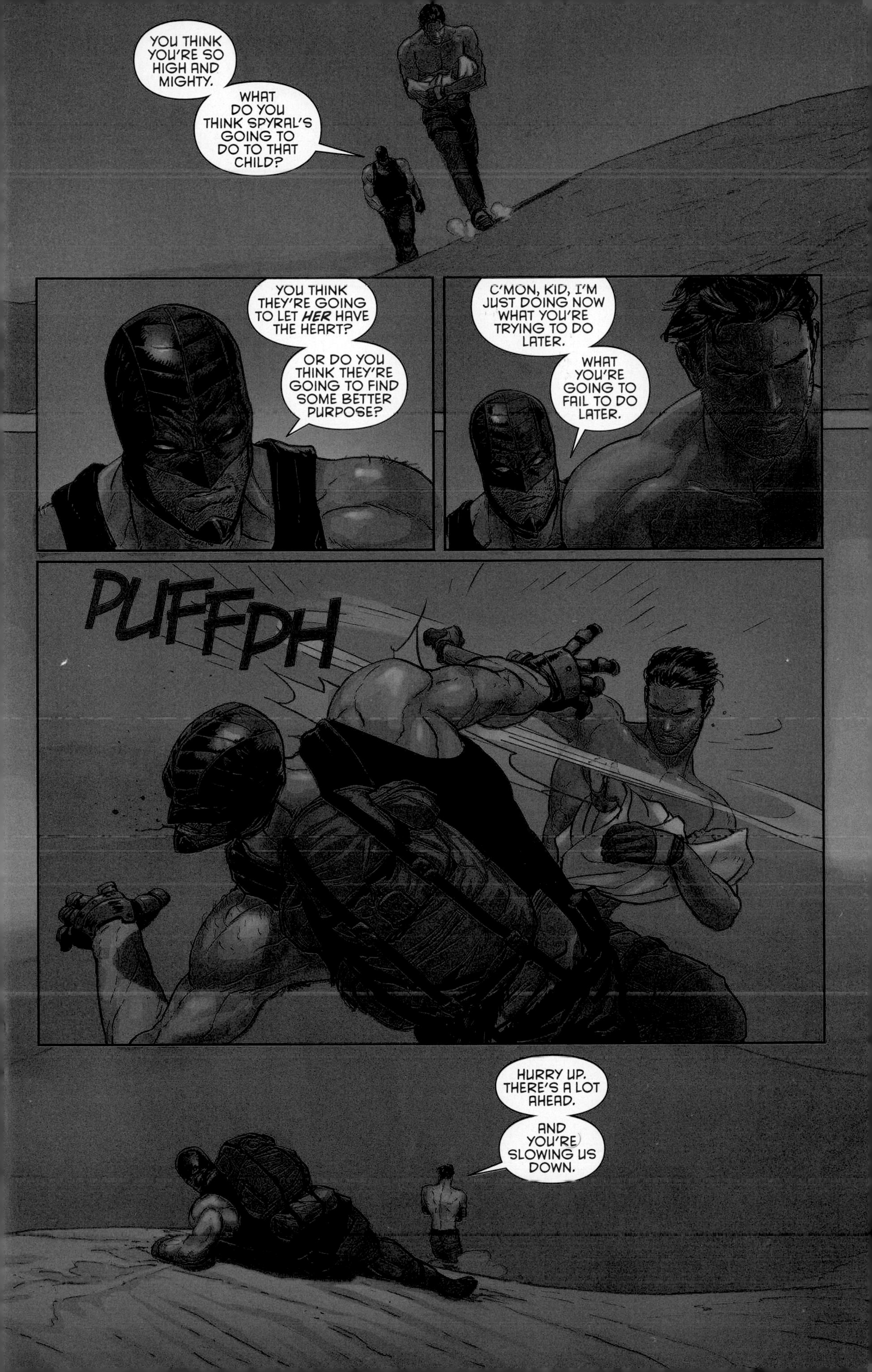
YOU THINK YOU'RE SO HIGH AND MIGHTY.
WHAT DO YOU THINK SPYRAL'S GOING TO DO TO THAT CHILD?
YOU THINK THEY'RE GOING TO LET HER HAVE THE HEART?
OR DO YOU THINK THEY'RE GOING TO FIND SOME BETTER PURPOSE?
C'MON, KID, I'M JUST DOING NOW WHAT YOU'RE TRYING TO DO LATER.
WHAT YOU'RE GOING TO FAIL TO DO LATER.
PUFFPH
HURRY UP. THERE'S A LOT AHEAD.
AND YOU'RE SLOWING US DOWN.

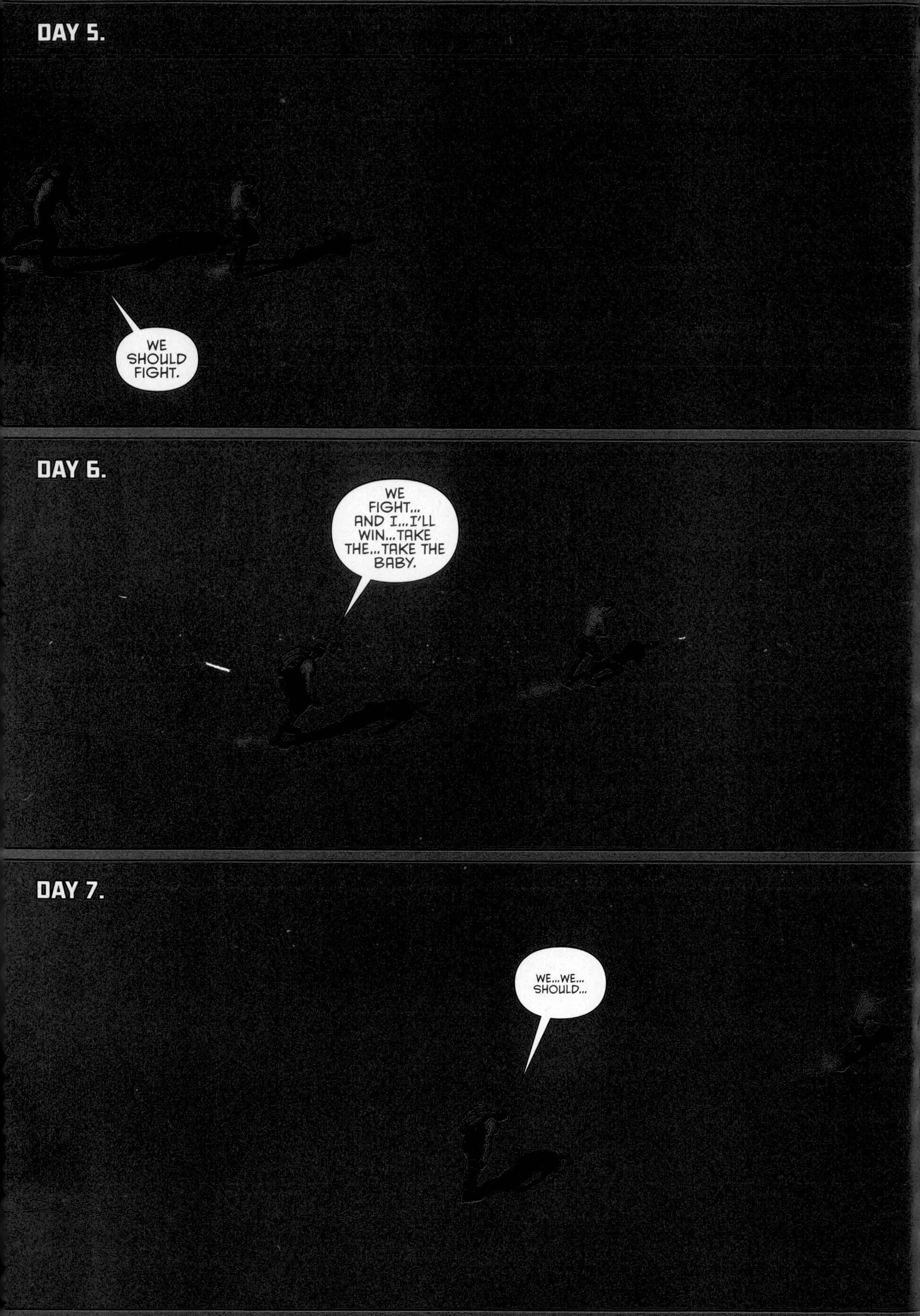
DAY 5.
WE SHOULD FIGHT.
DAY 6.
WE FIGHT... AND I...I'LL WIN...TAKE THE...TAKE THE BABY.
DAY 7.
WE...WE... SHOULD...

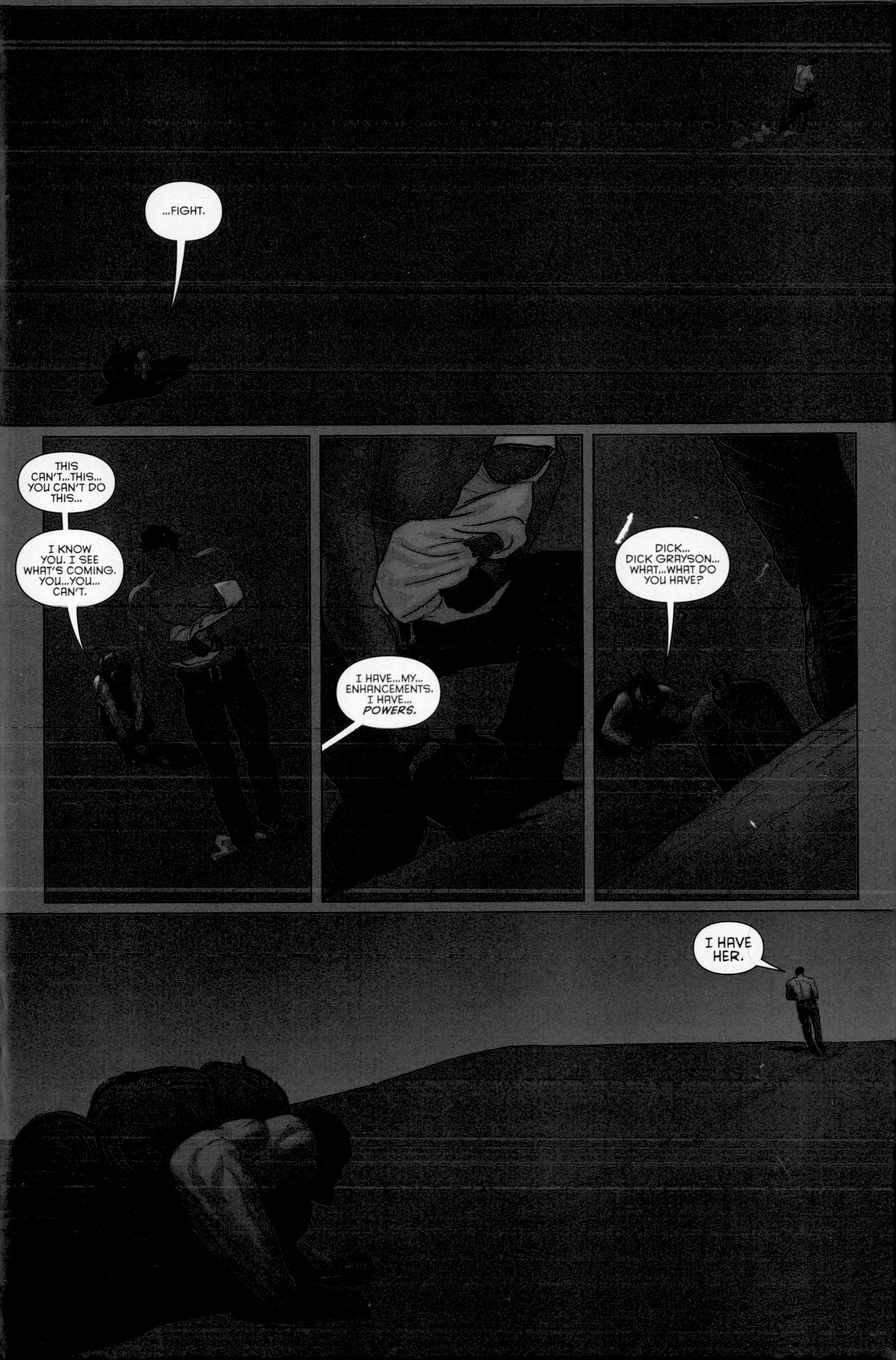
...FIGHT.
THIS CAN'T...THIS... YOU CAN'T DO THIS...
I KNOW YOU. I SEE WHAT'S COMING. YOU...YOU... CAN'T.
I HAVE...MY... ENHANCEMENTS. I HAVE... POWERS.
DICK... DICK GRAYSON... WHAT...WHAT DO YOU HAVE?
I HAVE HER.

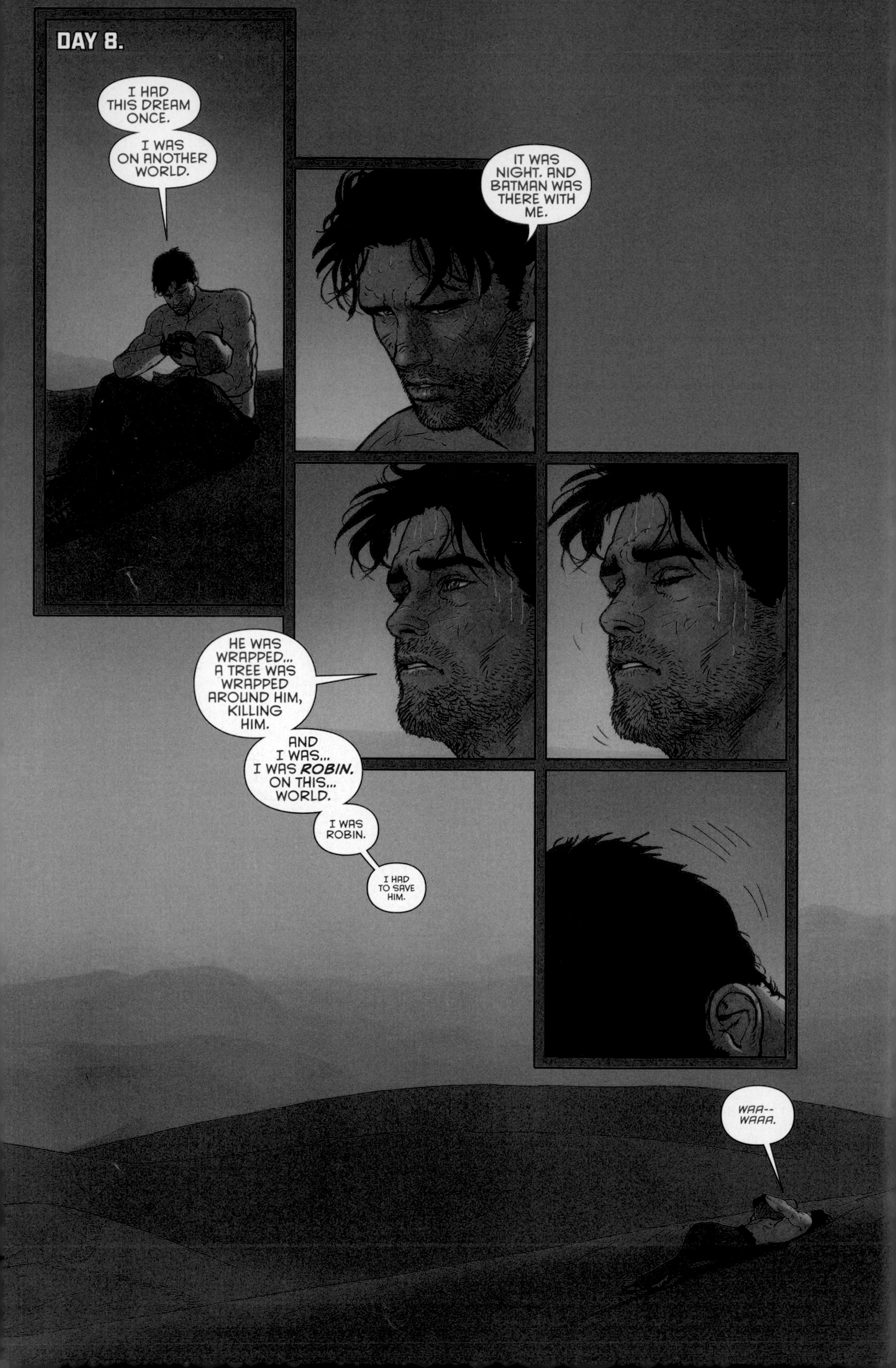
DAY 8.
I HAD THIS DREAM ONCE.
I WAS ON ANOTHER WORLD.
IT WAS NIGHT. AND BATMAN WAS THERE WITH ME.
HE WAS WRAPPED... A TREE WAS WRAPPED AROUND HIM, KILLING HIM.
AND I WAS... I WAS ROBIN. ON THIS... WORLD.
I WAS ROBIN.
I HAD TO SAVE HIM.
WAA-- WAAA.

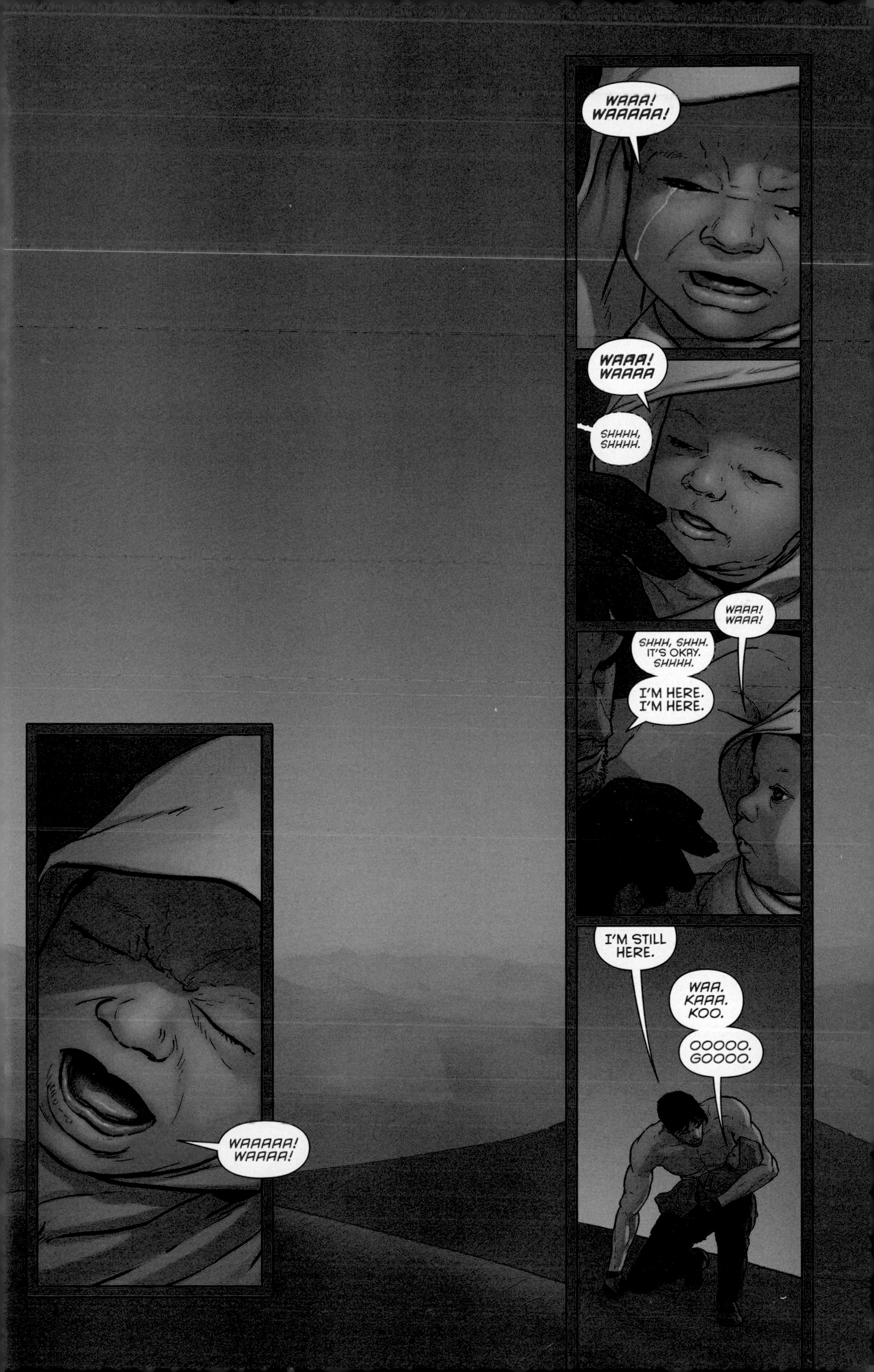
WAAA! WAAAAA!
WAAA! WAAAA
SHHHH, SHHHH.
WAAA! WAAA!
SHHH, SHHH. IT'S OKAY. SHHHH.
I'M HERE. I'M HERE.
I'M STILL HERE.
WAA. KAAA. KOO.
OOOOO. GOOOO.
WAAAAA! WAAAA!

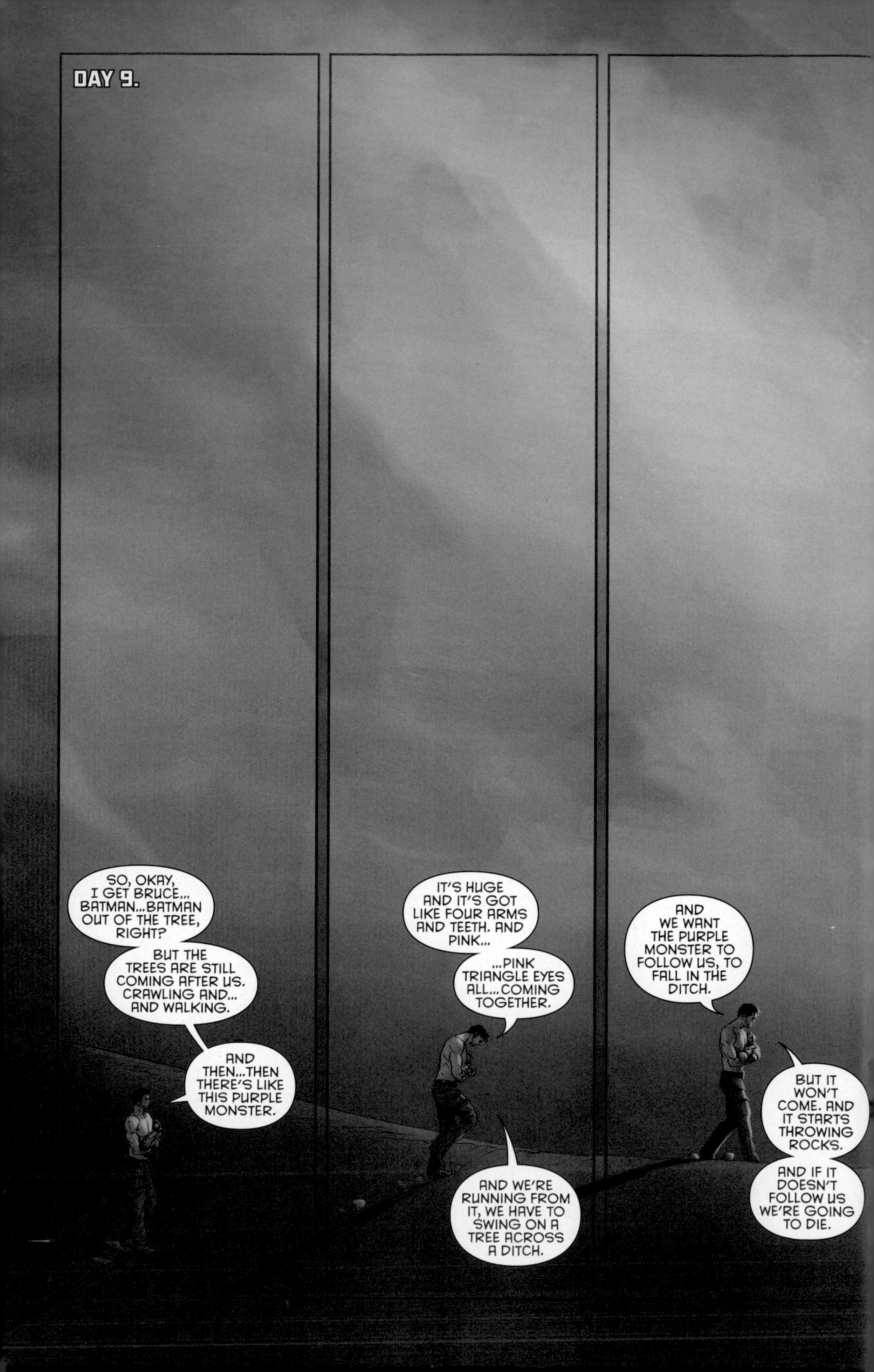
DAY 9.
SO, OKAY, I GET BRUCE... BATMAN...BATMAN OUT OF THE TREE, RIGHT?
BUT THE TREES ARE STILL COMING AFTER US. CRAWLING AND... AND WALKING.
AND THEN...THEN THERE'S LIKE THIS PURPLE MONSTER.
IT'S HUGE AND IT'S GOT LIKE FOUR ARMS AND TEETH. AND PINK...
...PINK TRIANGLE EYES ALL...COMING TOGETHER.
AND WE'RE RUNNING FROM IT, WE HAVE TO SWING ON A TREE ACROSS A DITCH.
AND WE WANT THE PURPLE MONSTER TO FOLLOW US, TO FALL IN THE DITCH.
BUT IT WON'T COME. AND IT STARTS THROWING ROCKS.
AND IF IT DOESN'T FOLLOW US WE'RE GOING TO DIE.

SO I RUSH UP TO THE EDGE. RIGHT ON THE EDGE OF THE FALL.
AND I... AND I SHOUT: *"COME ON, BIG BOY! I'M STILL WAITING FOR YOU!"*
AND THE MONSTER GETS MAD. AND HE COMES. AND HE FALLS.
AND WE WIN.
BUT THEN THERE WERE...ROCKS... ROCKS EVERY-WHERE.
AND A ROCK FELL... IT FELL...ON... IT FELL ON ME.
AND THE NIGHT WAS...WAS ENDING...BUT IT WAS ALL... ALL DARK.

BUT YOU GOT...GOT TO FORGET ABOUT THE ROCKS, OKAY?
PROMISE ME THAT, TO FORGET THAT.
YOU'RE TOO LITTLE.
YOU DON'T HAVE TO WORRY ABOUT THE ROCKS.
YOU ONLY HAVE TO...YOU JUST REMEMBER.
SOMETIMES YOU STAND ON THE EDGE.
AND THERE'S A MONSTER ON THE OTHER SIDE.
AND YOU TELL HIM...YOU JUST TELL THAT MONSTER:
COME ON...COME ON, BIG BOY!
I'M STILL WAITING FOR YOU!

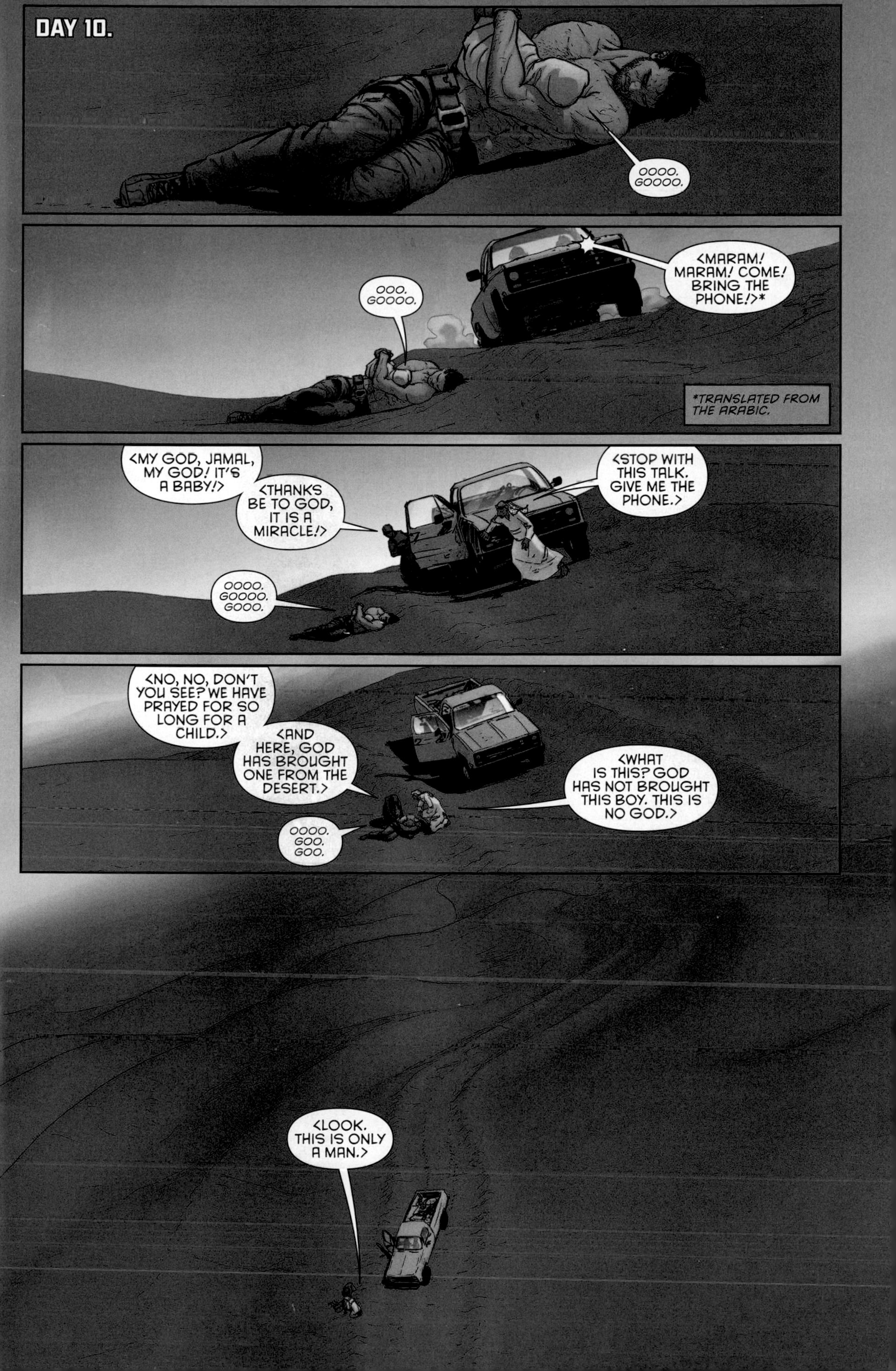
DAY 10.
OOOO. GOOOO.
OOO. GOOOO.
<MARAM! MARAM! COME! BRING THE PHONE!>*
*TRANSLATED FROM THE ARABIC.
<MY GOD, JAMAL, MY GOD! IT'S A BABY!>
<THANKS BE TO GOD, IT IS A MIRACLE!>
<STOP WITH THIS TALK. GIVE ME THE PHONE.>
OOOO. GOOOO. GOOO.
<NO, NO, DON'T YOU SEE? WE HAVE PRAYED FOR SO LONG FOR A CHILD.>
<AND HERE, GOD HAS BROUGHT ONE FROM THE DESERT.>
<WHAT IS THIS? GOD HAS NOT BROUGHT THIS BOY. THIS IS NO GOD.>
OOOO. GOO. GOO.
<LOOK. THIS IS ONLY A MAN.>

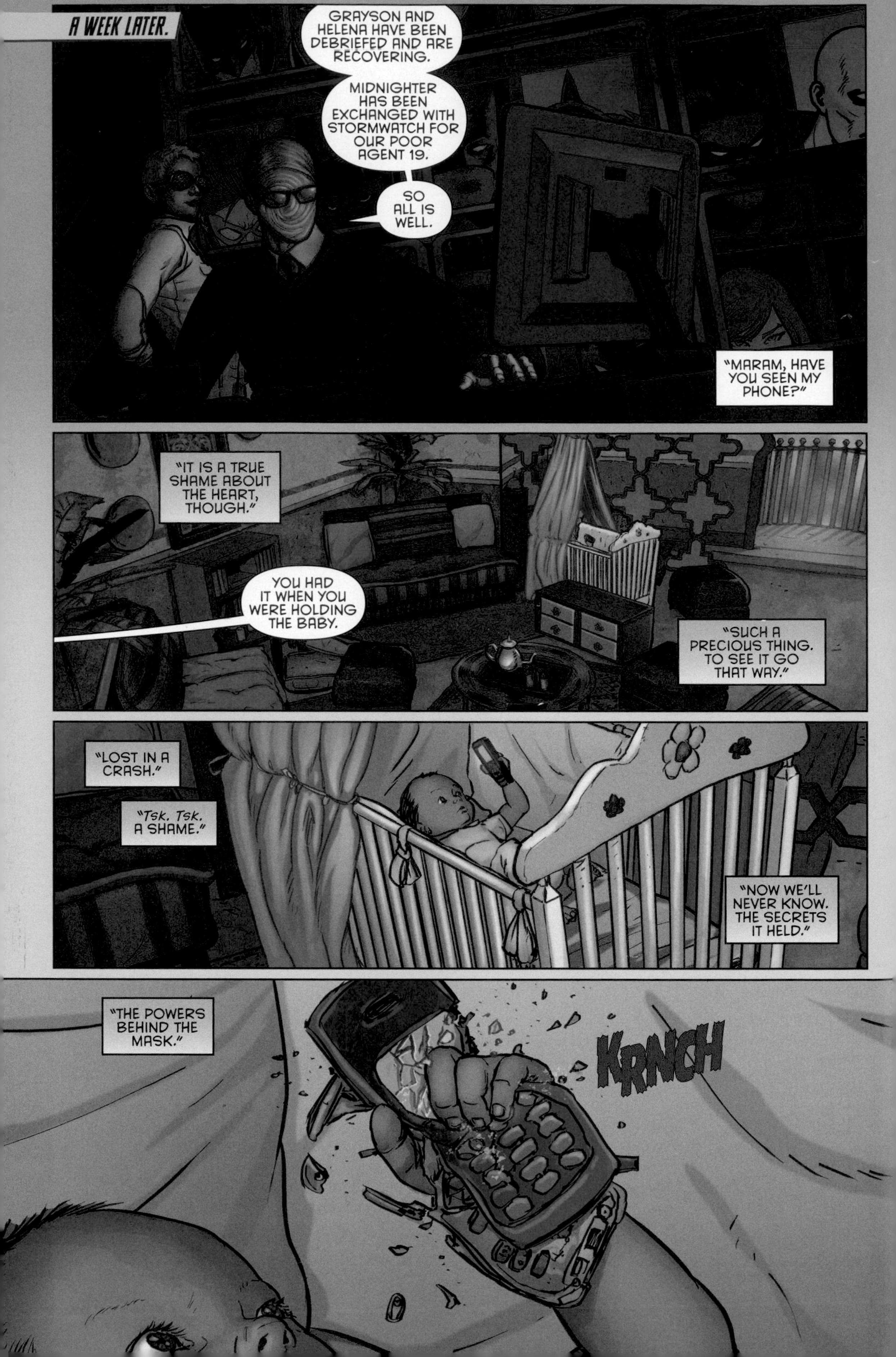
A WEEK LATER.
GRAYSON AND HELENA HAVE BEEN DEBRIEFED AND ARE RECOVERING.
MIDNIGHTER HAS BEEN EXCHANGED WITH STORMWATCH FOR OUR POOR AGENT 19.
SO ALL IS WELL.
"MARAM, HAVE YOU SEEN MY PHONE?"
"IT IS A TRUE SHAME ABOUT THE HEART, THOUGH."
YOU HAD IT WHEN YOU WERE HOLDING THE BABY.
"SUCH A PRECIOUS THING. TO SEE IT GO THAT WAY."
"LOST IN A CRASH."
"Tsk. Tsk. A SHAME."
"NOW WE'LL NEVER KNOW. THE SECRETS IT HELD."
"THE POWERS BEHIND THE MASK."
KRNCH

THE BRAINS OF OPERATION

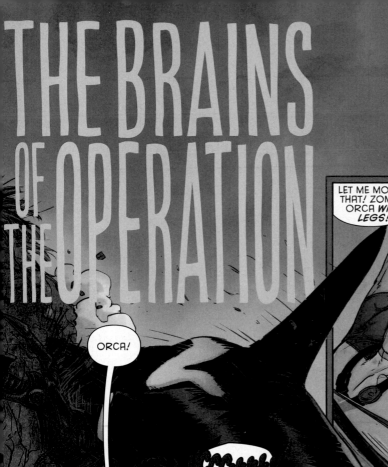

ORCA!

LET ME MODIFY THAT! ZOMBIE ORCA *WITH LEGS!*

DESPITE THE PRISON'S DESTRUCTION AT THE HANDS OF *MOTHER MACHINE,* THE *SECURITY NANOCYTES* ARE STILL ACTIVE. LACKING HUMAN HOSTS...

CCCHHH

TAK

...THEY BOND WITH THE NEXT DEADLIEST CREATURE THEY CAN FIND.

SKRCH

RETURN TO THE OCEAN AND SWIM FREE, WILLY.

WRITER / TIM SEELEY   PLOT BY TIM SEELEY & TOM KING   ARTIST / MIKEL JANÍN
COLORIST / JEROMY COX   LETTERER / CARLOS M. MANGUAL   COVER / MIKEL JANÍN

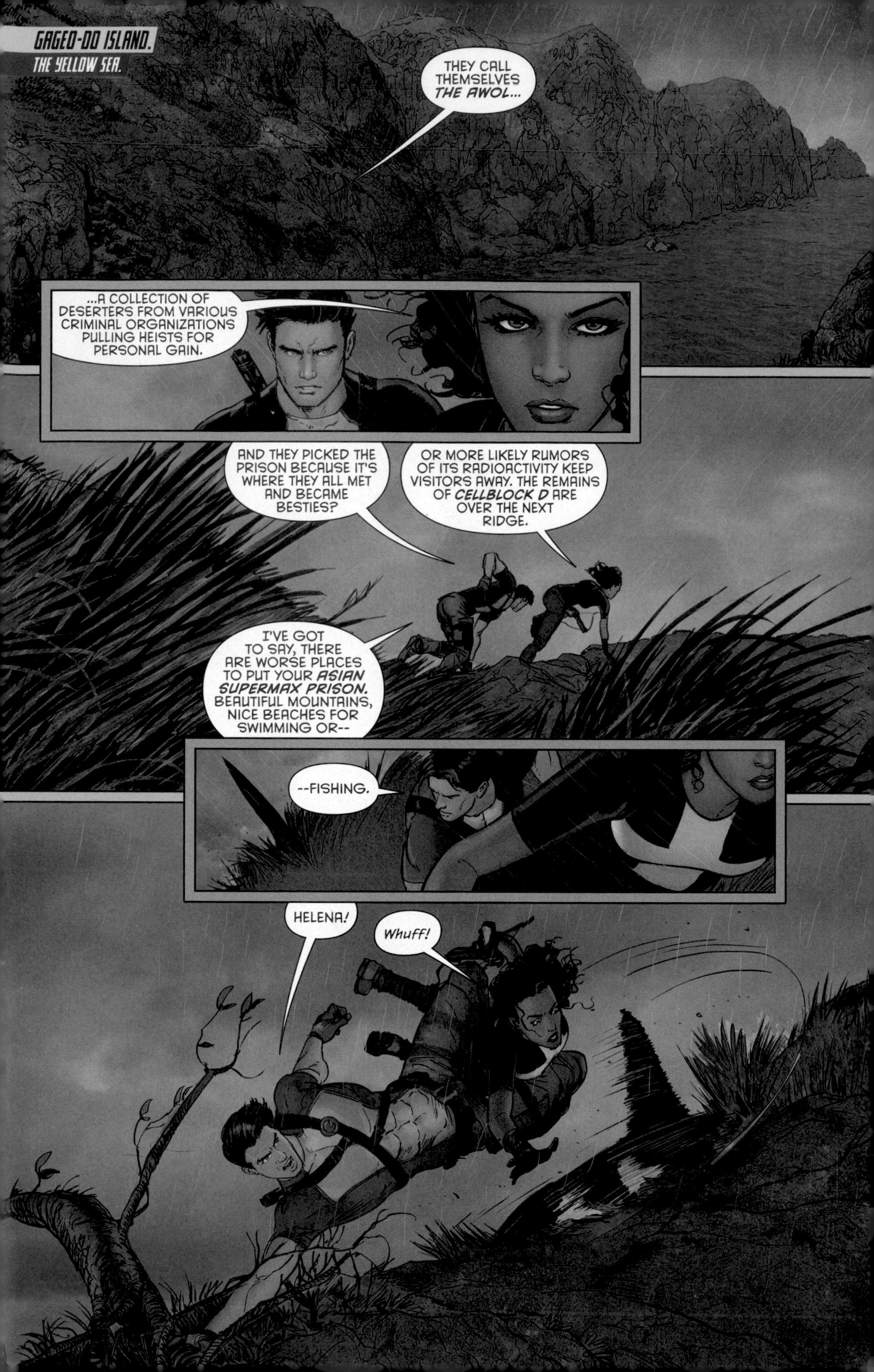
GAGED-DO ISLAND.
THE YELLOW SEA.
THEY CALL THEMSELVES THE AWOL...
...A COLLECTION OF DESERTERS FROM VARIOUS CRIMINAL ORGANIZATIONS PULLING HEISTS FOR PERSONAL GAIN.
AND THEY PICKED THE PRISON BECAUSE IT'S WHERE THEY ALL MET AND BECAME BESTIES?
OR MORE LIKELY RUMORS OF ITS RADIOACTIVITY KEEP VISITORS AWAY. THE REMAINS OF CELLBLOCK D ARE OVER THE NEXT RIDGE.
I'VE GOT TO SAY, THERE ARE WORSE PLACES TO PUT YOUR ASIAN SUPERMAX PRISON. BEAUTIFUL MOUNTAINS, NICE BEACHES FOR SWIMMING OR--
--FISHING.
HELENA!
Whuff!

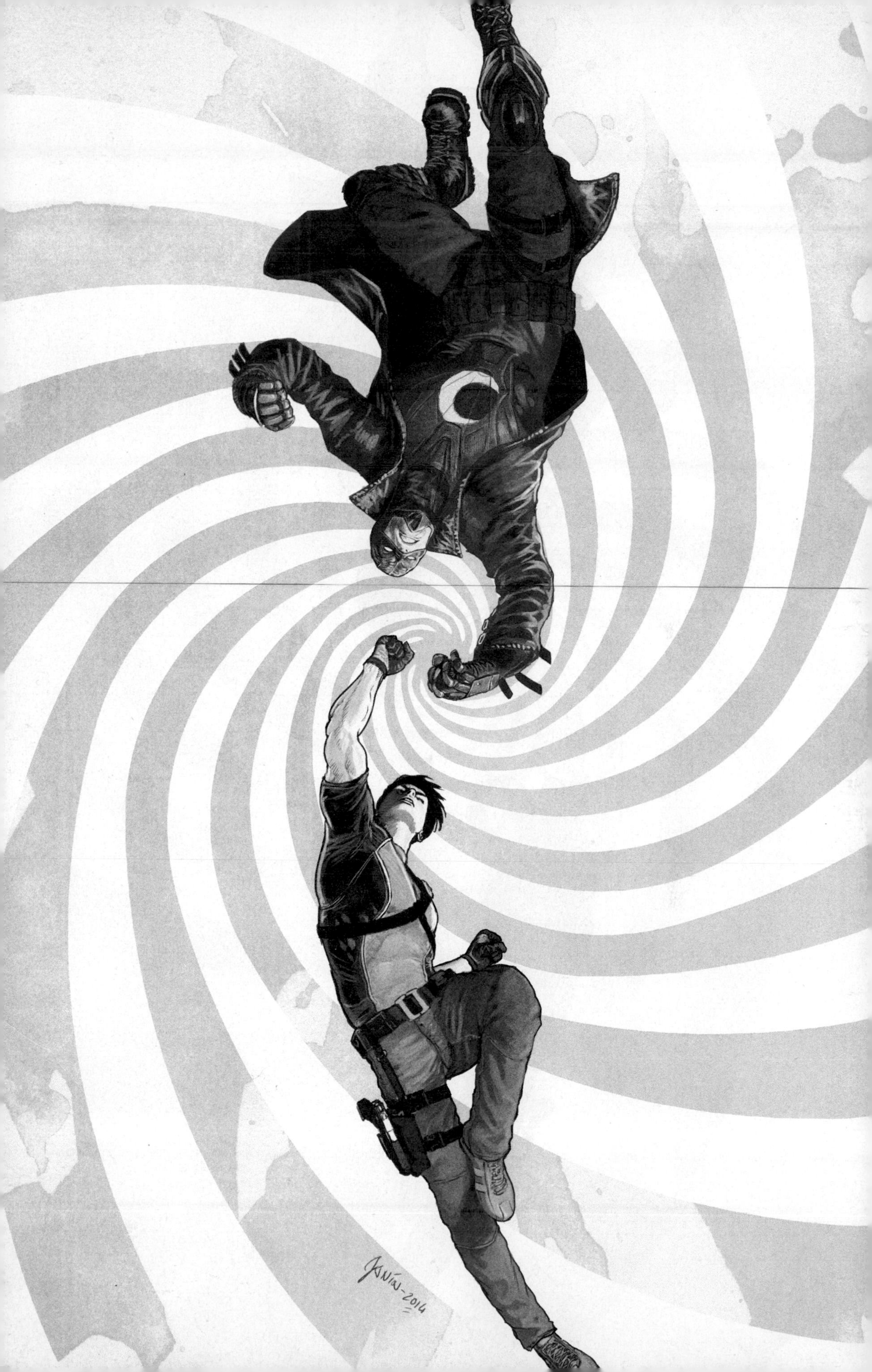

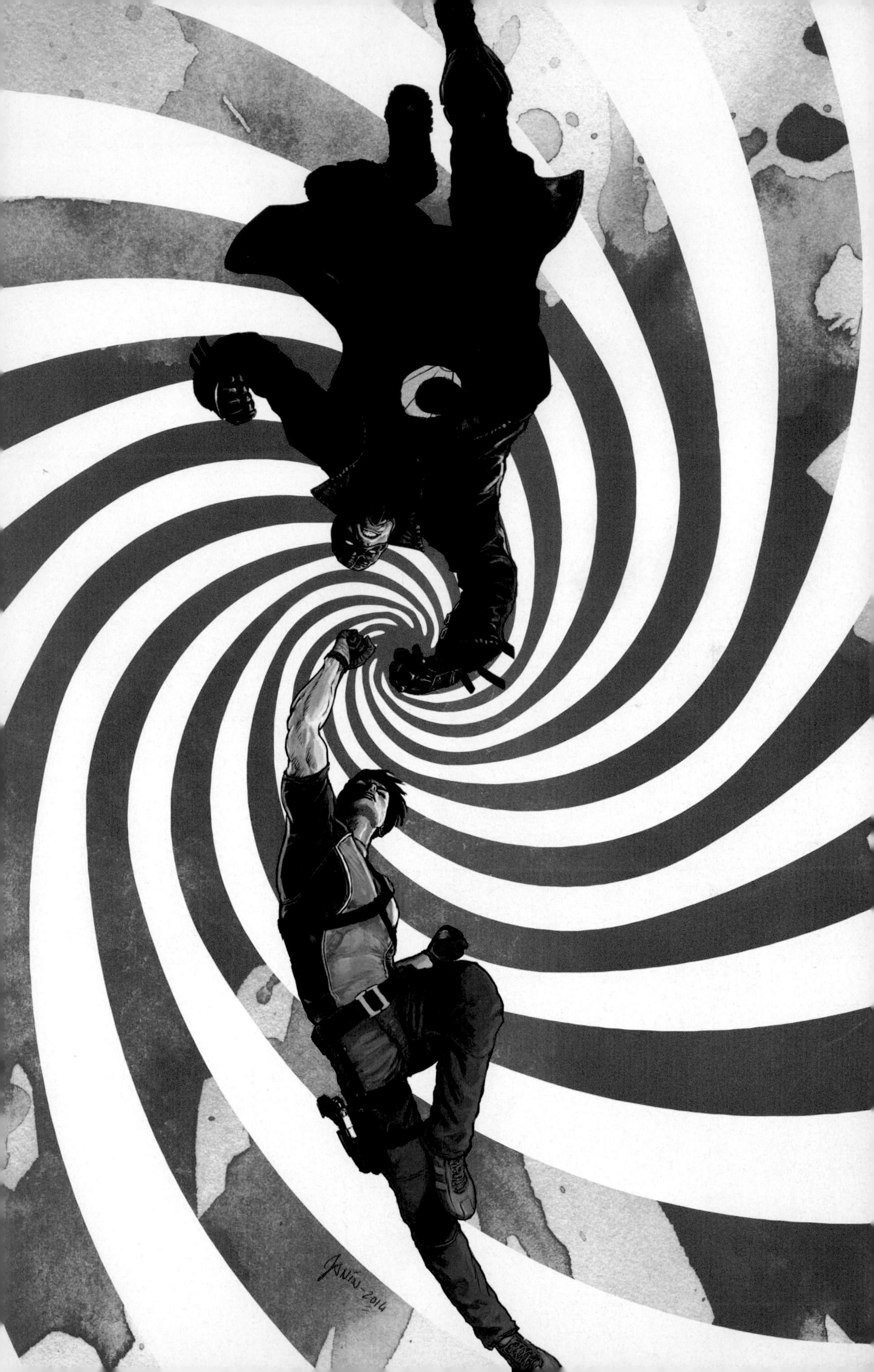

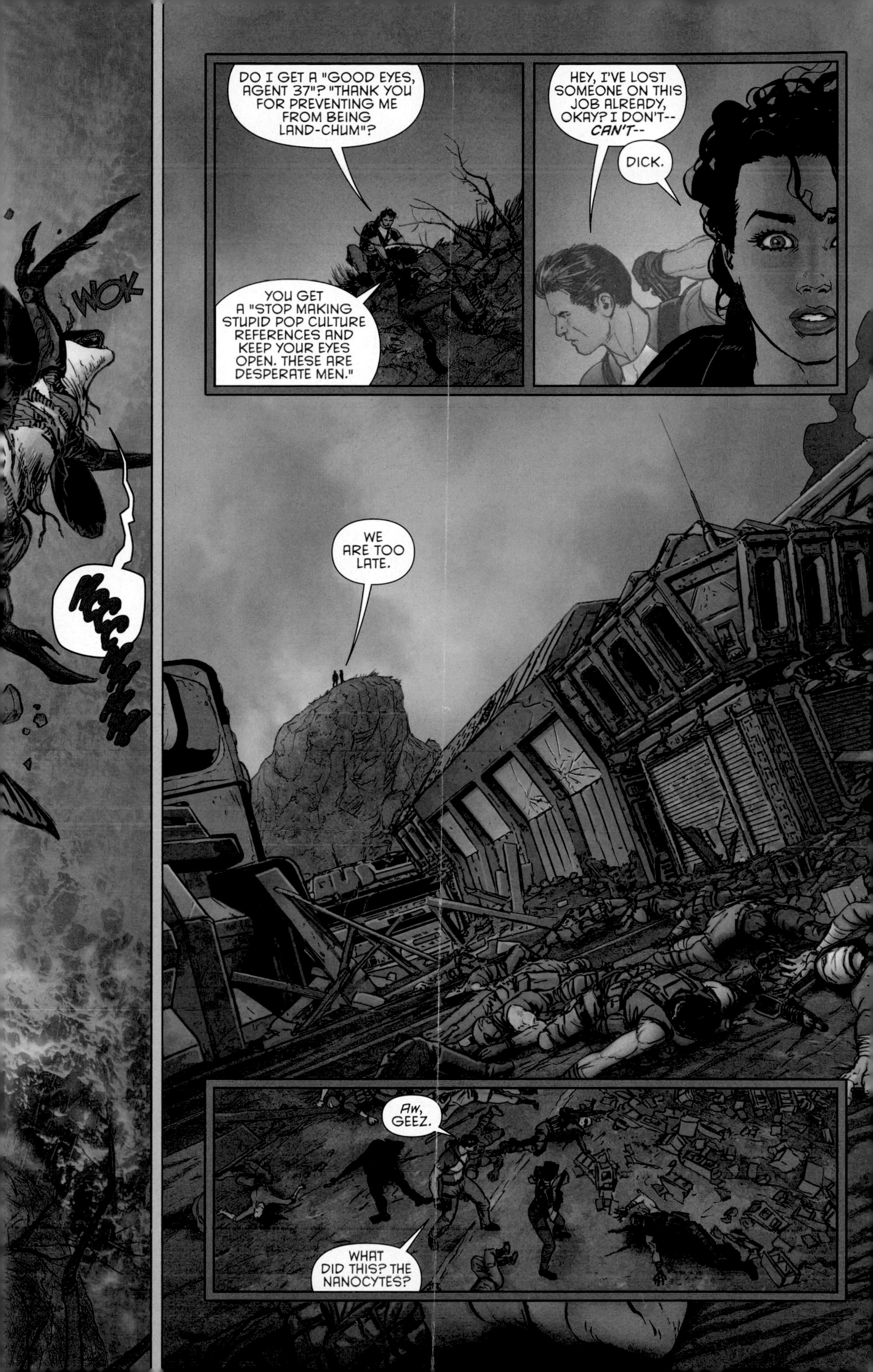
WOK
KRRCHHHH
DO I GET A "GOOD EYES, AGENT 37"? "THANK YOU FOR PREVENTING ME FROM BEING LAND-CHUM"?
YOU GET A "STOP MAKING STUPID POP CULTURE REFERENCES AND KEEP YOUR EYES OPEN. THESE ARE DESPERATE MEN."
HEY, I'VE LOST SOMEONE ON THIS JOB ALREADY, OKAY? I DON'T-- CAN'T--
DICK.
WE ARE TOO LATE.
AW, GEEZ.
WHAT DID THIS? THE NANOCYTES?

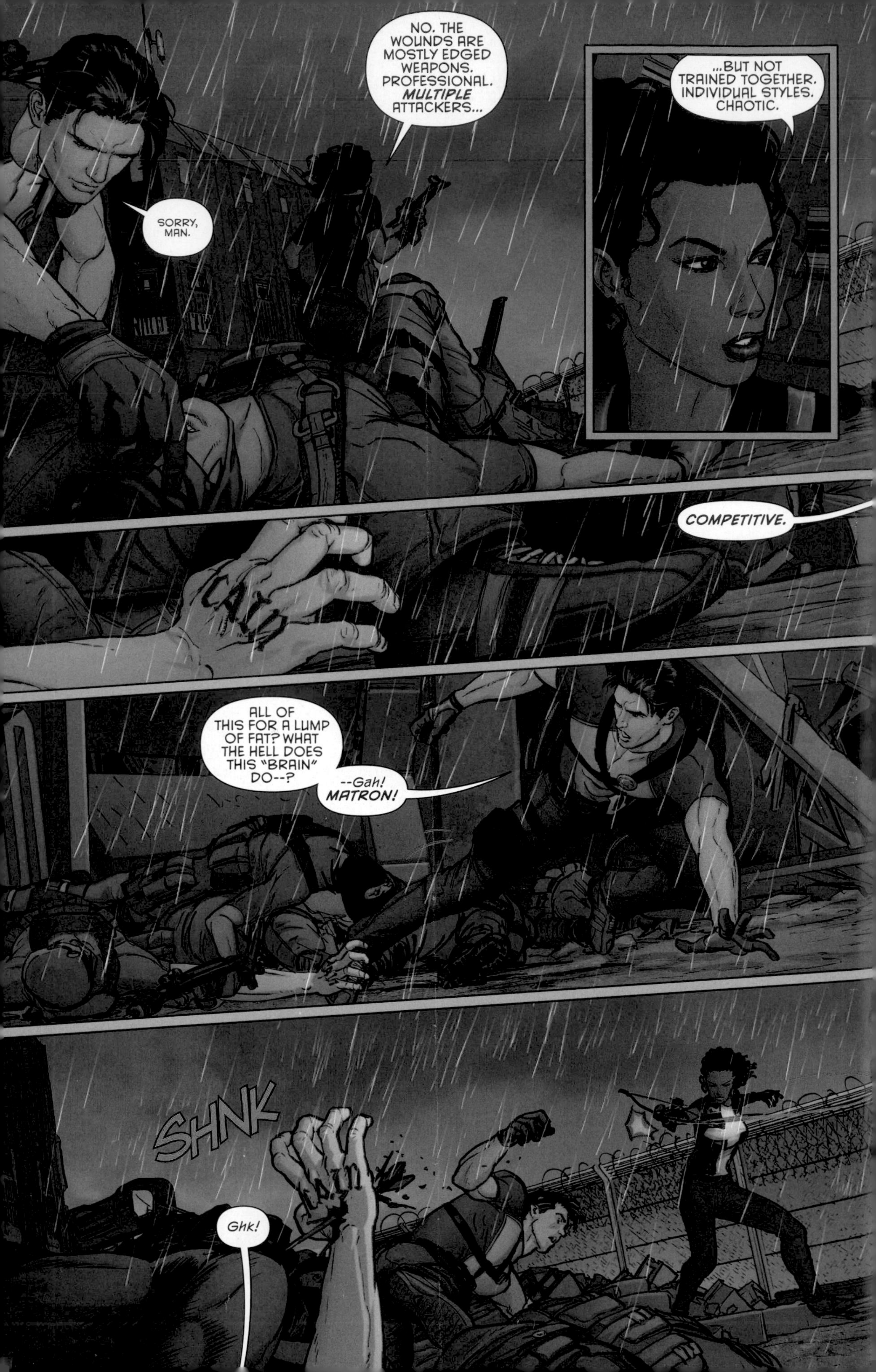
NO. THE WOUNDS ARE MOSTLY EDGED WEAPONS. PROFESSIONAL. *MULTIPLE* ATTACKERS...
SORRY, MAN.
...BUT NOT TRAINED TOGETHER. INDIVIDUAL STYLES. CHAOTIC.
COMPETITIVE.
CAIN
ALL OF THIS FOR A LUMP OF FAT? WHAT THE HELL DOES THIS "BRAIN" DO--?
--Gah! *MATRON!*
SHNK
Ghk!

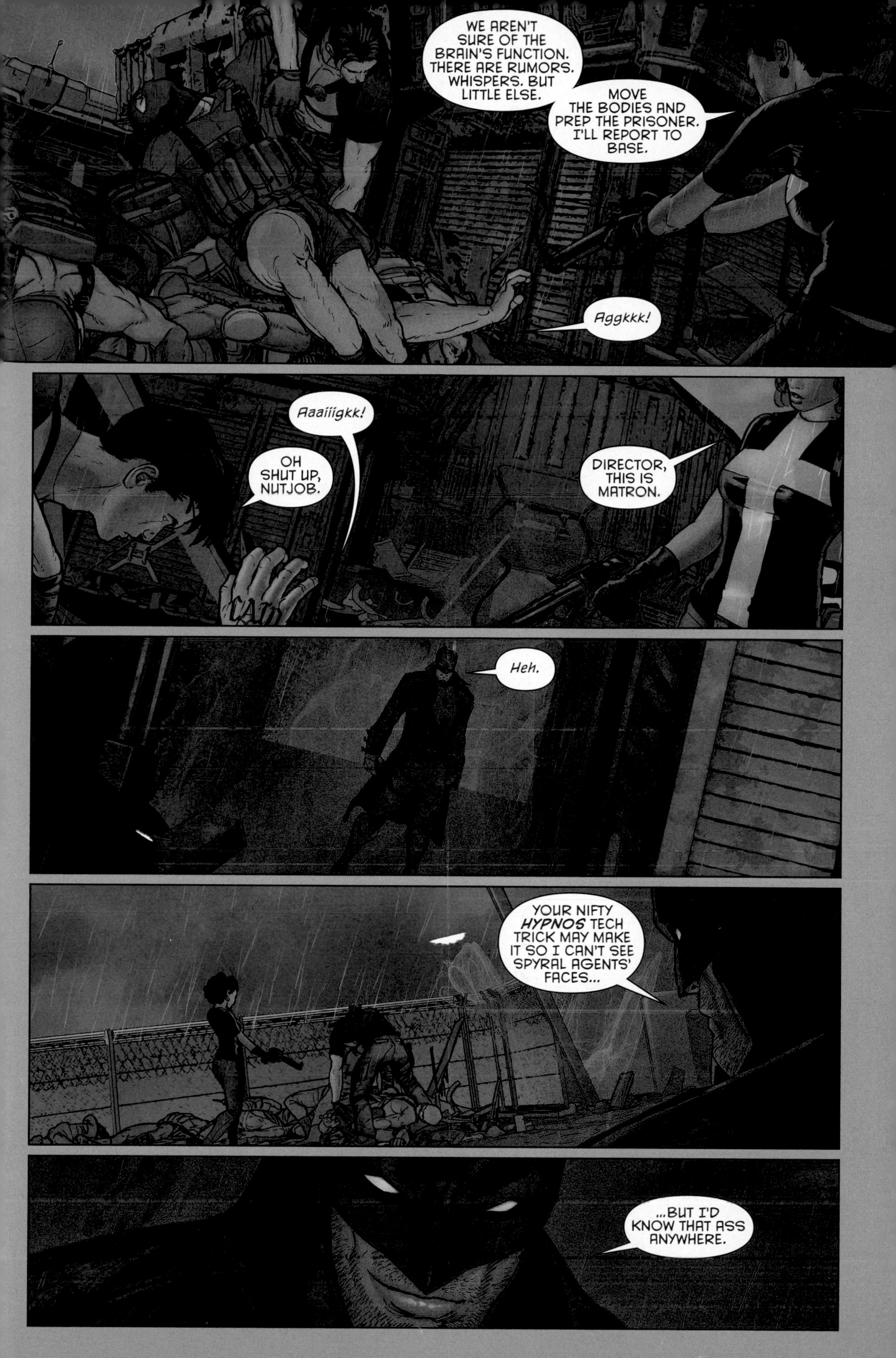

WE AREN'T SURE OF THE BRAIN'S FUNCTION. THERE ARE RUMORS. WHISPERS. BUT LITTLE ELSE.
MOVE THE BODIES AND PREP THE PRISONER. I'LL REPORT TO BASE.
Aggkkk!
Aaaiiigkk!
OH SHUT UP, NUTJOB.
DIRECTOR, THIS IS MATRON.
Heh.
YOUR NIFTY HYPNOS TECH TRICK MAY MAKE IT SO I CAN'T SEE SPYRAL AGENTS' FACES...
...BUT I'D KNOW THAT ASS ANYWHERE.

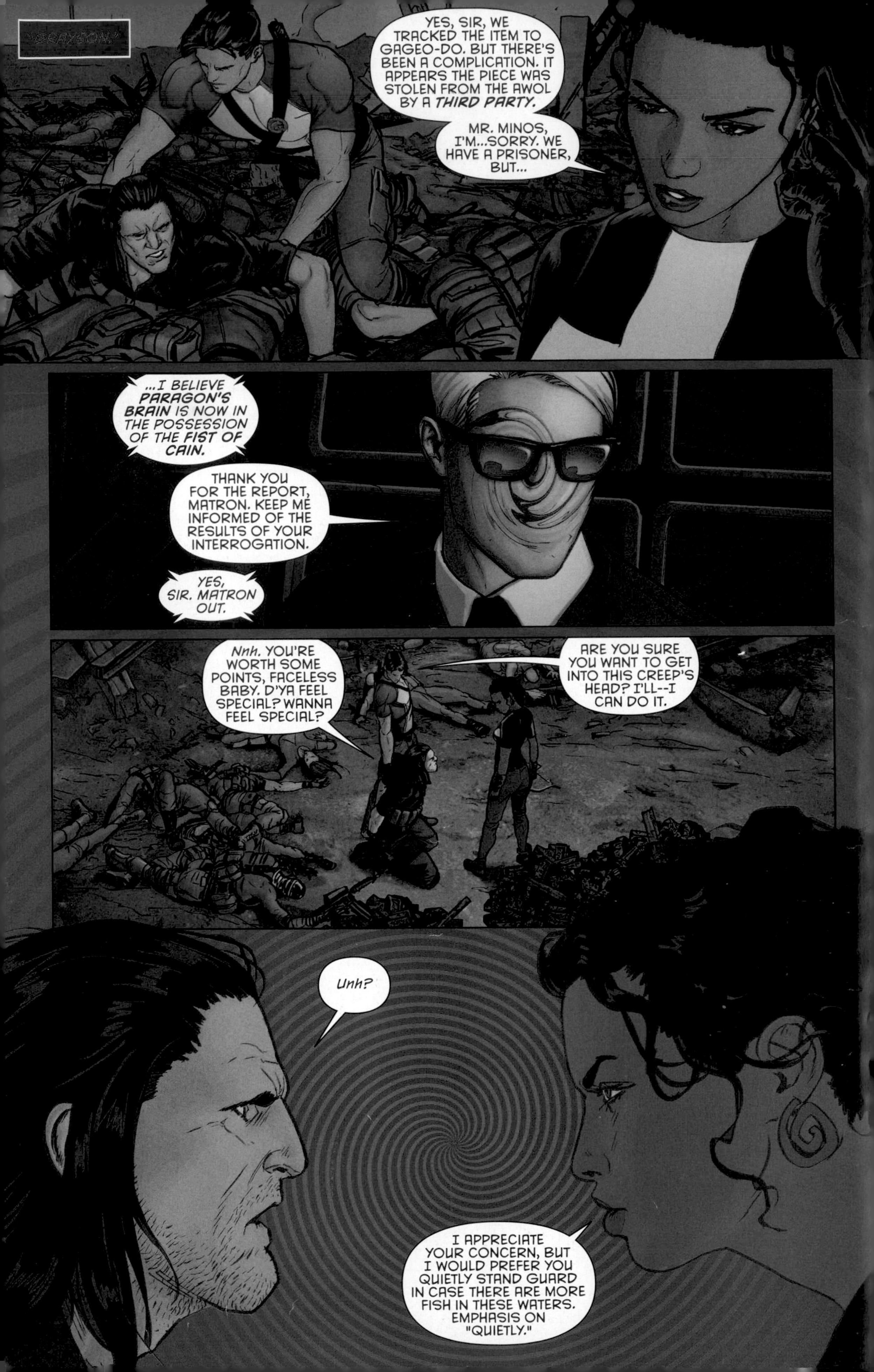
YES, SIR, WE TRACKED THE ITEM TO GAGEO-DO. BUT THERE'S BEEN A COMPLICATION. IT APPEARS THE PIECE WAS STOLEN FROM THE AWOL BY A THIRD PARTY.
MR. MINOS, I'M...SORRY. WE HAVE A PRISONER, BUT...
...I BELIEVE PARAGON'S BRAIN IS NOW IN THE POSSESSION OF THE FIST OF CAIN.
THANK YOU FOR THE REPORT, MATRON. KEEP ME INFORMED OF THE RESULTS OF YOUR INTERROGATION.
YES, SIR. MATRON OUT.
Nnh. YOU'RE WORTH SOME POINTS, FACELESS BABY. D'YA FEEL SPECIAL? WANNA FEEL SPECIAL?
ARE YOU SURE YOU WANT TO GET INTO THIS CREEP'S HEAD? I'LL--I CAN DO IT.
Unh?
I APPRECIATE YOUR CONCERN, BUT I WOULD PREFER YOU QUIETLY STAND GUARD IN CASE THERE ARE MORE FISH IN THESE WATERS. EMPHASIS ON "QUIETLY."

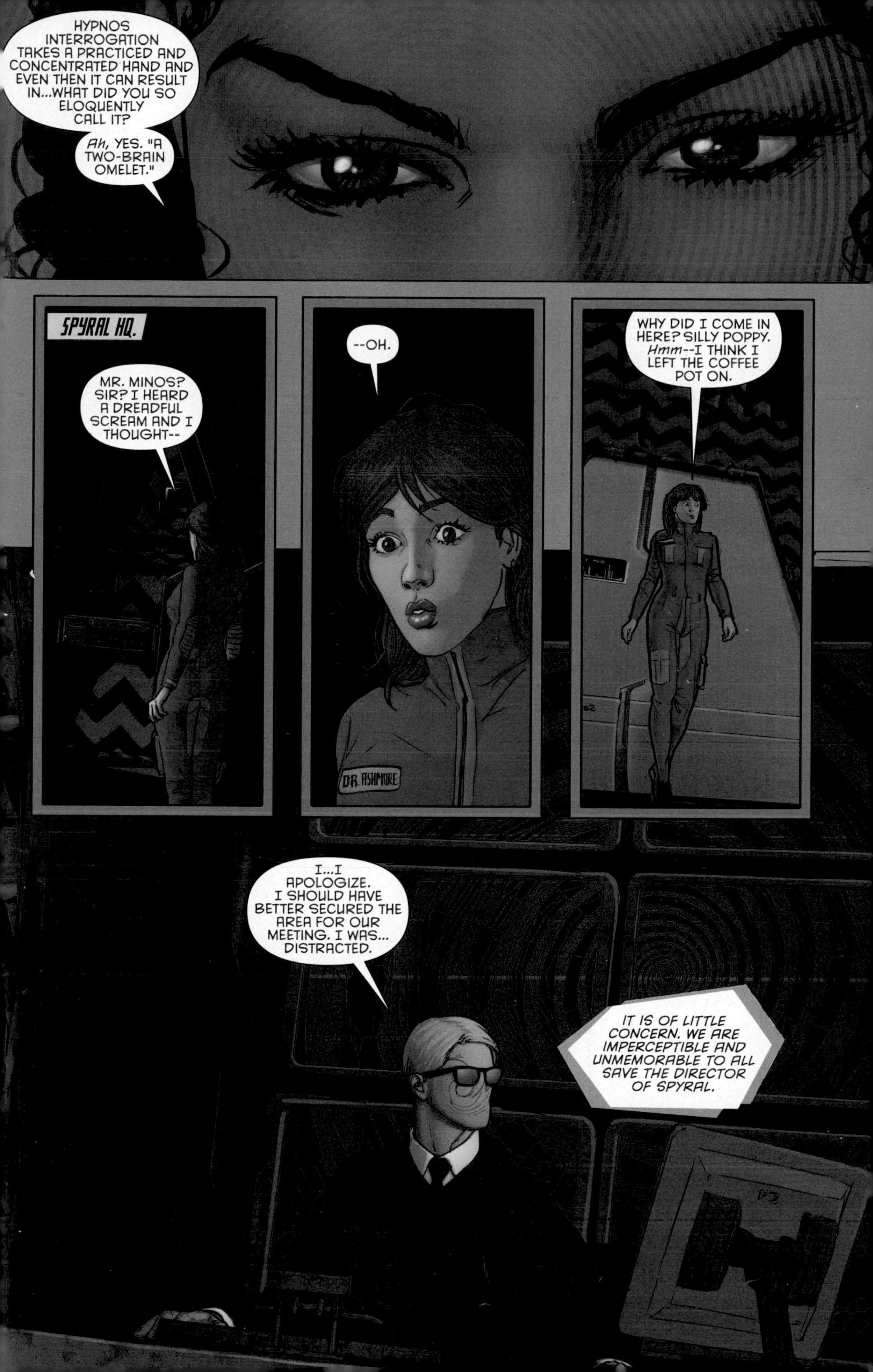
HYPNOS INTERROGATION TAKES A PRACTICED AND CONCENTRATED HAND AND EVEN THEN IT CAN RESULT IN...WHAT DID YOU SO ELOQUENTLY CALL IT?
Ah, YES. "A TWO-BRAIN OMELET."
SPYRAL HQ.
MR. MINOS? SIR? I HEARD A DREADFUL SCREAM AND I THOUGHT--
--OH.
DR. ASHMORE
WHY DID I COME IN HERE? SILLY POPPY. Hmm--I THINK I LEFT THE COFFEE POT ON.
I...I APOLOGIZE. I SHOULD HAVE BETTER SECURED THE AREA FOR OUR MEETING. I WAS... DISTRACTED.
IT IS OF LITTLE CONCERN. WE ARE IMPERCEPTIBLE AND UNMEMORABLE TO ALL SAVE THE DIRECTOR OF SPYRAL.

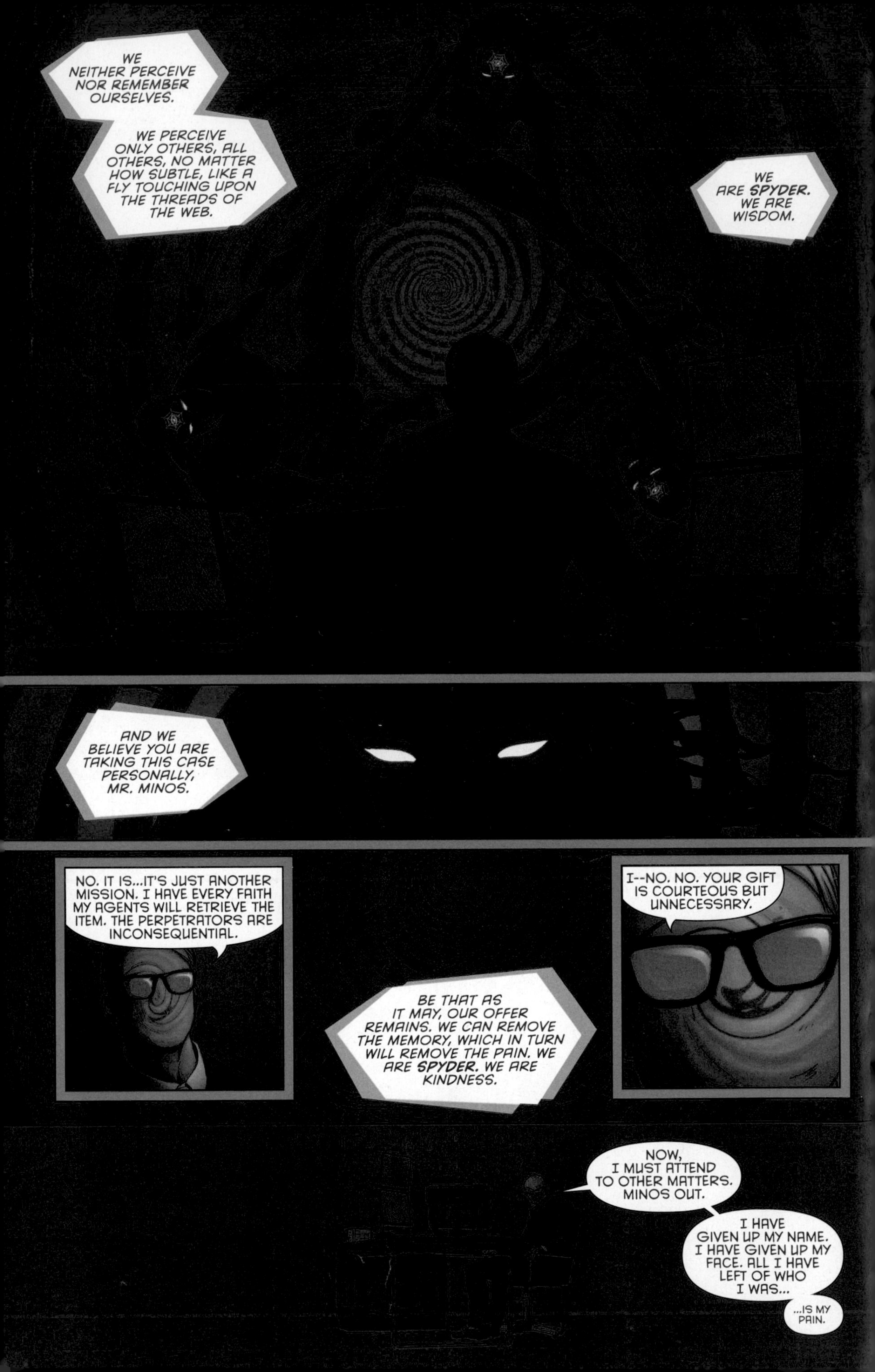
WE NEITHER PERCEIVE NOR REMEMBER OURSELVES.
WE PERCEIVE ONLY OTHERS, ALL OTHERS, NO MATTER HOW SUBTLE, LIKE A FLY TOUCHING UPON THE THREADS OF THE WEB.
WE ARE SPYDER. WE ARE WISDOM.
AND WE BELIEVE YOU ARE TAKING THIS CASE PERSONALLY, MR. MINOS.
NO. IT IS...IT'S JUST ANOTHER MISSION. I HAVE EVERY FAITH MY AGENTS WILL RETRIEVE THE ITEM. THE PERPETRATORS ARE INCONSEQUENTIAL.
BE THAT AS IT MAY, OUR OFFER REMAINS. WE CAN REMOVE THE MEMORY, WHICH IN TURN WILL REMOVE THE PAIN. WE ARE SPYDER. WE ARE KINDNESS.
I--NO. NO. YOUR GIFT IS COURTEOUS BUT UNNECESSARY.
NOW, I MUST ATTEND TO OTHER MATTERS. MINOS OUT.
I HAVE GIVEN UP MY NAME. I HAVE GIVEN UP MY FACE. ALL I HAVE LEFT OF WHO I WAS...
...IS MY PAIN.

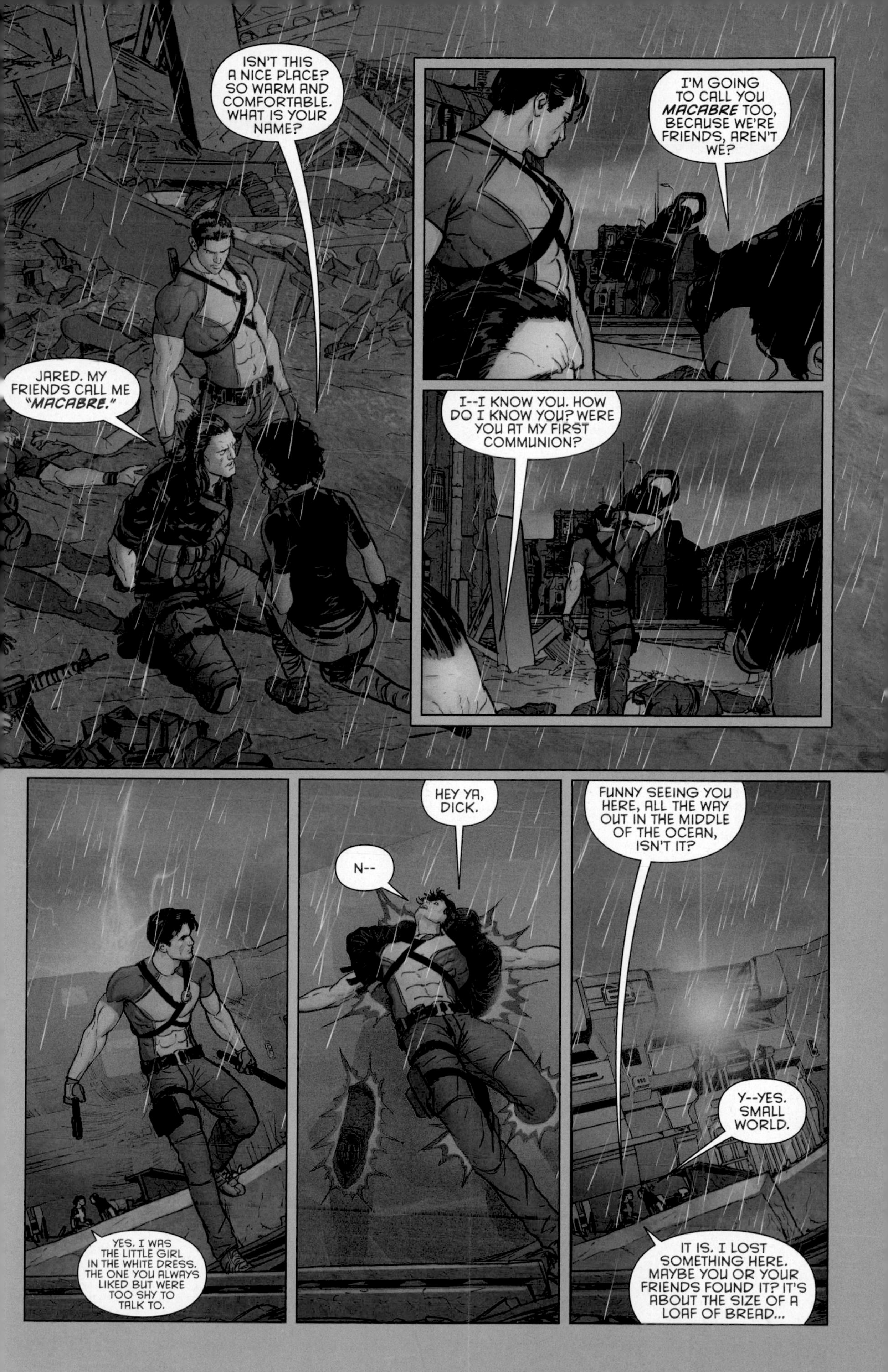
ISN'T THIS A NICE PLACE? SO WARM AND COMFORTABLE. WHAT IS YOUR NAME?
JARED. MY FRIENDS CALL ME "MACABRE."
I'M GOING TO CALL YOU MACABRE TOO, BECAUSE WE'RE FRIENDS, AREN'T WE?
I--I KNOW YOU. HOW DO I KNOW YOU? WERE YOU AT MY FIRST COMMUNION?
YES. I WAS THE LITTLE GIRL IN THE WHITE DRESS. THE ONE YOU ALWAYS LIKED BUT WERE TOO SHY TO TALK TO.
HEY YA, DICK.
N--
FUNNY SEEING YOU HERE, ALL THE WAY OUT IN THE MIDDLE OF THE OCEAN, ISN'T IT?
Y--YES. SMALL WORLD.
IT IS. I LOST SOMETHING HERE. MAYBE YOU OR YOUR FRIENDS FOUND IT? IT'S ABOUT THE SIZE OF A LOAF OF BREAD...

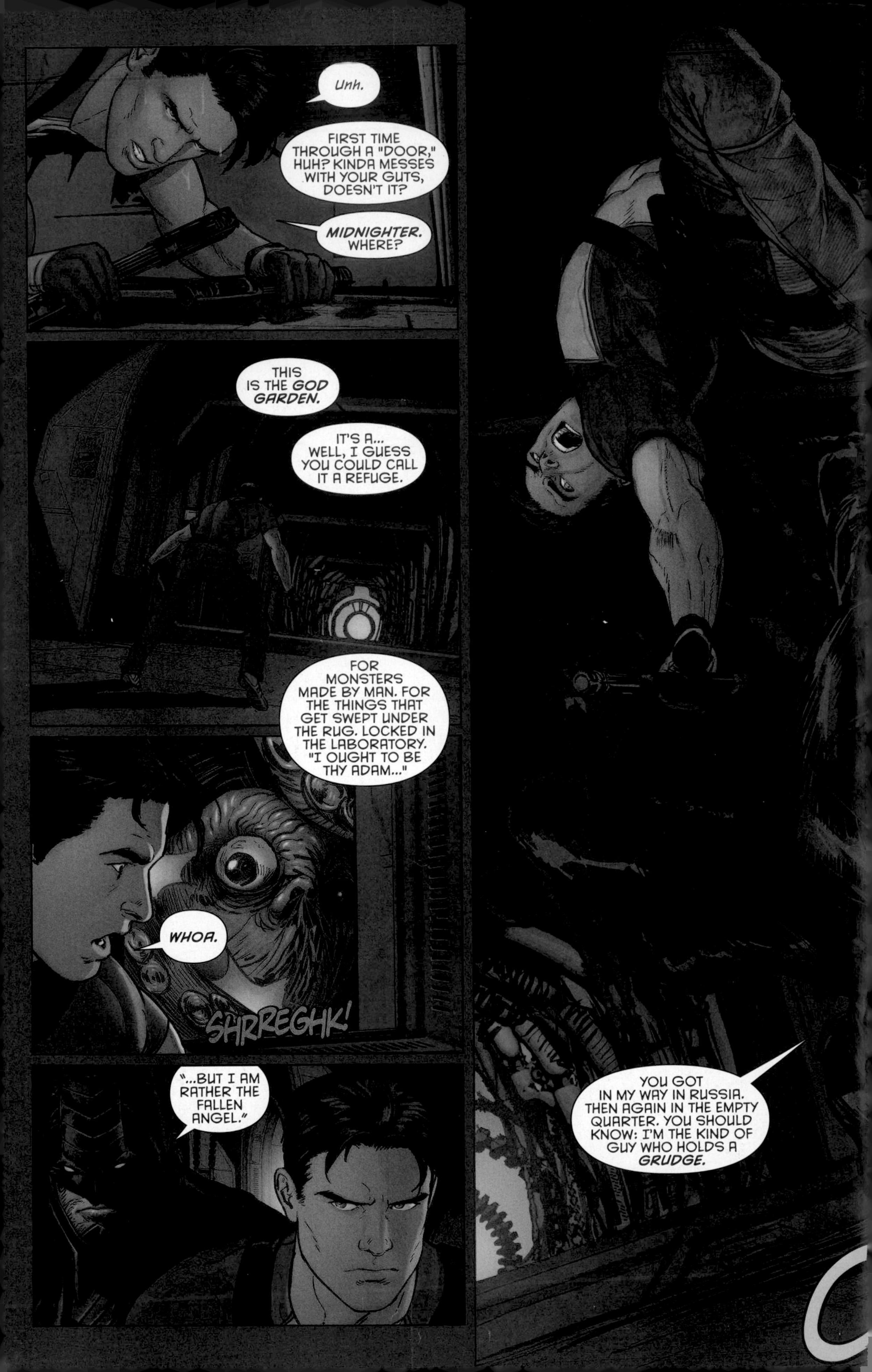
Unh.
FIRST TIME THROUGH A "DOOR," HUH? KINDA MESSES WITH YOUR GUTS, DOESN'T IT?
MIDNIGHTER. WHERE?
THIS IS THE GOD GARDEN.
IT'S A... WELL, I GUESS YOU COULD CALL IT A REFUGE.
FOR MONSTERS MADE BY MAN. FOR THE THINGS THAT GET SWEPT UNDER THE RUG. LOCKED IN THE LABORATORY. "I OUGHT TO BE THY ADAM..."
WHOA.
SHRREGHK!
"...BUT I AM RATHER THE FALLEN ANGEL."
YOU GOT IN MY WAY IN RUSSIA. THEN AGAIN IN THE EMPTY QUARTER. YOU SHOULD KNOW: I'M THE KIND OF GUY WHO HOLDS A GRUDGE.

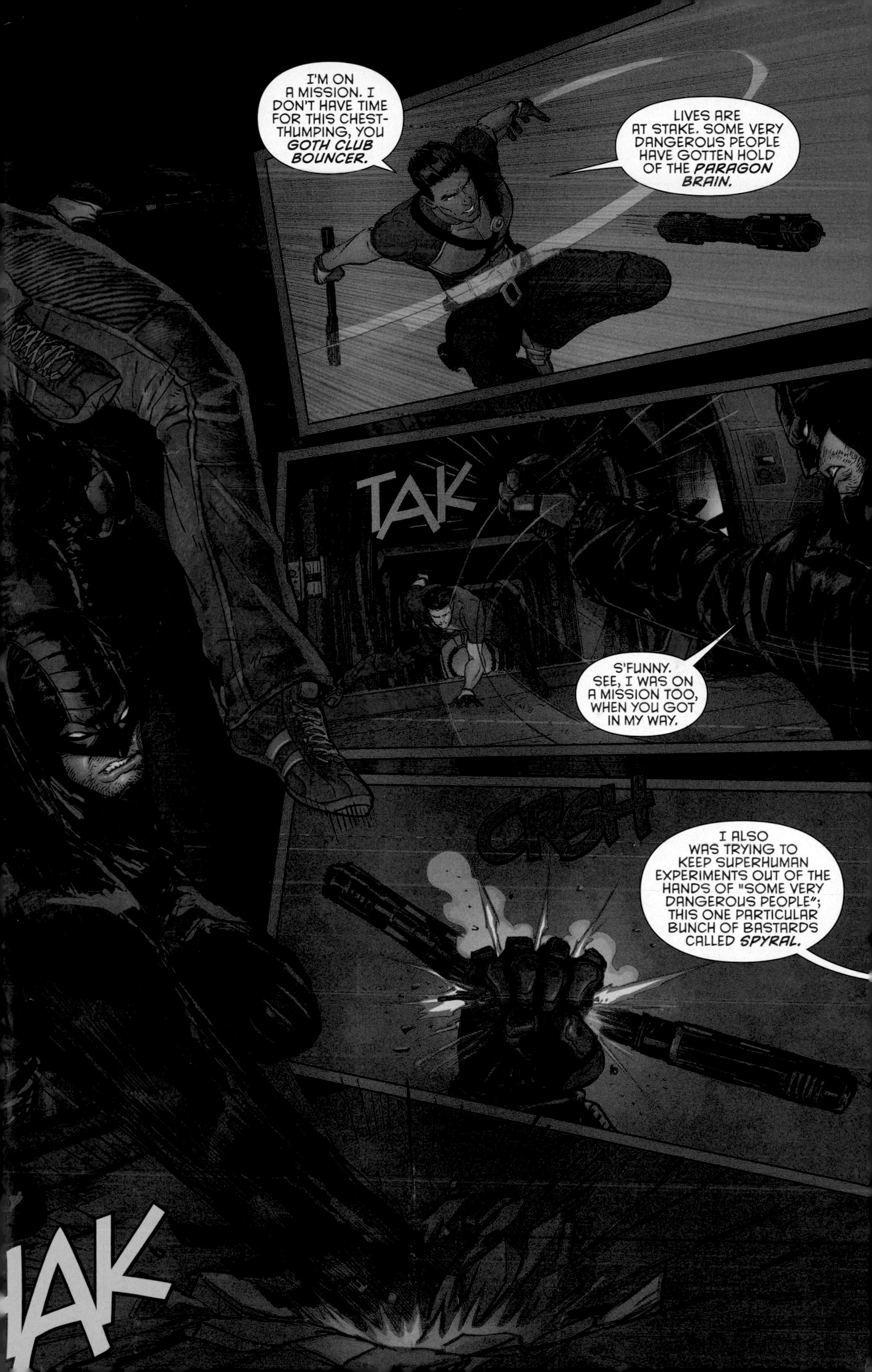
I'M ON A MISSION. I DON'T HAVE TIME FOR THIS CHEST-THUMPING, YOU GOTH CLUB BOUNCER.
LIVES ARE AT STAKE. SOME VERY DANGEROUS PEOPLE HAVE GOTTEN HOLD OF THE PARAGON BRAIN.
TAK
S'FUNNY. SEE, I WAS ON A MISSION TOO, WHEN YOU GOT IN MY WAY.
CRSH
I ALSO WAS TRYING TO KEEP SUPERHUMAN EXPERIMENTS OUT OF THE HANDS OF "SOME VERY DANGEROUS PEOPLE"; THIS ONE PARTICULAR BUNCH OF BASTARDS CALLED SPYRAL.
HAK

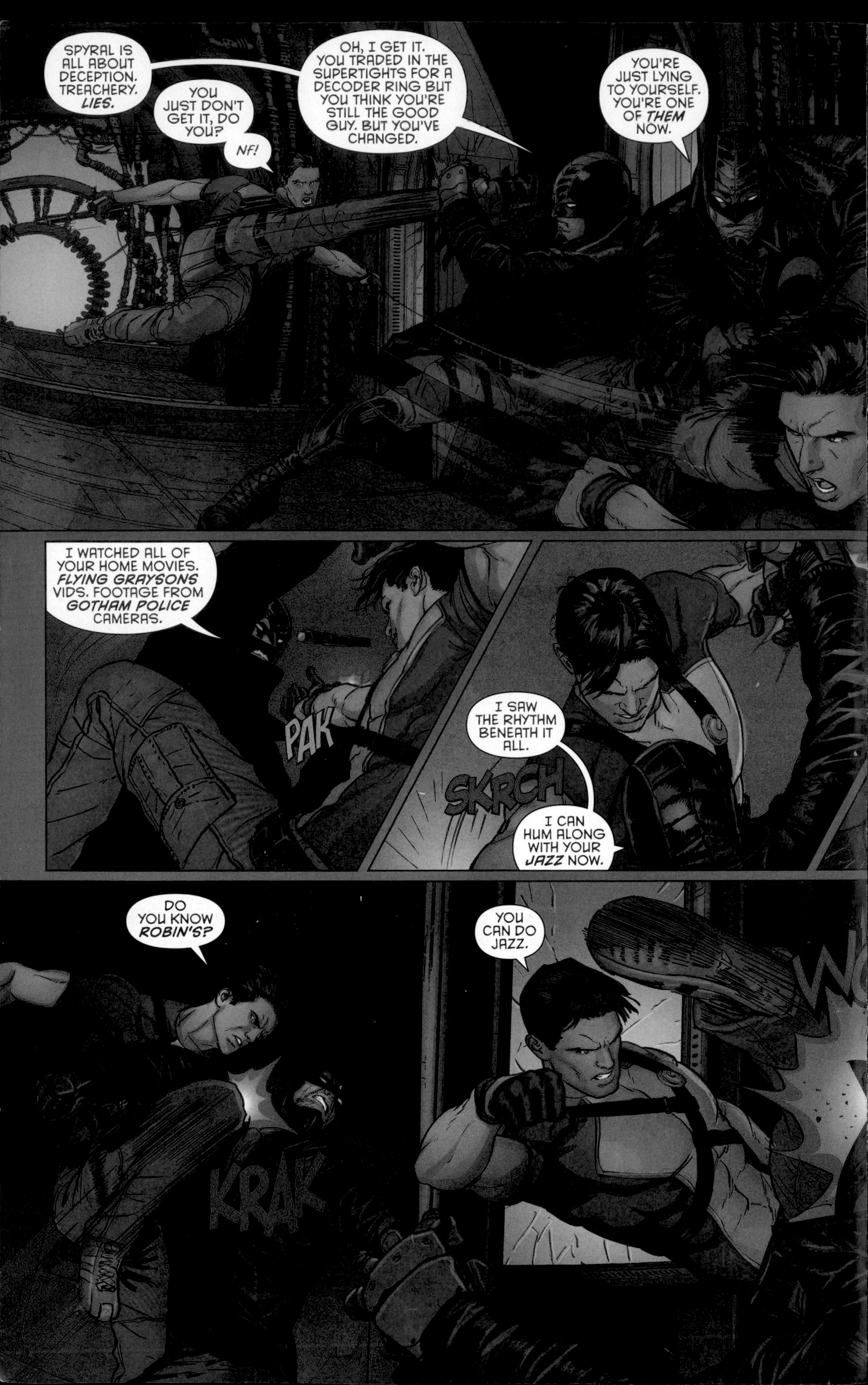
SPYRAL IS ALL ABOUT DECEPTION. TREACHERY. LIES.
YOU JUST DON'T GET IT, DO YOU?
NF!
OH, I GET IT. YOU TRADED IN THE SUPERTIGHTS FOR A DECODER RING BUT YOU THINK YOU'RE STILL THE GOOD GUY. BUT YOU'VE CHANGED.
YOU'RE JUST LYING TO YOURSELF. YOU'RE ONE OF THEM NOW.
I WATCHED ALL OF YOUR HOME MOVIES. FLYING GRAYSONS VIDS. FOOTAGE FROM GOTHAM POLICE CAMERAS.
PAK
I SAW THE RHYTHM BENEATH IT ALL.
SKRCH
I CAN HUM ALONG WITH YOUR JAZZ NOW.
DO YOU KNOW ROBIN'S?
KRAK
YOU CAN DO JAZZ.

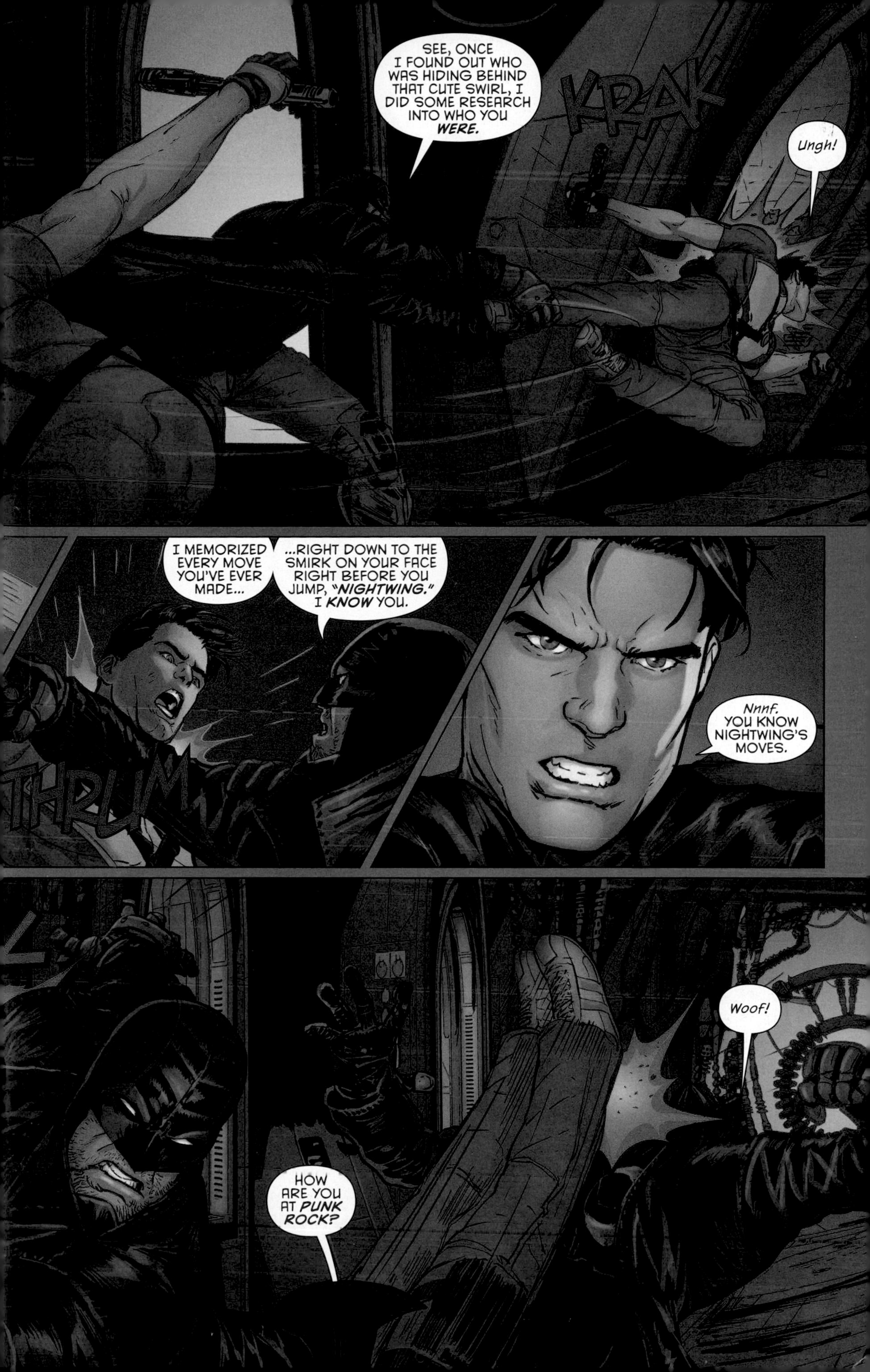
SEE, ONCE I FOUND OUT WHO WAS HIDING BEHIND THAT CUTE SWIRL, I DID SOME RESEARCH INTO WHO YOU *WERE.*
KRAK
Ungh!
I MEMORIZED EVERY MOVE YOU'VE EVER MADE...
...RIGHT DOWN TO THE SMIRK ON YOUR FACE RIGHT BEFORE YOU JUMP, *"NIGHTWING."* I *KNOW* YOU.
THRUM
Nnnf. YOU KNOW NIGHTWING'S MOVES.
Woof!
HOW ARE YOU AT *PUNK ROCK?*

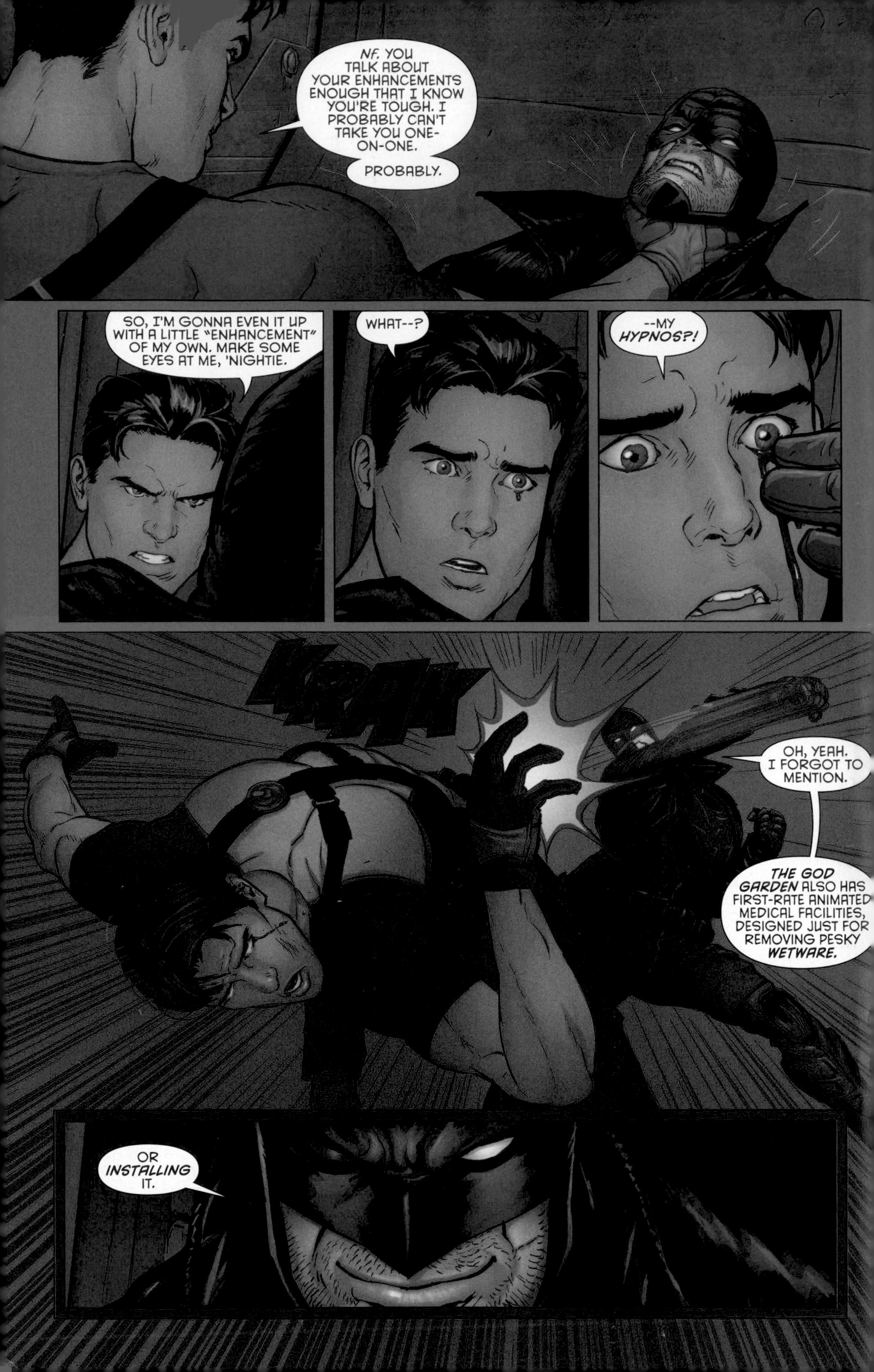
NF, YOU TALK ABOUT YOUR ENHANCEMENTS ENOUGH THAT I KNOW YOU'RE TOUGH. I PROBABLY CAN'T TAKE YOU ONE-ON-ONE.
PROBABLY.
SO, I'M GONNA EVEN IT UP WITH A LITTLE "ENHANCEMENT" OF MY OWN. MAKE SOME EYES AT ME, 'NIGHTIE.
WHAT--?
--MY HYPNOS?!
KRAK
OH, YEAH. I FORGOT TO MENTION.
THE GOD GARDEN ALSO HAS FIRST-RATE ANIMATED MEDICAL FACILITIES, DESIGNED JUST FOR REMOVING PESKY WETWARE.
OR INSTALLING IT.

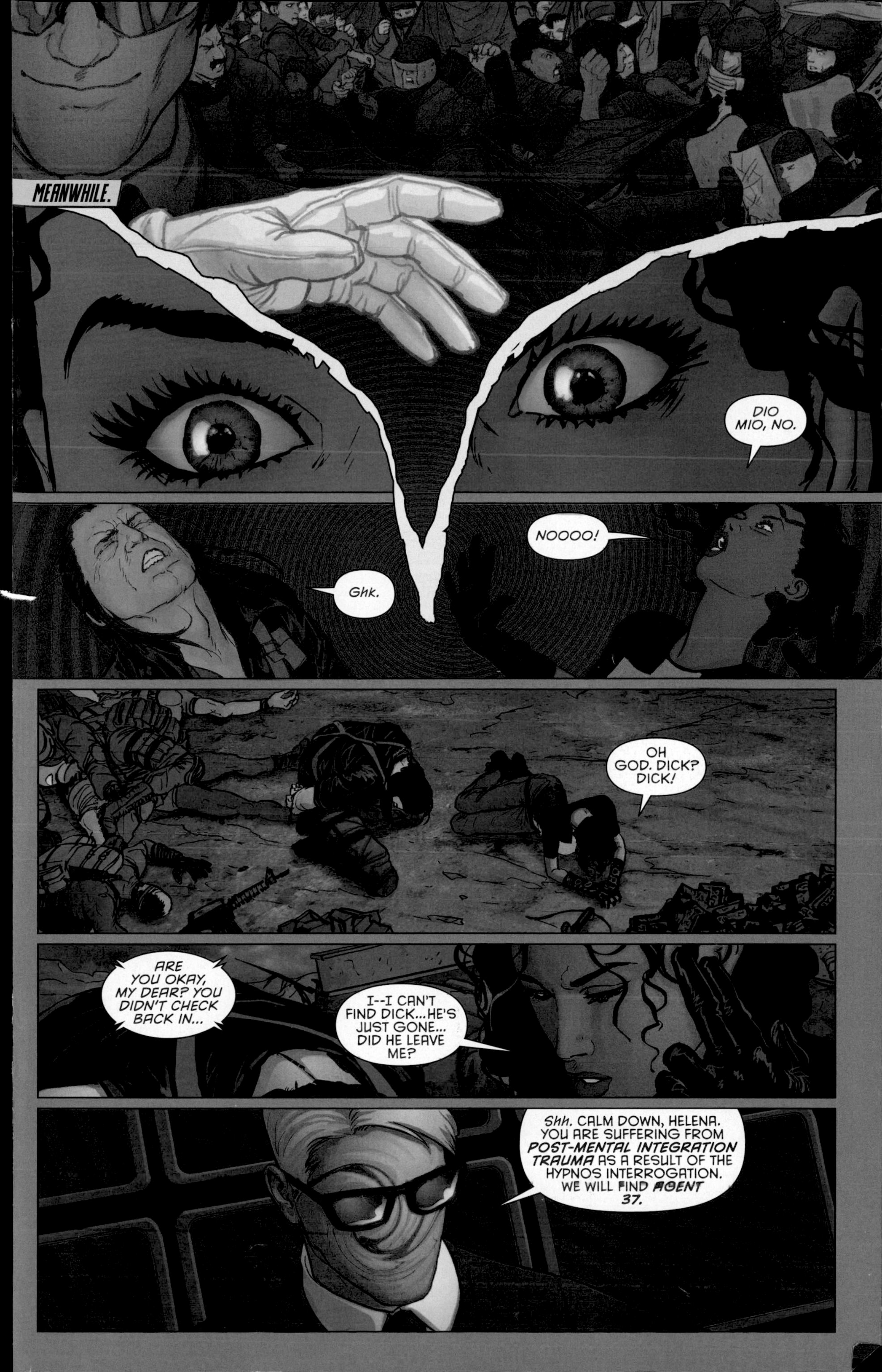

MEANWHILE.
DIO MIO, NO.
NOOOO!
Ghk.
OH GOD. DICK? DICK!
ARE YOU OKAY, MY DEAR? YOU DIDN'T CHECK BACK IN...
I--I CAN'T FIND DICK...HE'S JUST GONE... DID HE LEAVE ME?
Shh. CALM DOWN, HELENA. YOU ARE SUFFERING FROM POST-MENTAL INTEGRATION TRAUMA AS A RESULT OF THE HYPNOS INTERROGATION. WE WILL FIND AGENT 37.

NOW, TELL ME, WHAT HAVE YOU FOUND?

I--I KNOW WHAT THE *FIST OF CAIN* INTENDS TO DO WITH THE *PARAGON BRAIN*...

I SAW...I SAW WHAT THEY WANT. SO VIVID AND RED. SOMEHOW, THEY'RE GOING TO USE THE POWERS OF THE BRAIN...

...THEY'RE GOING TO FILL IT WITH HATE AND ANGER UNTIL IT'S BURSTING...AND THEY'RE GOING TO UNLEASH A PSYCHIC ATTACK AT THE *TEL-AVIV RALLY FOR PEACE.*

Name: MANHUNTER
DNA Identification:
Secret Identity: UNKNOWN
Superhuman Power Set: Telepath/Empath

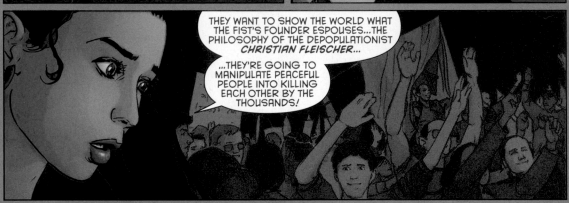

THEY WANT TO SHOW THE WORLD WHAT THE FIST'S FOUNDER ESPOUSES...THE PHILOSOPHY OF THE DEPOPULATIONIST *CHRISTIAN FLEISCHER*...

...THEY'RE GOING TO MANIPULATE PEACEFUL PEOPLE INTO KILLING EACH OTHER BY THE THOUSANDS!

THEY WANT TO SHOW THAT HUMANITY IS JUST AN ANIMAL BACKED INTO A CORNER, PREPARED TO FIGHT FOR SCRAPS.

THEY'RE GOING TO SHOW THE WORLD THAT THERE'S NO LOVE, NO COMPASSION, NO PEACE...

CAIN

"...THERE IS ONLY MURDER."

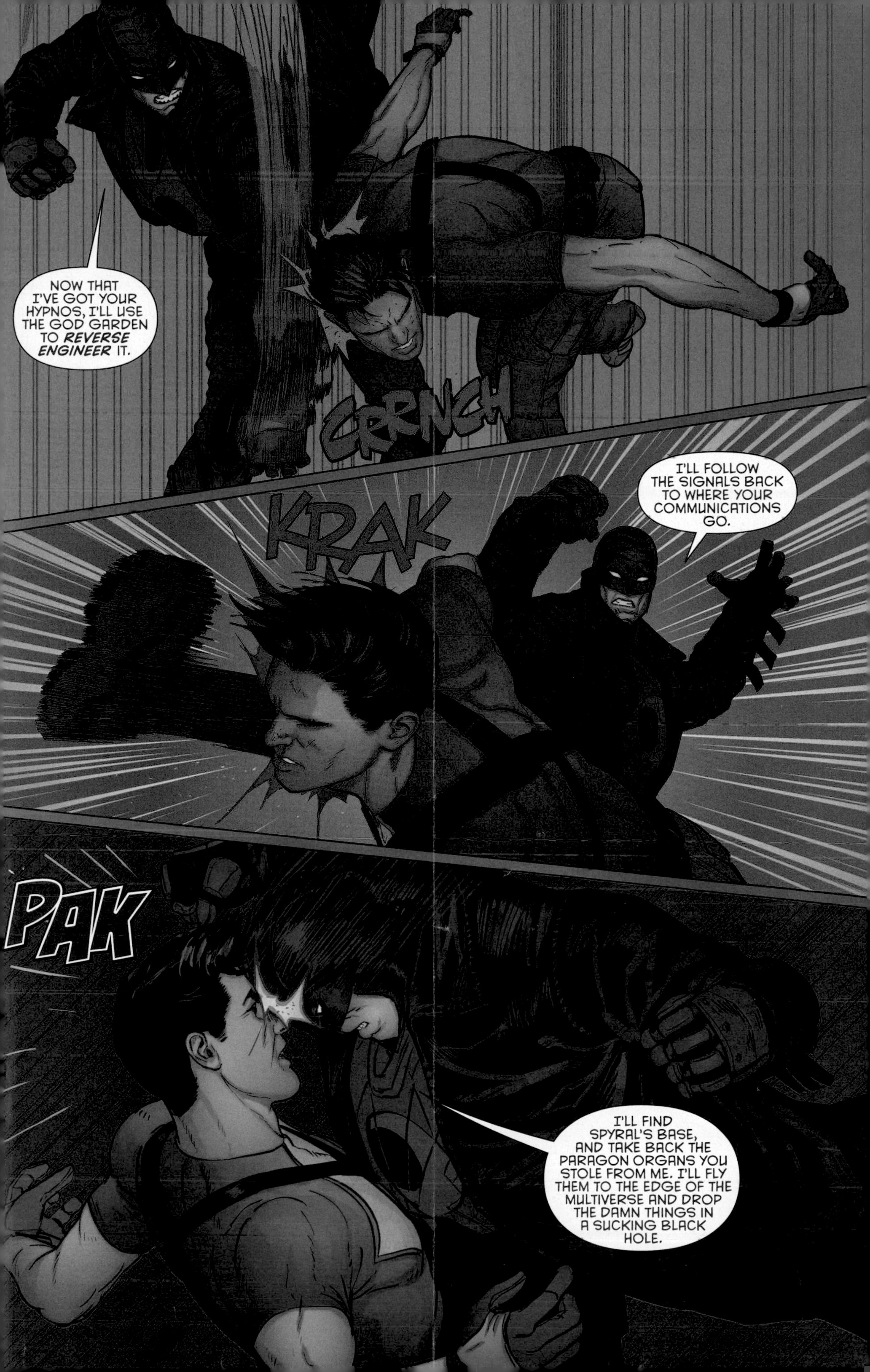
NOW THAT I'VE GOT YOUR HYPNOS, I'LL USE THE GOD GARDEN TO REVERSE ENGINEER IT.
CRRNCH
I'LL FOLLOW THE SIGNALS BACK TO WHERE YOUR COMMUNICATIONS GO.
KRAK
PAK
I'LL FIND SPYRAL'S BASE, AND TAKE BACK THE PARAGON ORGANS YOU STOLE FROM ME. I'LL FLY THEM TO THE EDGE OF THE MULTIVERSE AND DROP THE DAMN THINGS IN A SUCKING BLACK HOLE.

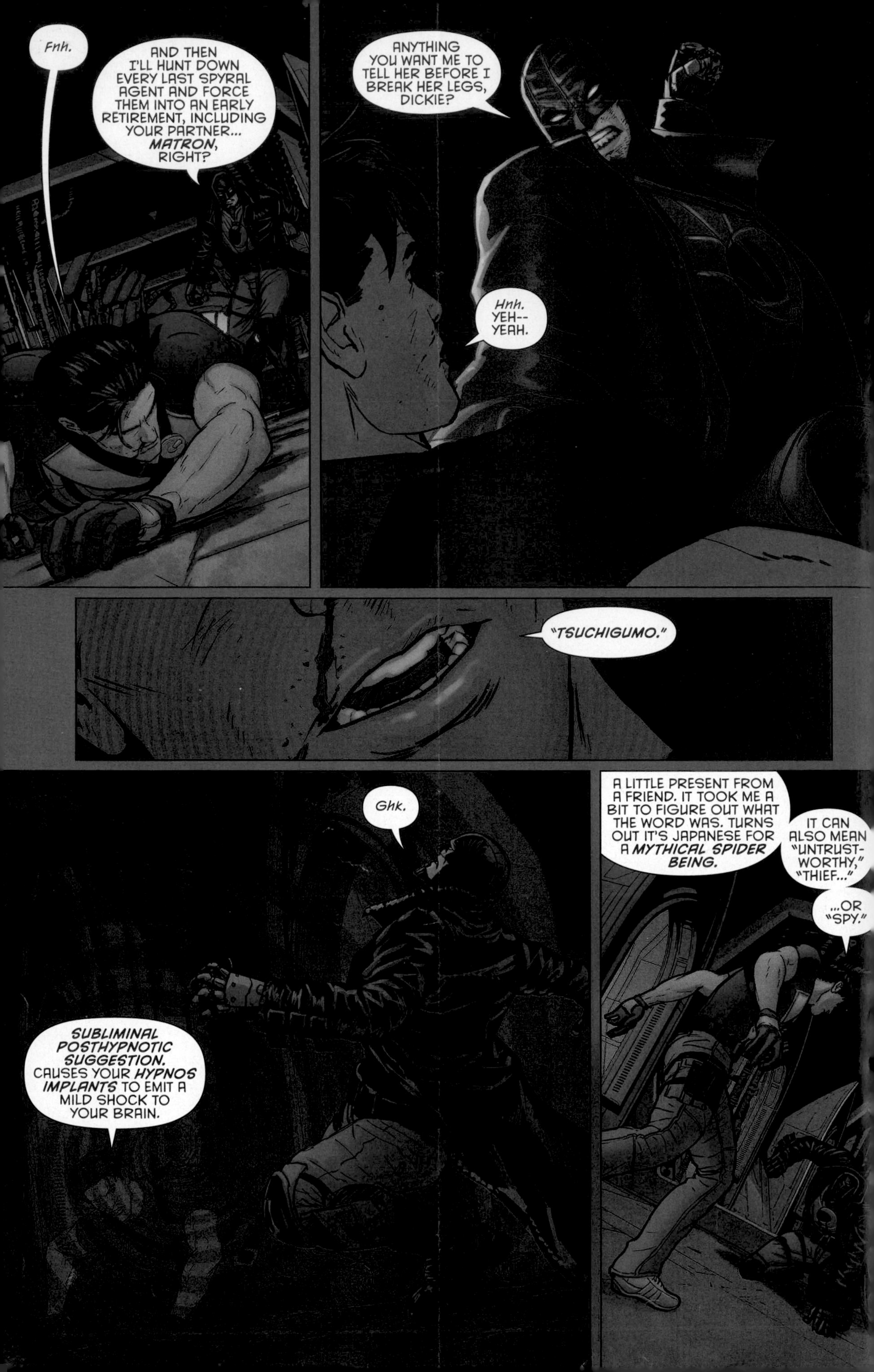
Fnh.
AND THEN I'LL HUNT DOWN EVERY LAST SPYRAL AGENT AND FORCE THEM INTO AN EARLY RETIREMENT, INCLUDING YOUR PARTNER... MATRON, RIGHT?
ANYTHING YOU WANT ME TO TELL HER BEFORE I BREAK HER LEGS, DICKIE?
Hnh. YEH-- YEAH.
"TSUCHIGUMO."
Ghk.
SUBLIMINAL POSTHYPNOTIC SUGGESTION. CAUSES YOUR HYPNOS IMPLANTS TO EMIT A MILD SHOCK TO YOUR BRAIN.
A LITTLE PRESENT FROM A FRIEND. IT TOOK ME A BIT TO FIGURE OUT WHAT THE WORD WAS. TURNS OUT IT'S JAPANESE FOR A MYTHICAL SPIDER BEING.
IT CAN ALSO MEAN "UNTRUST-WORTHY," "THIEF..."
...OR "SPY."

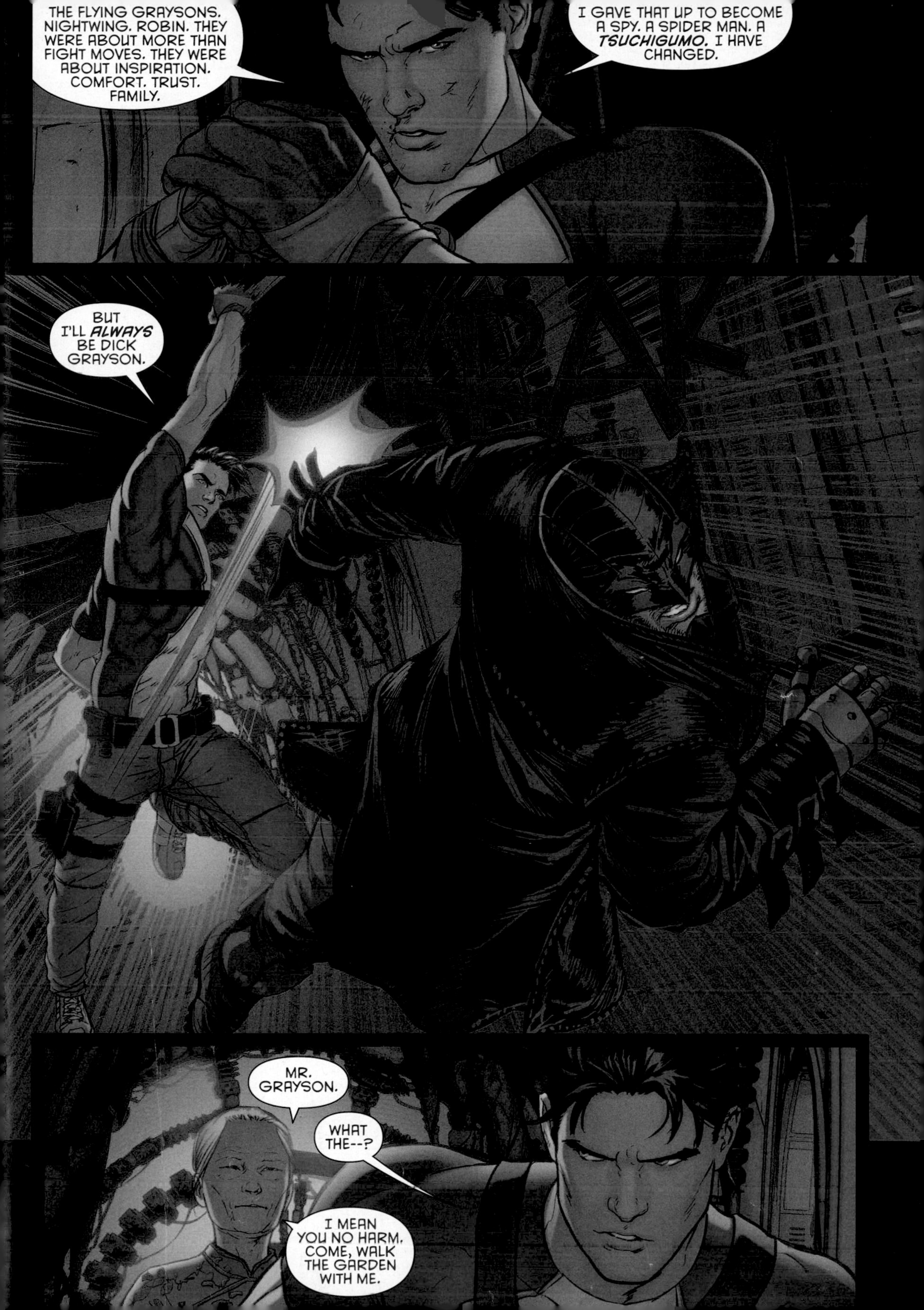
THE FLYING GRAYSONS. NIGHTWING. ROBIN. THEY WERE ABOUT MORE THAN FIGHT MOVES. THEY WERE ABOUT INSPIRATION. COMFORT. TRUST. FAMILY.
I GAVE THAT UP TO BECOME A SPY. A SPIDER MAN. A TSUCHIGUMO. I HAVE CHANGED.
BUT I'LL ALWAYS BE DICK GRAYSON.
MR. GRAYSON.
WHAT THE--?
I MEAN YOU NO HARM. COME, WALK THE GARDEN WITH ME.

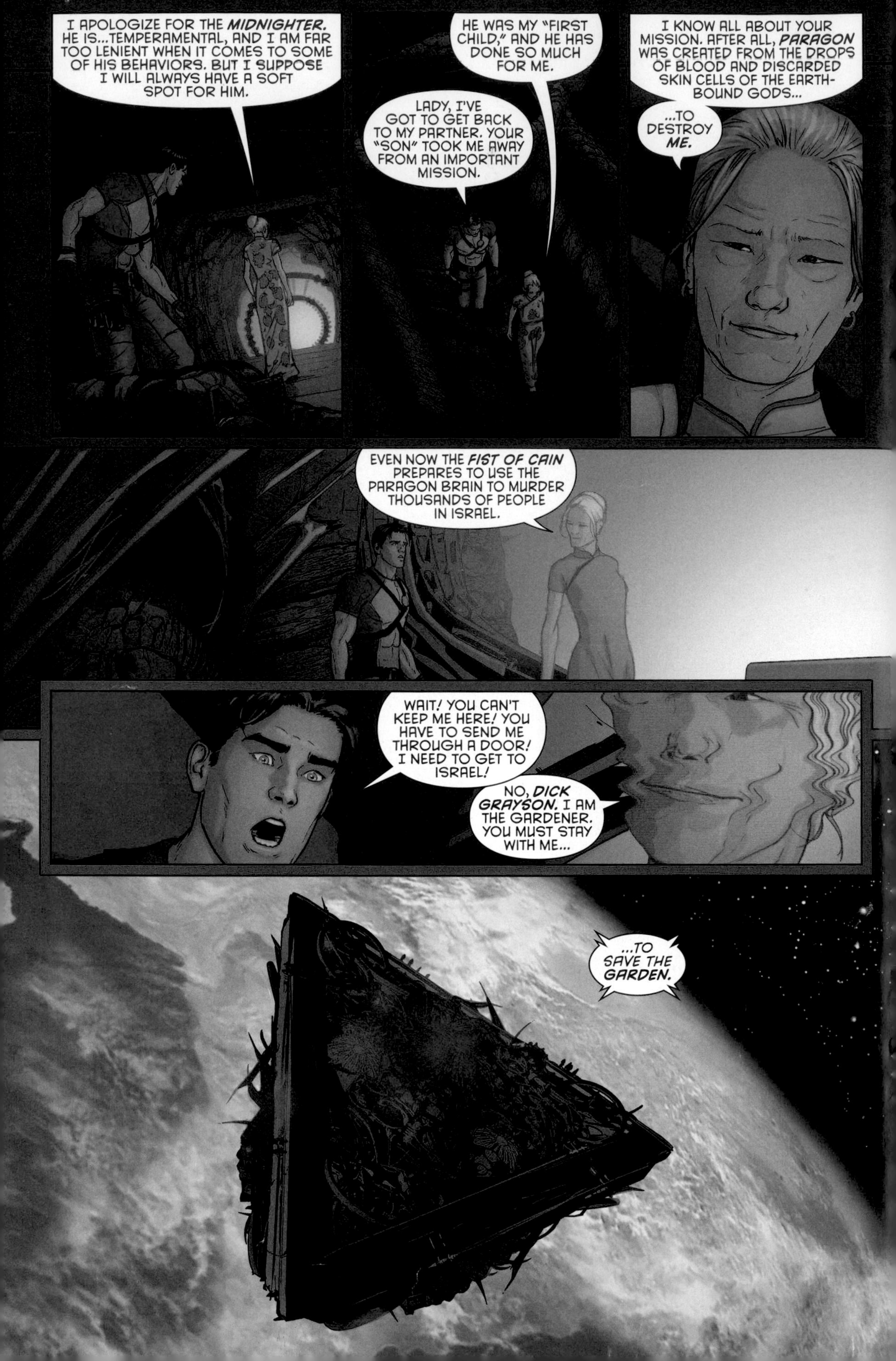
I APOLOGIZE FOR THE MIDNIGHTER. HE IS...TEMPERAMENTAL, AND I AM FAR TOO LENIENT WHEN IT COMES TO SOME OF HIS BEHAVIORS. BUT I SUPPOSE I WILL ALWAYS HAVE A SOFT SPOT FOR HIM.
HE WAS MY "FIRST CHILD," AND HE HAS DONE SO MUCH FOR ME.
LADY, I'VE GOT TO GET BACK TO MY PARTNER. YOUR "SON" TOOK ME AWAY FROM AN IMPORTANT MISSION.
I KNOW ALL ABOUT YOUR MISSION. AFTER ALL, PARAGON WAS CREATED FROM THE DROPS OF BLOOD AND DISCARDED SKIN CELLS OF THE EARTH-BOUND GODS...
...TO DESTROY ME.
EVEN NOW THE FIST OF CAIN PREPARES TO USE THE PARAGON BRAIN TO MURDER THOUSANDS OF PEOPLE IN ISRAEL.
WAIT! YOU CAN'T KEEP ME HERE! YOU HAVE TO SEND ME THROUGH A DOOR! I NEED TO GET TO ISRAEL!
NO, DICK GRAYSON. I AM THE GARDENER. YOU MUST STAY WITH ME...
...TO SAVE THE GARDEN.

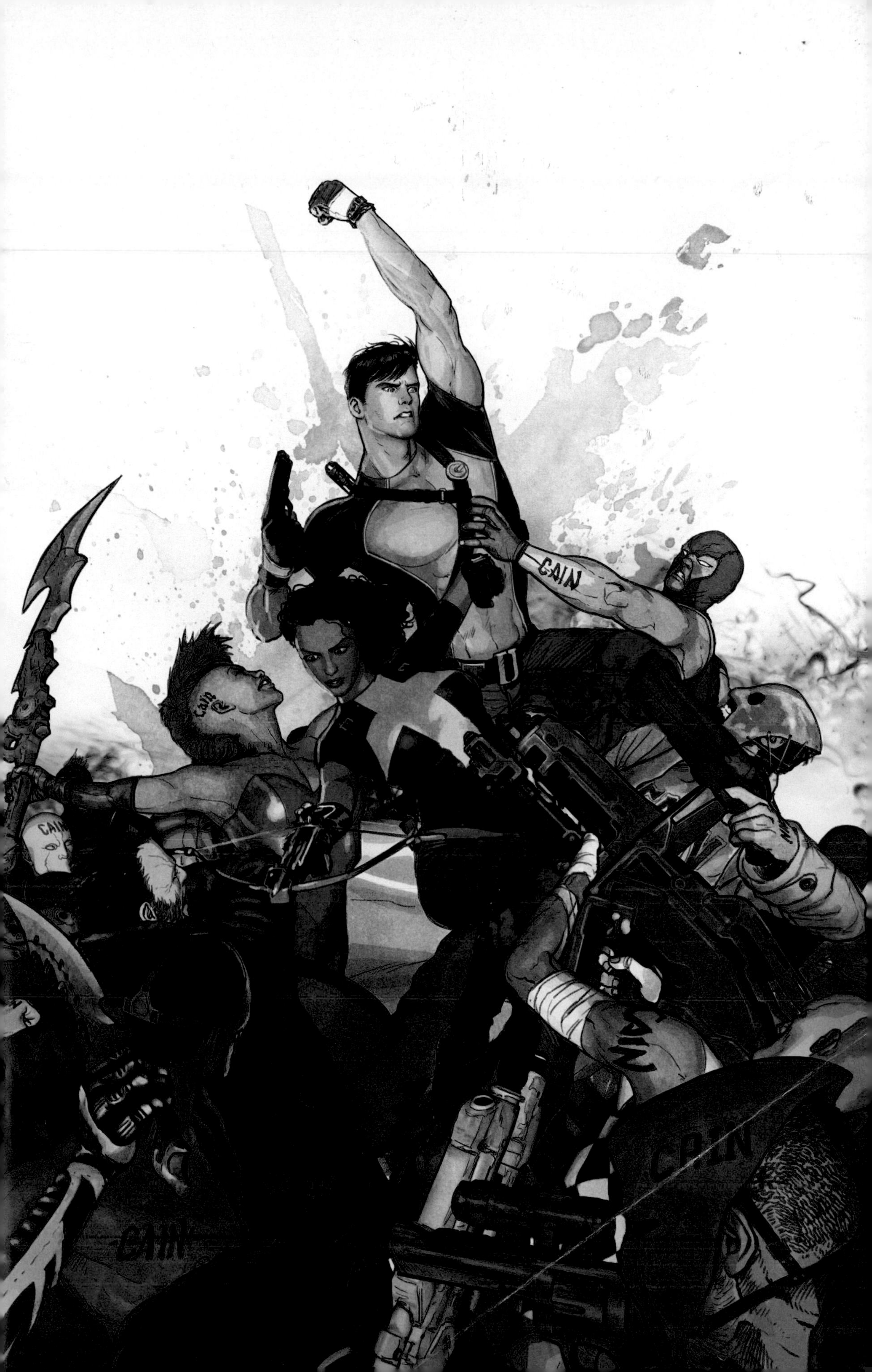

CAIN

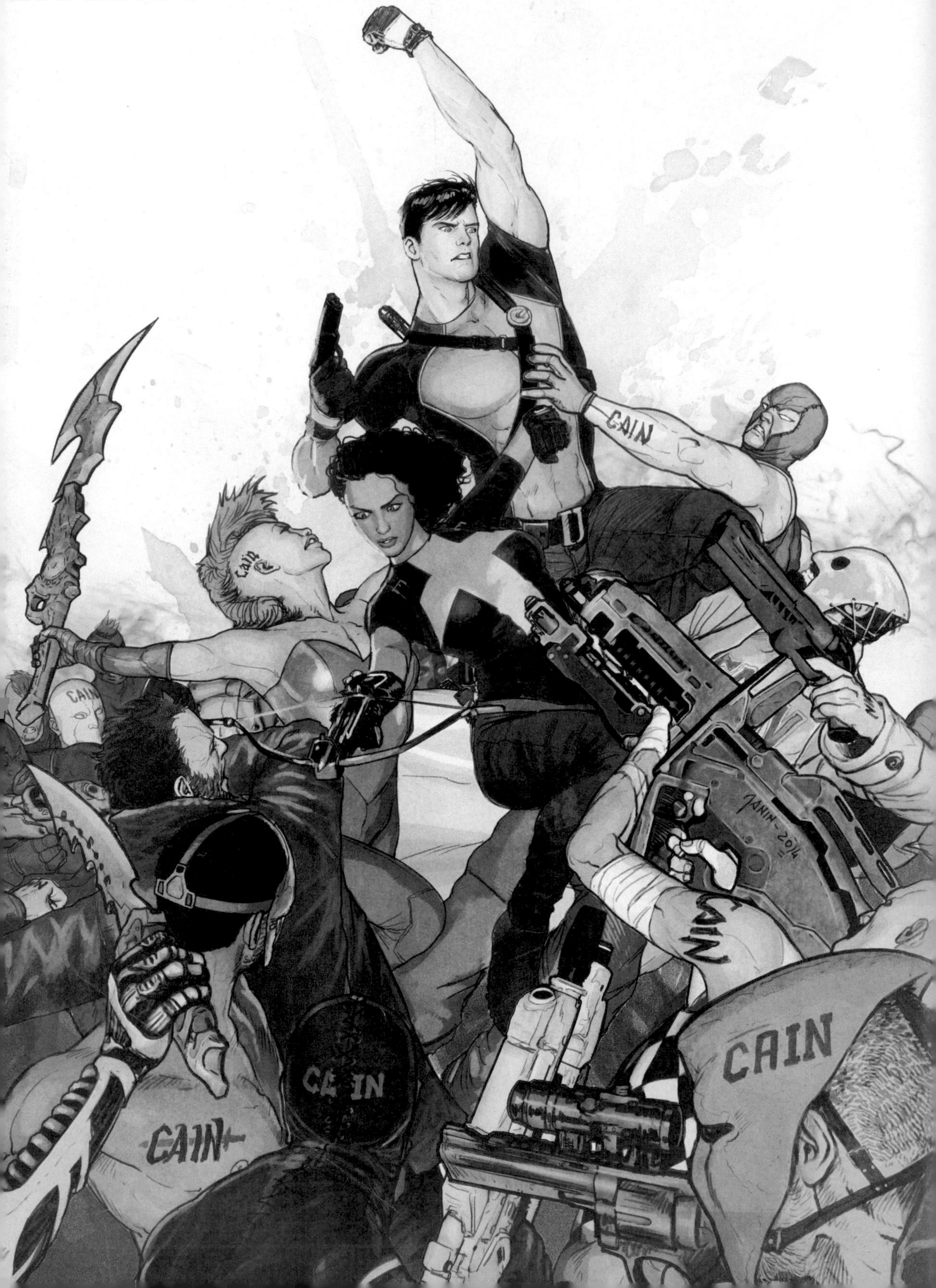

CAIN
Cain
CAIN
JANIN - 2014
CAIN
CAIN
CAIN
CAIN

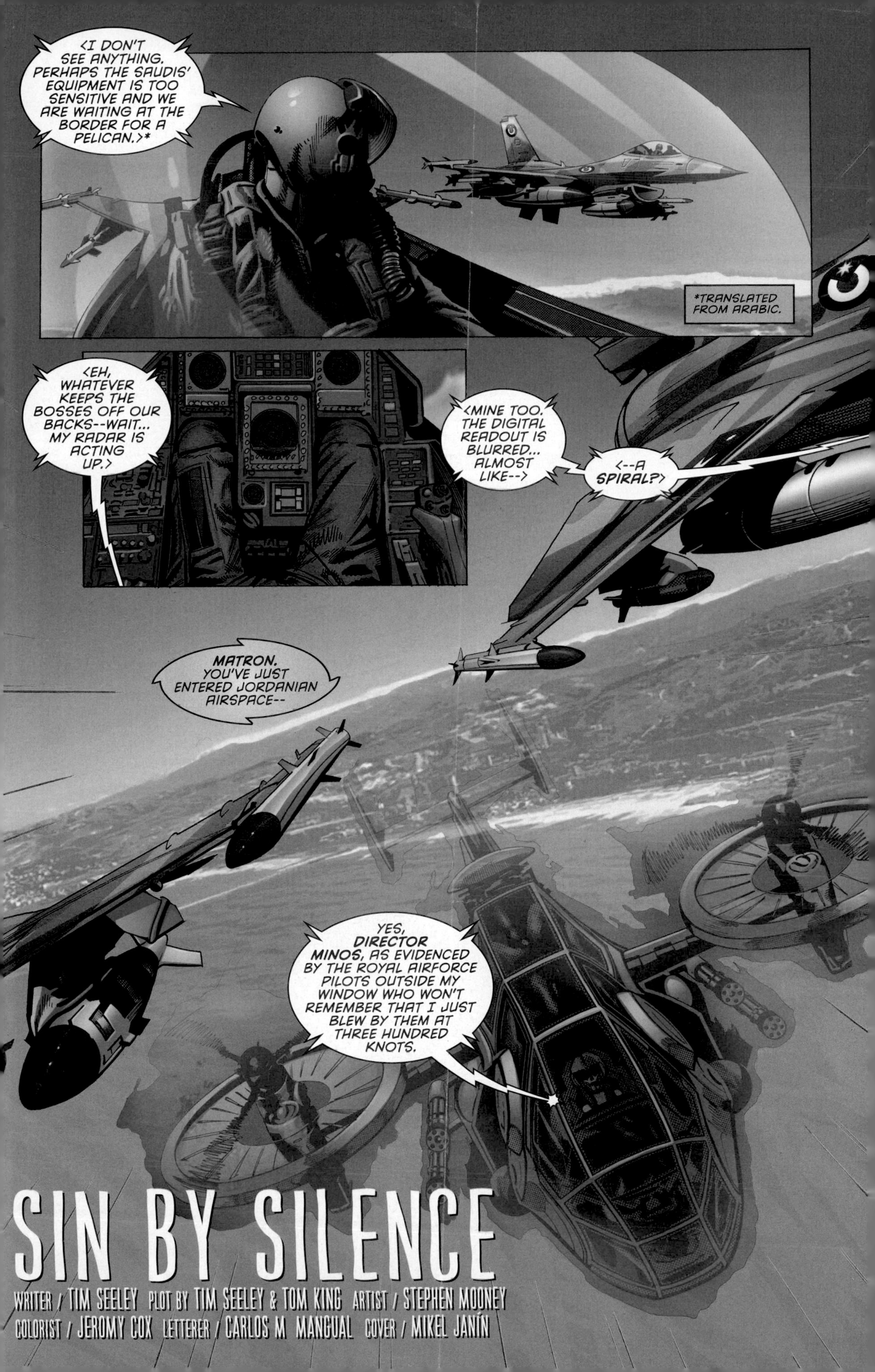
<I DON'T SEE ANYTHING. PERHAPS THE SAUDIS' EQUIPMENT IS TOO SENSITIVE AND WE ARE WAITING AT THE BORDER FOR A PELICAN.>*
*TRANSLATED FROM ARABIC.
<EH, WHATEVER KEEPS THE BOSSES OFF OUR BACKS--WAIT... MY RADAR IS ACTING UP.>
<MINE TOO. THE DIGITAL READOUT IS BLURRED... ALMOST LIKE-->
<--A SPIRAL?>
MATRON. YOU'VE JUST ENTERED JORDANIAN AIRSPACE--
YES, DIRECTOR MINOS, AS EVIDENCED BY THE ROYAL AIRFORCE PILOTS OUTSIDE MY WINDOW WHO WON'T REMEMBER THAT I JUST BLEW BY THEM AT THREE HUNDRED KNOTS.
SIN BY SILENCE
WRITER / TIM SEELEY PLOT BY TIM SEELEY & TOM KING ARTIST / STEPHEN MOONEY
COLORIST / JEROMY COX LETTERER / CARLOS M MANGUAL COVER / MIKEL JANÍN

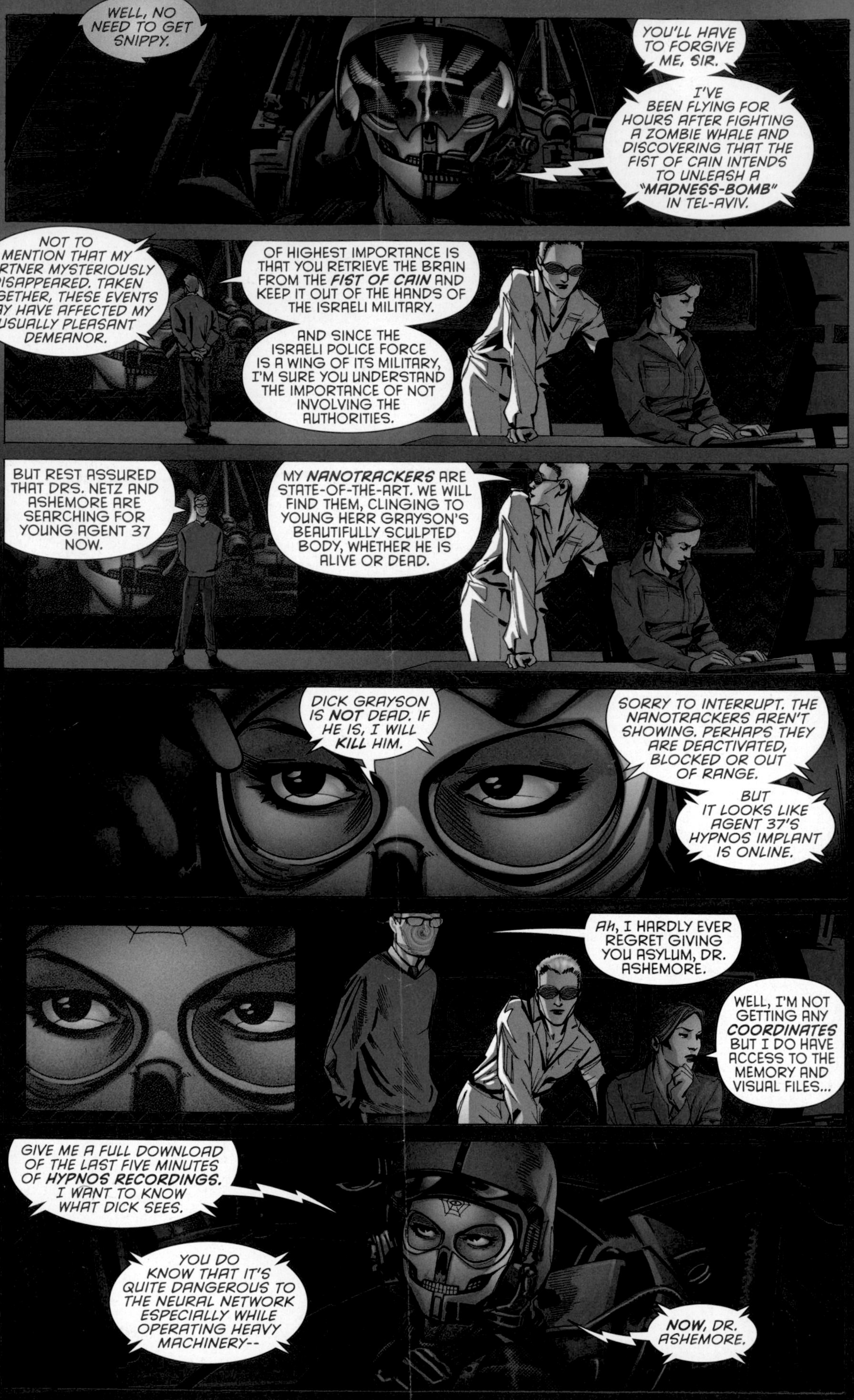
WELL, NO NEED TO GET SNIPPY.
YOU'LL HAVE TO FORGIVE ME, SIR.
I'VE BEEN FLYING FOR HOURS AFTER FIGHTING A ZOMBIE WHALE AND DISCOVERING THAT THE FIST OF CAIN INTENDS TO UNLEASH A "MADNESS-BOMB" IN TEL-AVIV.
NOT TO MENTION THAT MY PARTNER MYSTERIOUSLY DISAPPEARED. TAKEN TOGETHER, THESE EVENTS MAY HAVE AFFECTED MY USUALLY PLEASANT DEMEANOR.
OF HIGHEST IMPORTANCE IS THAT YOU RETRIEVE THE BRAIN FROM THE FIST OF CAIN AND KEEP IT OUT OF THE HANDS OF THE ISRAELI MILITARY.
AND SINCE THE ISRAELI POLICE FORCE IS A WING OF ITS MILITARY, I'M SURE YOU UNDERSTAND THE IMPORTANCE OF NOT INVOLVING THE AUTHORITIES.
BUT REST ASSURED THAT DRS. NETZ AND ASHEMORE ARE SEARCHING FOR YOUNG AGENT 37 NOW.
MY NANOTRACKERS ARE STATE-OF-THE-ART. WE WILL FIND THEM, CLINGING TO YOUNG HERR GRAYSON'S BEAUTIFULLY SCULPTED BODY, WHETHER HE IS ALIVE OR DEAD.
DICK GRAYSON IS NOT DEAD. IF HE IS, I WILL KILL HIM.
SORRY TO INTERRUPT. THE NANOTRACKERS AREN'T SHOWING. PERHAPS THEY ARE DEACTIVATED, BLOCKED OR OUT OF RANGE.
BUT IT LOOKS LIKE AGENT 37'S HYPNOS IMPLANT IS ONLINE.
Ah, I HARDLY EVER REGRET GIVING YOU ASYLUM, DR. ASHEMORE.
WELL, I'M NOT GETTING ANY COORDINATES BUT I DO HAVE ACCESS TO THE MEMORY AND VISUAL FILES...
GIVE ME A FULL DOWNLOAD OF THE LAST FIVE MINUTES OF HYPNOS RECORDINGS. I WANT TO KNOW WHAT DICK SEES.
YOU DO KNOW THAT IT'S QUITE DANGEROUS TO THE NEURAL NETWORK ESPECIALLY WHILE OPERATING HEAVY MACHINERY--
NOW, DR. ASHEMORE.

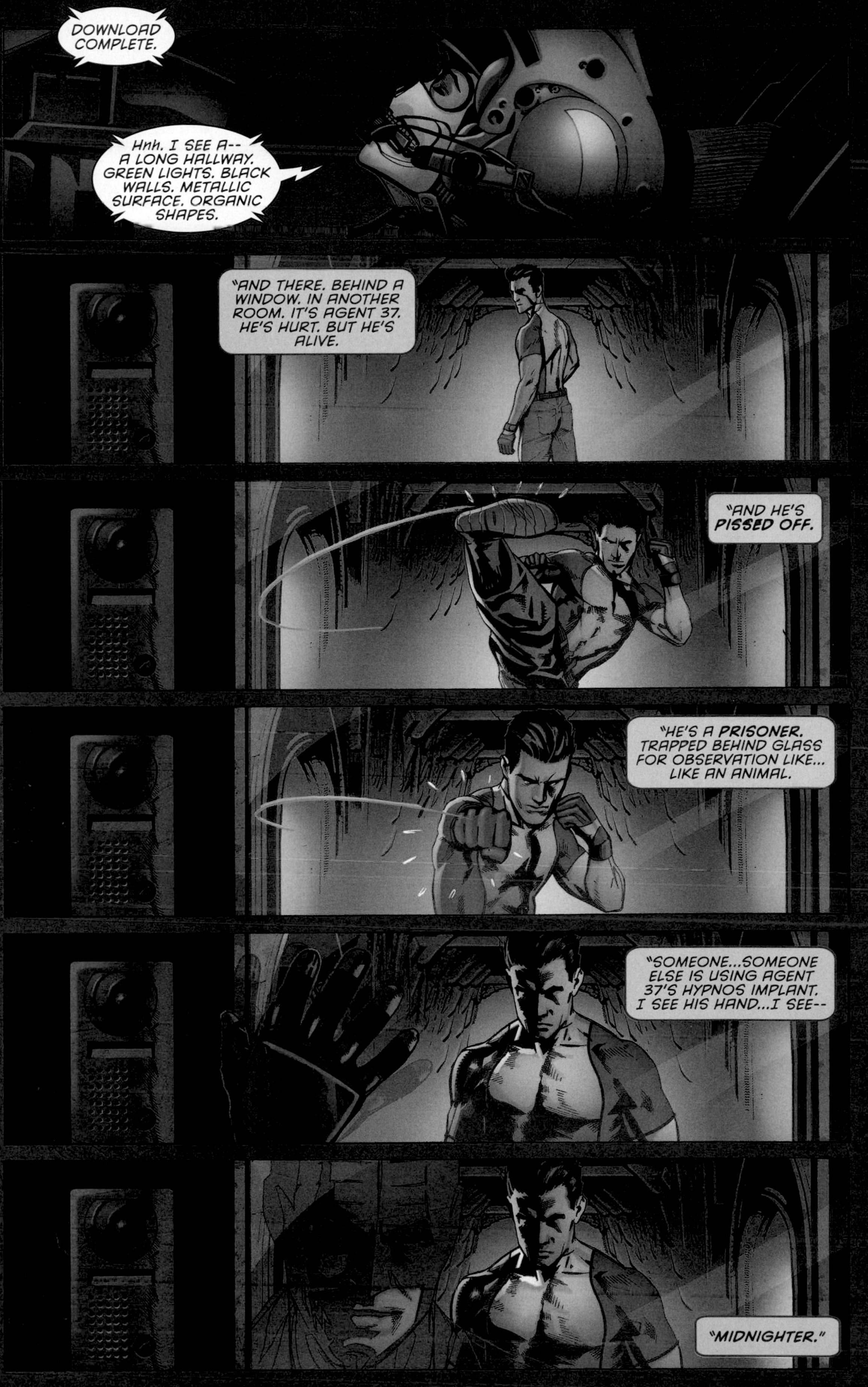
DOWNLOAD COMPLETE.
Hnh. I SEE A-- A LONG HALLWAY. GREEN LIGHTS. BLACK WALLS. METALLIC SURFACE. ORGANIC SHAPES.
"AND THERE. BEHIND A WINDOW. IN ANOTHER ROOM. IT'S AGENT 37. HE'S HURT. BUT HE'S ALIVE.
"AND HE'S PISSED OFF.
"HE'S A PRISONER. TRAPPED BEHIND GLASS FOR OBSERVATION LIKE... LIKE AN ANIMAL.
"SOMEONE...SOMEONE ELSE IS USING AGENT 37'S HYPNOS IMPLANT. I SEE HIS HAND...I SEE--
"MIDNIGHTER."

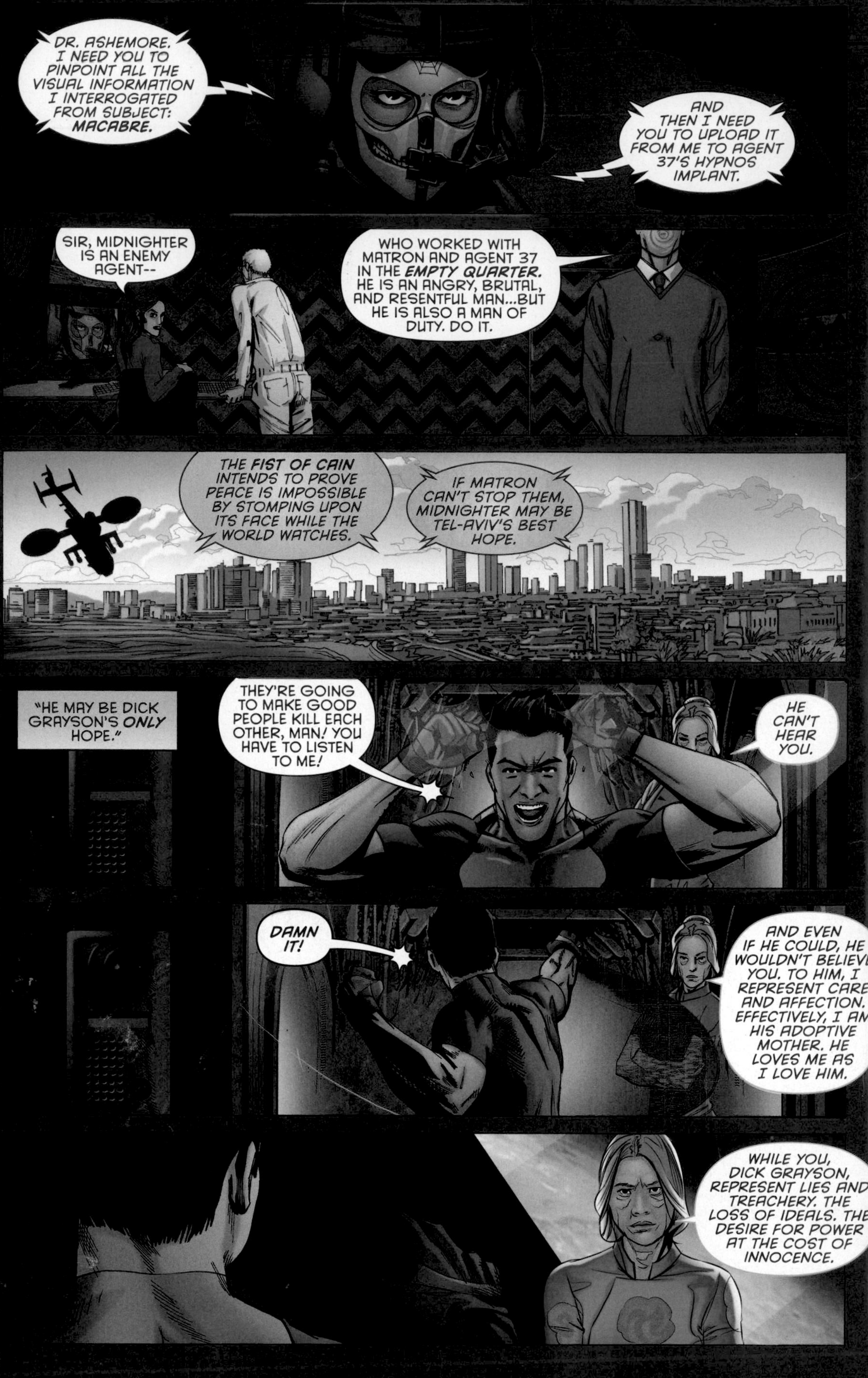
DR. ASHEMORE. I NEED YOU TO PINPOINT ALL THE VISUAL INFORMATION I INTERROGATED FROM SUBJECT: MACABRE.
AND THEN I NEED YOU TO UPLOAD IT FROM ME TO AGENT 37'S HYPNOS IMPLANT.
SIR, MIDNIGHTER IS AN ENEMY AGENT--
WHO WORKED WITH MATRON AND AGENT 37 IN THE EMPTY QUARTER. HE IS AN ANGRY, BRUTAL, AND RESENTFUL MAN...BUT HE IS ALSO A MAN OF DUTY. DO IT.
THE FIST OF CAIN INTENDS TO PROVE PEACE IS IMPOSSIBLE BY STOMPING UPON ITS FACE WHILE THE WORLD WATCHES.
IF MATRON CAN'T STOP THEM, MIDNIGHTER MAY BE TEL-AVIV'S BEST HOPE.
"HE MAY BE DICK GRAYSON'S ONLY HOPE."
THEY'RE GOING TO MAKE GOOD PEOPLE KILL EACH OTHER, MAN! YOU HAVE TO LISTEN TO ME!
HE CAN'T HEAR YOU.
DAMN IT!
AND EVEN IF HE COULD, HE WOULDN'T BELIEVE YOU. TO HIM, I REPRESENT CARE AND AFFECTION. EFFECTIVELY, I AM HIS ADOPTIVE MOTHER. HE LOVES ME AS I LOVE HIM.
WHILE YOU, DICK GRAYSON, REPRESENT LIES AND TREACHERY. THE LOSS OF IDEALS. THE DESIRE FOR POWER AT THE COST OF INNOCENCE.

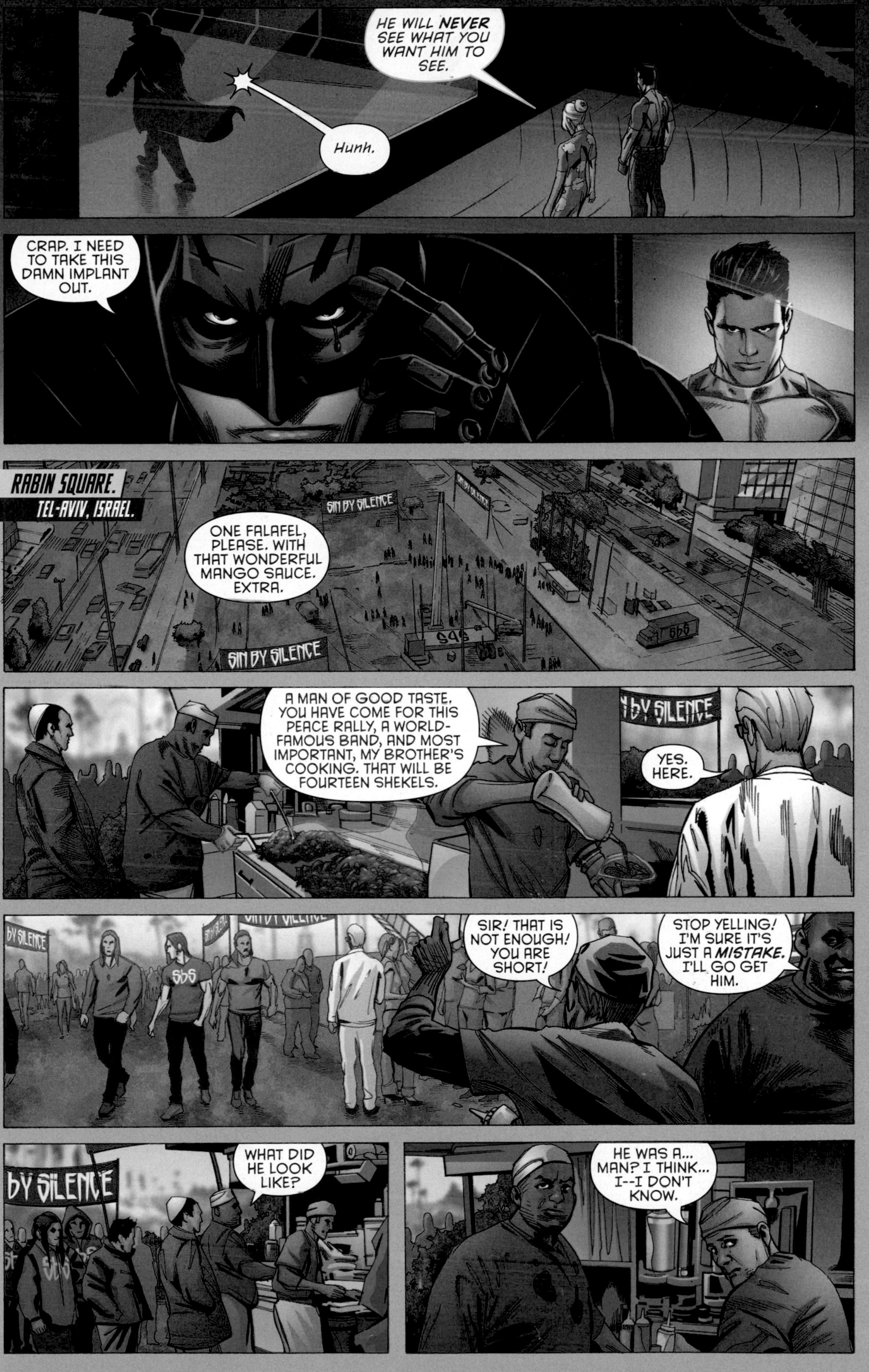

HE WILL NEVER SEE WHAT YOU WANT HIM TO SEE.
Hunh.
CRAP. I NEED TO TAKE THIS DAMN IMPLANT OUT.
RABIN SQUARE.
TEL-AVIV, ISRAEL.
SIN BY SILENCE
SIN BY SILENCE
ONE FALAFEL, PLEASE. WITH THAT WONDERFUL MANGO SAUCE. EXTRA.
SIN BY SILENCE
A MAN OF GOOD TASTE. YOU HAVE COME FOR THIS PEACE RALLY, A WORLD-FAMOUS BAND, AND MOST IMPORTANT, MY BROTHER'S COOKING. THAT WILL BE FOURTEEN SHEKELS.
YES. HERE.
SIR! THAT IS NOT ENOUGH! YOU ARE SHORT!
STOP YELLING! I'M SURE IT'S JUST A MISTAKE. I'LL GO GET HIM.
WHAT DID HE LOOK LIKE?
HE WAS A... MAN? I THINK... I--I DON'T KNOW.

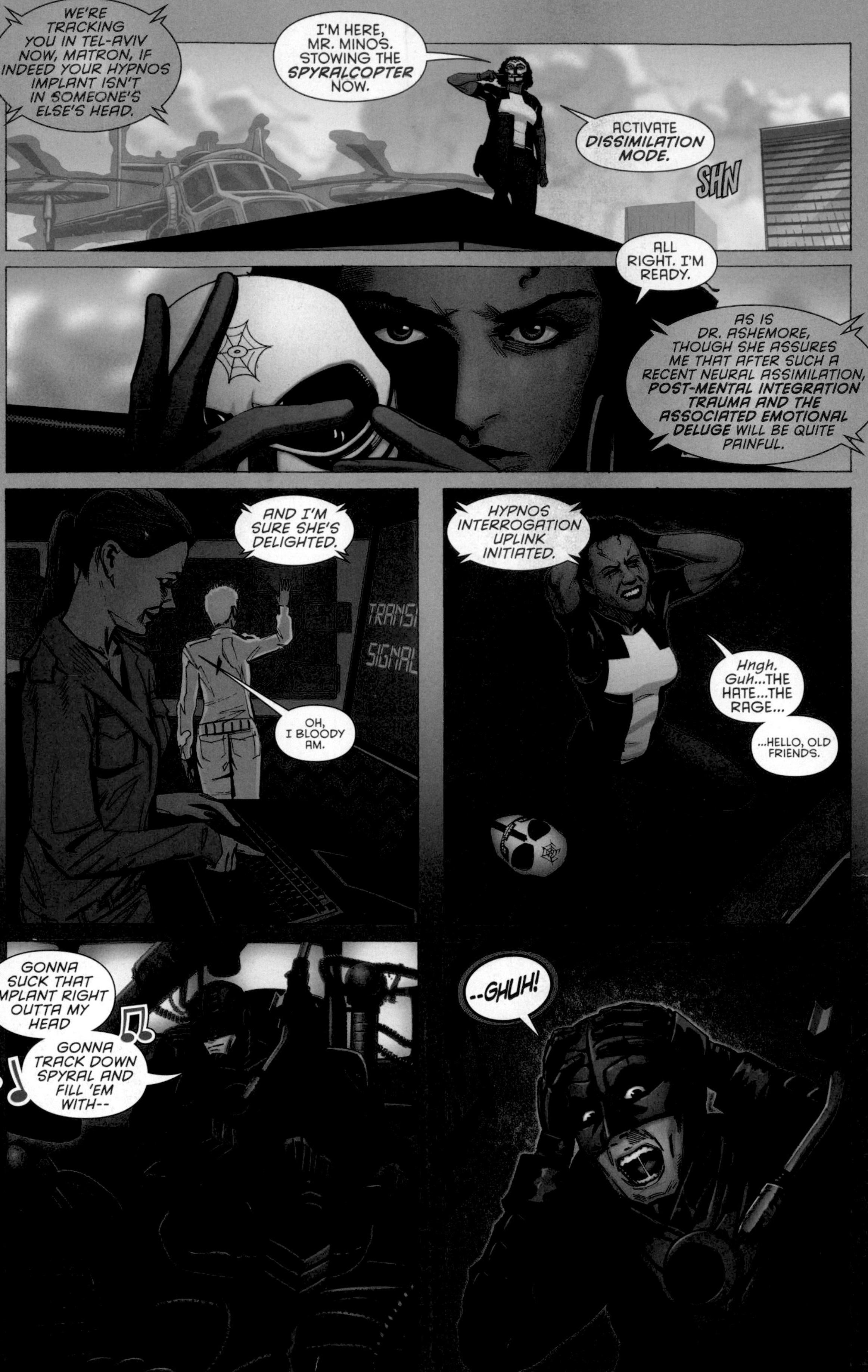
WE'RE TRACKING YOU IN TEL-AVIV NOW, MATRON, IF INDEED YOUR HYPNOS IMPLANT ISN'T IN SOMEONE'S ELSE'S HEAD.
I'M HERE, MR. MINOS. STOWING THE SPYRALCOPTER NOW.
ACTIVATE DISSIMILATION MODE.
SHN
ALL RIGHT. I'M READY.
AS IS DR. ASHEMORE, THOUGH SHE ASSURES ME THAT AFTER SUCH A RECENT NEURAL ASSIMILATION, POST-MENTAL INTEGRATION TRAUMA AND THE ASSOCIATED EMOTIONAL DELUGE WILL BE QUITE PAINFUL.
AND I'M SURE SHE'S DELIGHTED.
TRANSI
SIGNAL
OH, I BLOODY AM.
HYPNOS INTERROGATION UPLINK INITIATED.
Hngh. Guh...THE HATE...THE RAGE...
...HELLO, OLD FRIENDS.
GONNA SUCK THAT IMPLANT RIGHT OUTTA MY HEAD
GONNA TRACK DOWN SPYRAL AND FILL 'EM WITH--
--GHUH!

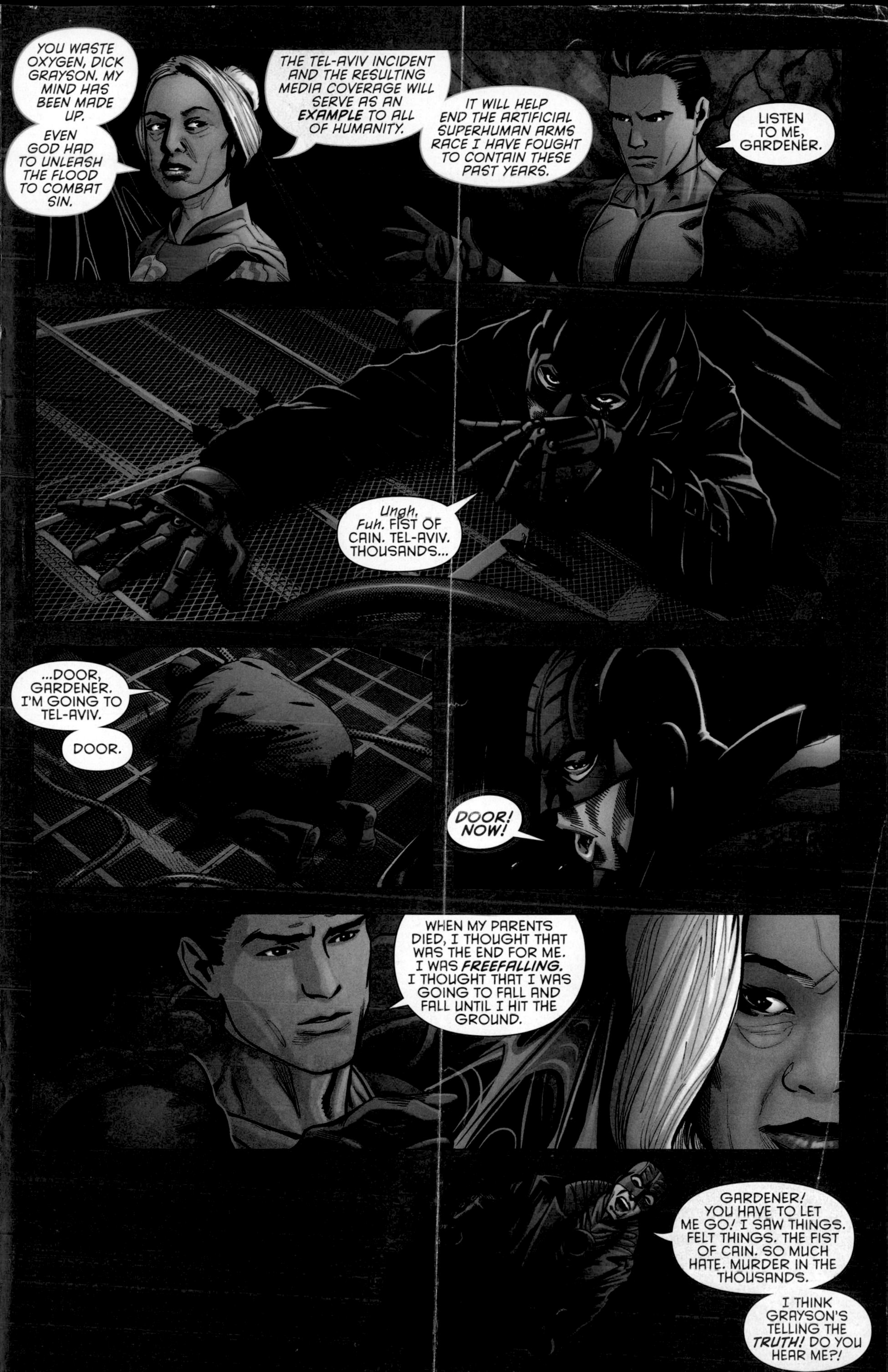
YOU WASTE OXYGEN, DICK GRAYSON. MY MIND HAS BEEN MADE UP.
EVEN GOD HAD TO UNLEASH THE FLOOD TO COMBAT SIN.
THE TEL-AVIV INCIDENT AND THE RESULTING MEDIA COVERAGE WILL SERVE AS AN EXAMPLE TO ALL OF HUMANITY.
IT WILL HELP END THE ARTIFICIAL SUPERHUMAN ARMS RACE I HAVE FOUGHT TO CONTAIN THESE PAST YEARS.
LISTEN TO ME, GARDENER.
Ungh. Fuh. FIST OF CAIN. TEL-AVIV. THOUSANDS...
...DOOR, GARDENER. I'M GOING TO TEL-AVIV.
DOOR.
DOOR! NOW!
WHEN MY PARENTS DIED, I THOUGHT THAT WAS THE END FOR ME. I WAS FREEFALLING. I THOUGHT THAT I WAS GOING TO FALL AND FALL UNTIL I HIT THE GROUND.
GARDENER! YOU HAVE TO LET ME GO! I SAW THINGS. FELT THINGS. THE FIST OF CAIN. SO MUCH HATE. MURDER IN THE THOUSANDS.
I THINK GRAYSON'S TELLING THE TRUTH! DO YOU HEAR ME?!

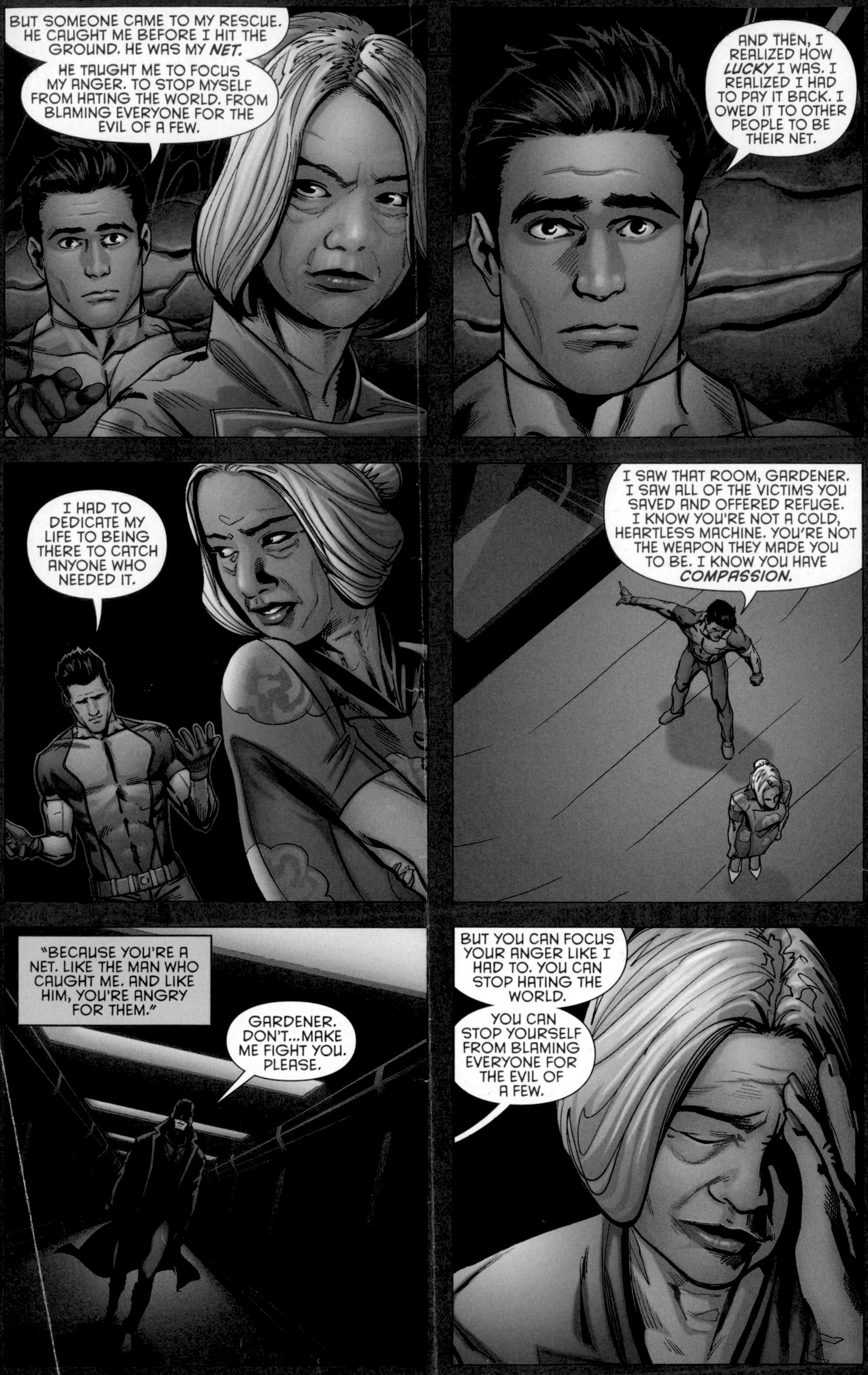
BUT SOMEONE CAME TO MY RESCUE. HE CAUGHT ME BEFORE I HIT THE GROUND. HE WAS MY NET.
HE TAUGHT ME TO FOCUS MY ANGER. TO STOP MYSELF FROM HATING THE WORLD. FROM BLAMING EVERYONE FOR THE EVIL OF A FEW.
AND THEN, I REALIZED HOW LUCKY I WAS. I REALIZED I HAD TO PAY IT BACK. I OWED IT TO OTHER PEOPLE TO BE THEIR NET.
I HAD TO DEDICATE MY LIFE TO BEING THERE TO CATCH ANYONE WHO NEEDED IT.
I SAW THAT ROOM, GARDENER. I SAW ALL OF THE VICTIMS YOU SAVED AND OFFERED REFUGE. I KNOW YOU'RE NOT A COLD, HEARTLESS MACHINE. YOU'RE NOT THE WEAPON THEY MADE YOU TO BE. I KNOW YOU HAVE COMPASSION.
"BECAUSE YOU'RE A NET. LIKE THE MAN WHO CAUGHT ME. AND LIKE HIM, YOU'RE ANGRY FOR THEM."
GARDENER. DON'T...MAKE ME FIGHT YOU. PLEASE.
BUT YOU CAN FOCUS YOUR ANGER LIKE I HAD TO. YOU CAN STOP HATING THE WORLD.
YOU CAN STOP YOURSELF FROM BLAMING EVERYONE FOR THE EVIL OF A FEW.

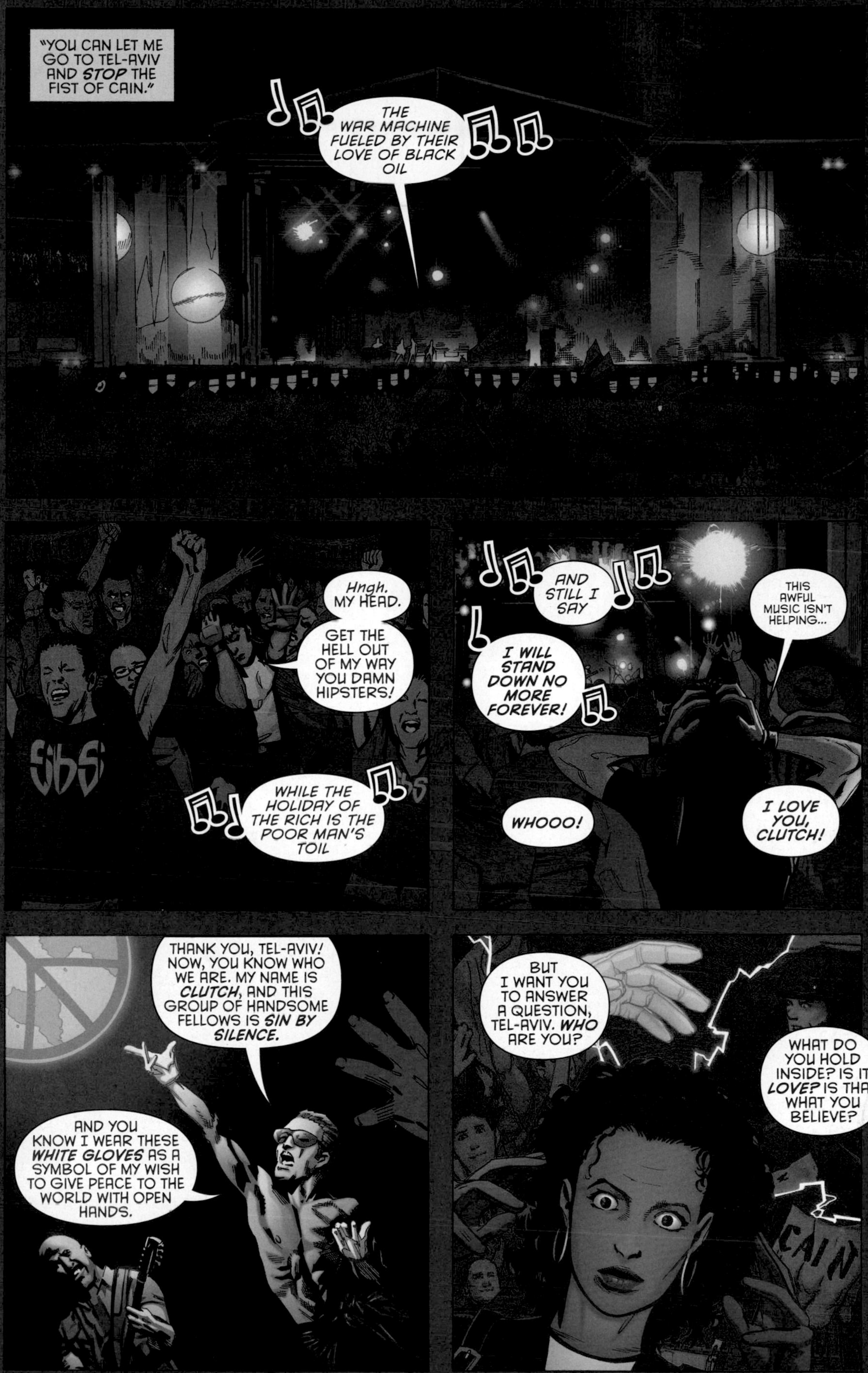
"YOU CAN LET ME GO TO TEL-AVIV AND STOP THE FIST OF CAIN."
THE WAR MACHINE FUELED BY THEIR LOVE OF BLACK OIL
Hngh. MY HEAD.
GET THE HELL OUT OF MY WAY YOU DAMN HIPSTERS!
WHILE THE HOLIDAY OF THE RICH IS THE POOR MAN'S TOIL
AND STILL I SAY
THIS AWFUL MUSIC ISN'T HELPING...
I WILL STAND DOWN NO MORE FOREVER!
WHOOO!
I LOVE YOU, CLUTCH!
THANK YOU, TEL-AVIV! NOW, YOU KNOW WHO WE ARE. MY NAME IS CLUTCH, AND THIS GROUP OF HANDSOME FELLOWS IS SIN BY SILENCE.
AND YOU KNOW I WEAR THESE WHITE GLOVES AS A SYMBOL OF MY WISH TO GIVE PEACE TO THE WORLD WITH OPEN HANDS.
BUT I WANT YOU TO ANSWER A QUESTION, TEL-AVIV. WHO ARE YOU?
WHAT DO YOU HOLD INSIDE? IS IT LOVE? IS THAT WHAT YOU BELIEVE?
CAIN

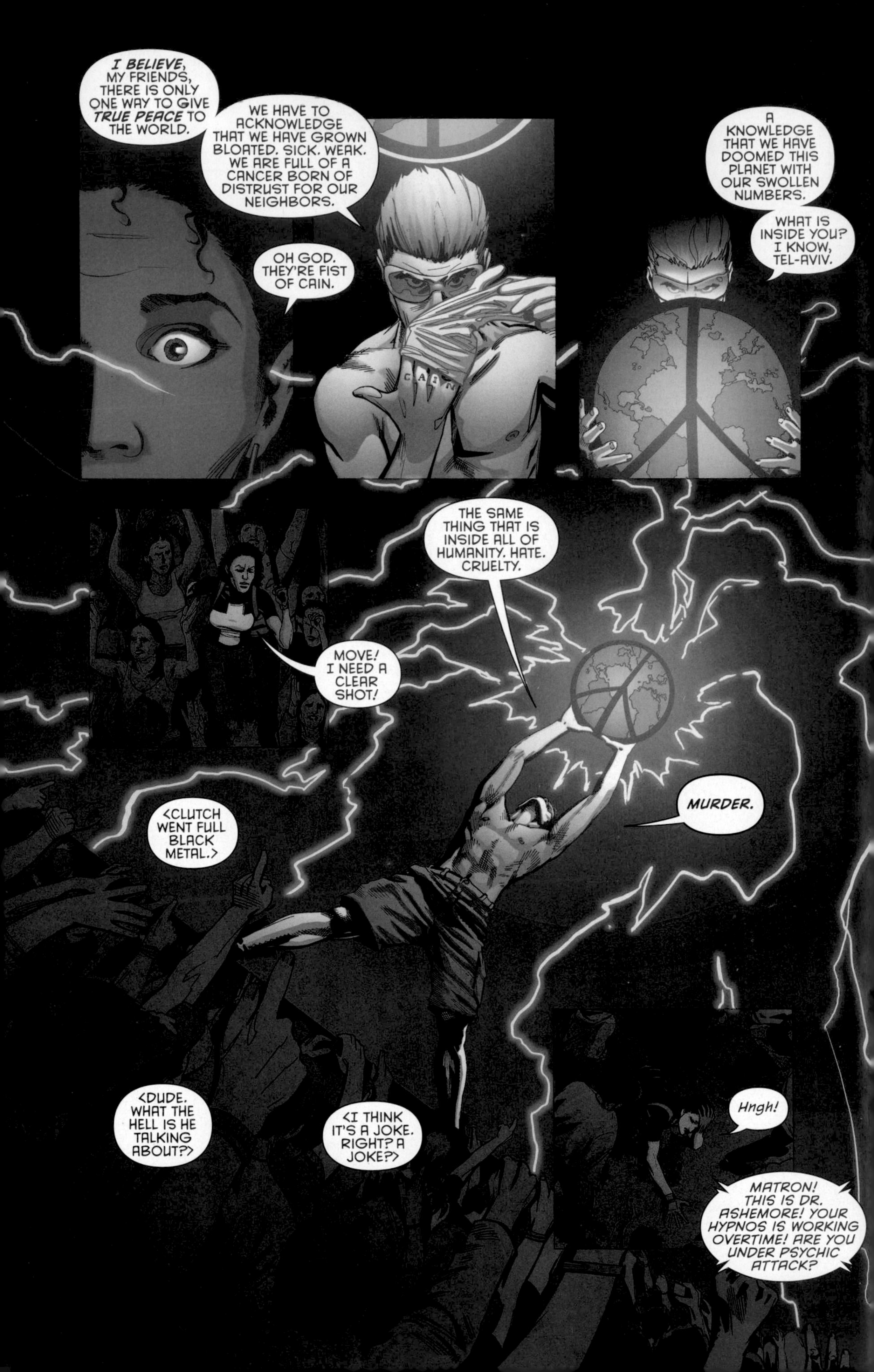
I BELIEVE, MY FRIENDS, THERE IS ONLY ONE WAY TO GIVE TRUE PEACE TO THE WORLD.
WE HAVE TO ACKNOWLEDGE THAT WE HAVE GROWN BLOATED. SICK. WEAK. WE ARE FULL OF A CANCER BORN OF DISTRUST FOR OUR NEIGHBORS.
OH GOD. THEY'RE FIST OF CAIN.
CAIN
A KNOWLEDGE THAT WE HAVE DOOMED THIS PLANET WITH OUR SWOLLEN NUMBERS.
WHAT IS INSIDE YOU? I KNOW, TEL-AVIV.
THE SAME THING THAT IS INSIDE ALL OF HUMANITY. HATE. CRUELTY.
MOVE! I NEED A CLEAR SHOT!
MURDER.
<CLUTCH WENT FULL BLACK METAL.>
<DUDE. WHAT THE HELL IS HE TALKING ABOUT?>
<I THINK IT'S A JOKE. RIGHT? A JOKE?>
Hngh!
MATRON! THIS IS DR. ASHEMORE! YOUR HYPNOS IS WORKING OVERTIME! ARE YOU UNDER PSYCHIC ATTACK?

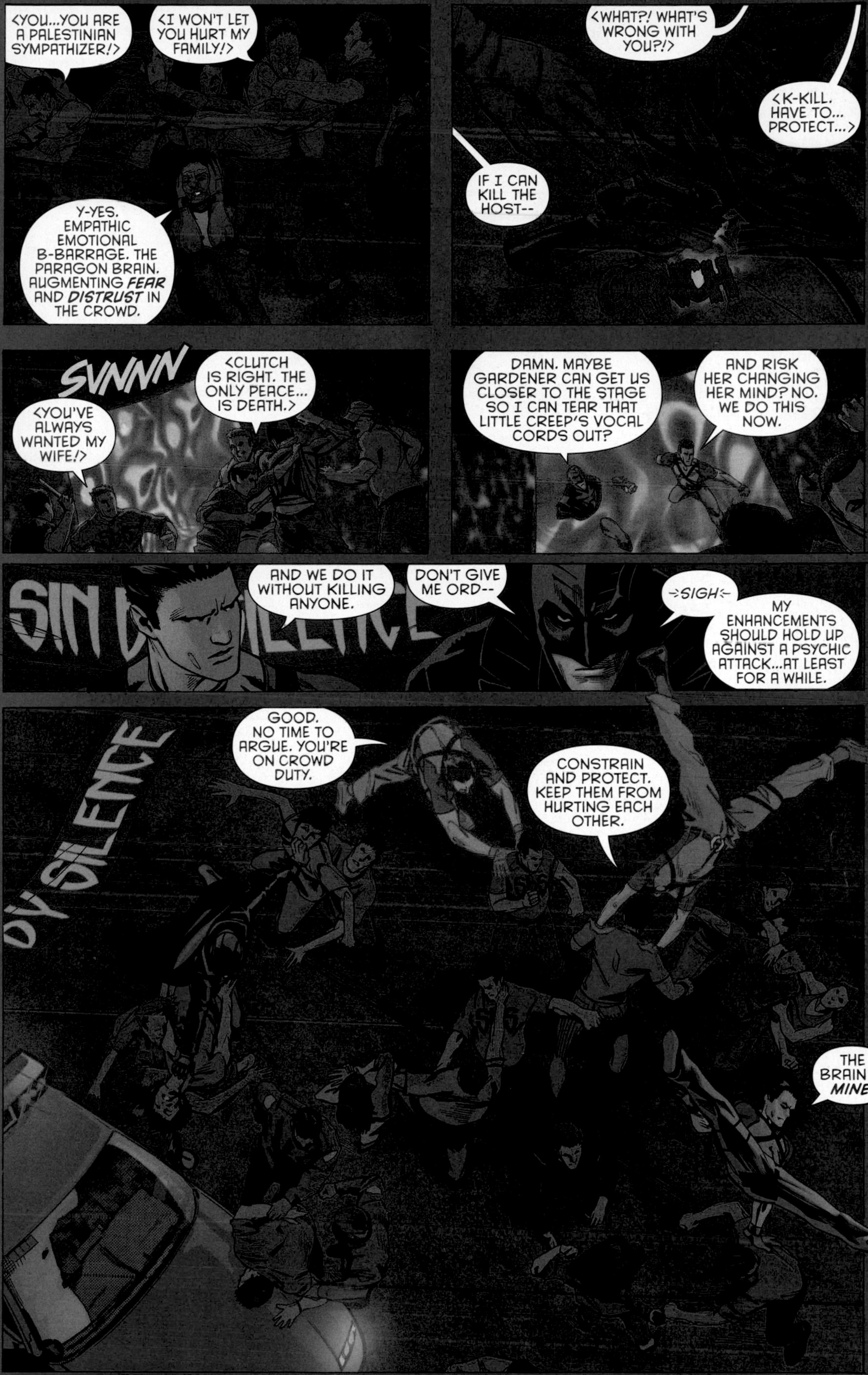
<YOU...YOU ARE A PALESTINIAN SYMPATHIZER!>
<I WON'T LET YOU HURT MY FAMILY!>
Y-YES. EMPATHIC EMOTIONAL B-BARRAGE. THE PARAGON BRAIN. AUGMENTING *FEAR* AND *DISTRUST* IN THE CROWD.
<WHAT?! WHAT'S WRONG WITH YOU?!>
<K-KILL. HAVE TO... PROTECT...>
IF I CAN KILL THE HOST--
SVNNN
<CLUTCH IS RIGHT. THE ONLY PEACE... IS DEATH.>
<YOU'VE ALWAYS WANTED MY WIFE!>
DAMN. MAYBE GARDENER CAN GET US CLOSER TO THE STAGE SO I CAN TEAR THAT LITTLE CREEP'S VOCAL CORDS OUT?
AND RISK HER CHANGING HER MIND? NO. WE DO THIS NOW.
AND WE DO IT WITHOUT KILLING ANYONE.
DON'T GIVE ME ORD--
SIGH
MY ENHANCEMENTS SHOULD HOLD UP AGAINST A PSYCHIC ATTACK...AT LEAST FOR A WHILE.
GOOD. NO TIME TO ARGUE. YOU'RE ON CROWD DUTY.
CONSTRAIN AND PROTECT. KEEP THEM FROM HURTING EACH OTHER.
THE BRAIN IS *MINE.*

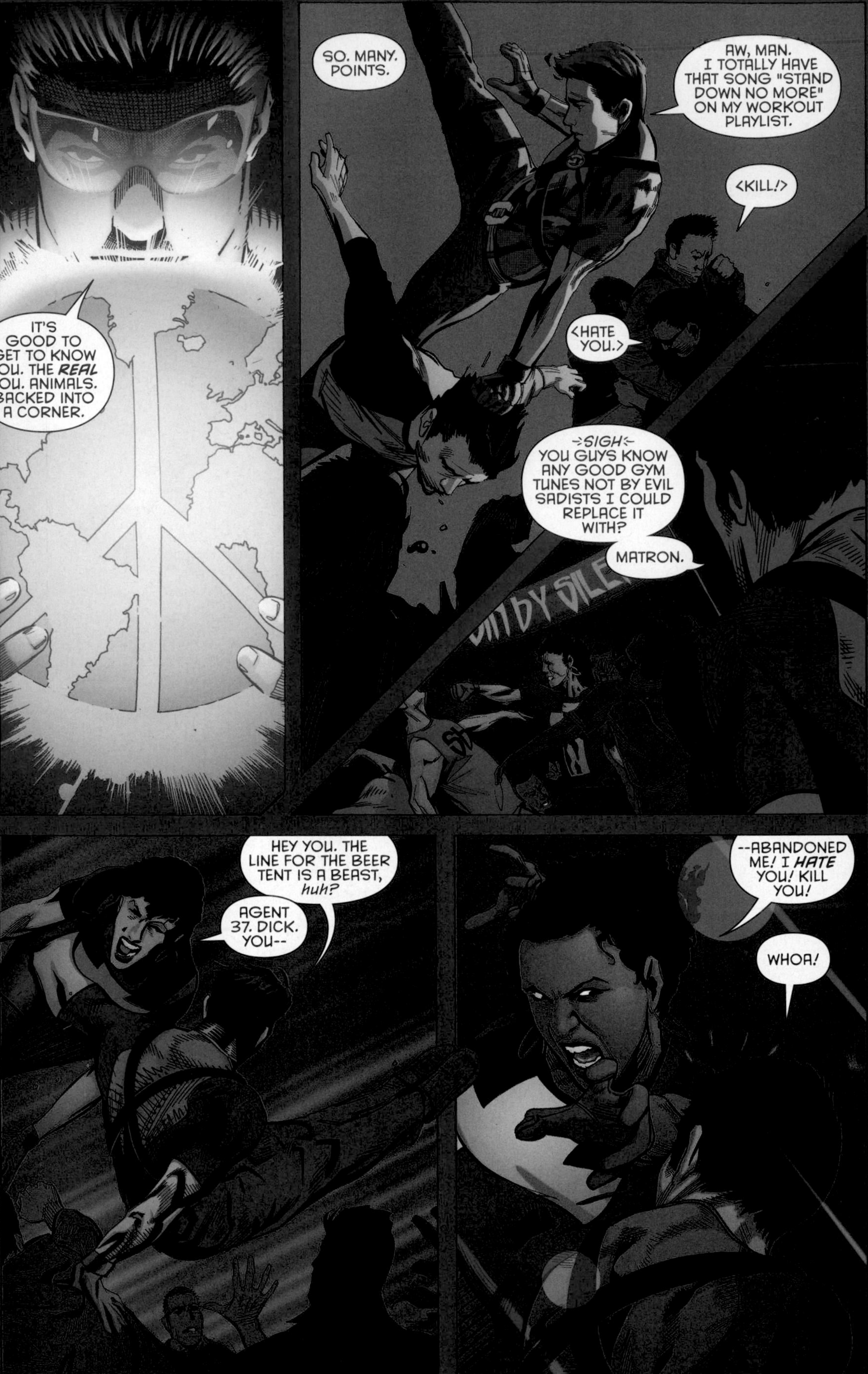
IT'S GOOD TO GET TO KNOW YOU. THE *REAL* YOU. ANIMALS. BACKED INTO A CORNER.
SO. MANY. POINTS.
AW, MAN. I TOTALLY HAVE THAT SONG "STAND DOWN NO MORE" ON MY WORKOUT PLAYLIST.
<KILL!>
<HATE YOU.>
-*SIGH*- YOU GUYS KNOW ANY GOOD GYM TUNES NOT BY EVIL SADISTS I COULD REPLACE IT WITH?
MATRON.
HEY YOU. THE LINE FOR THE BEER TENT IS A BEAST, *huh?*
AGENT 37. DICK. YOU--
--ABANDONED ME! I *HATE* YOU! KILL YOU!
WHOA!

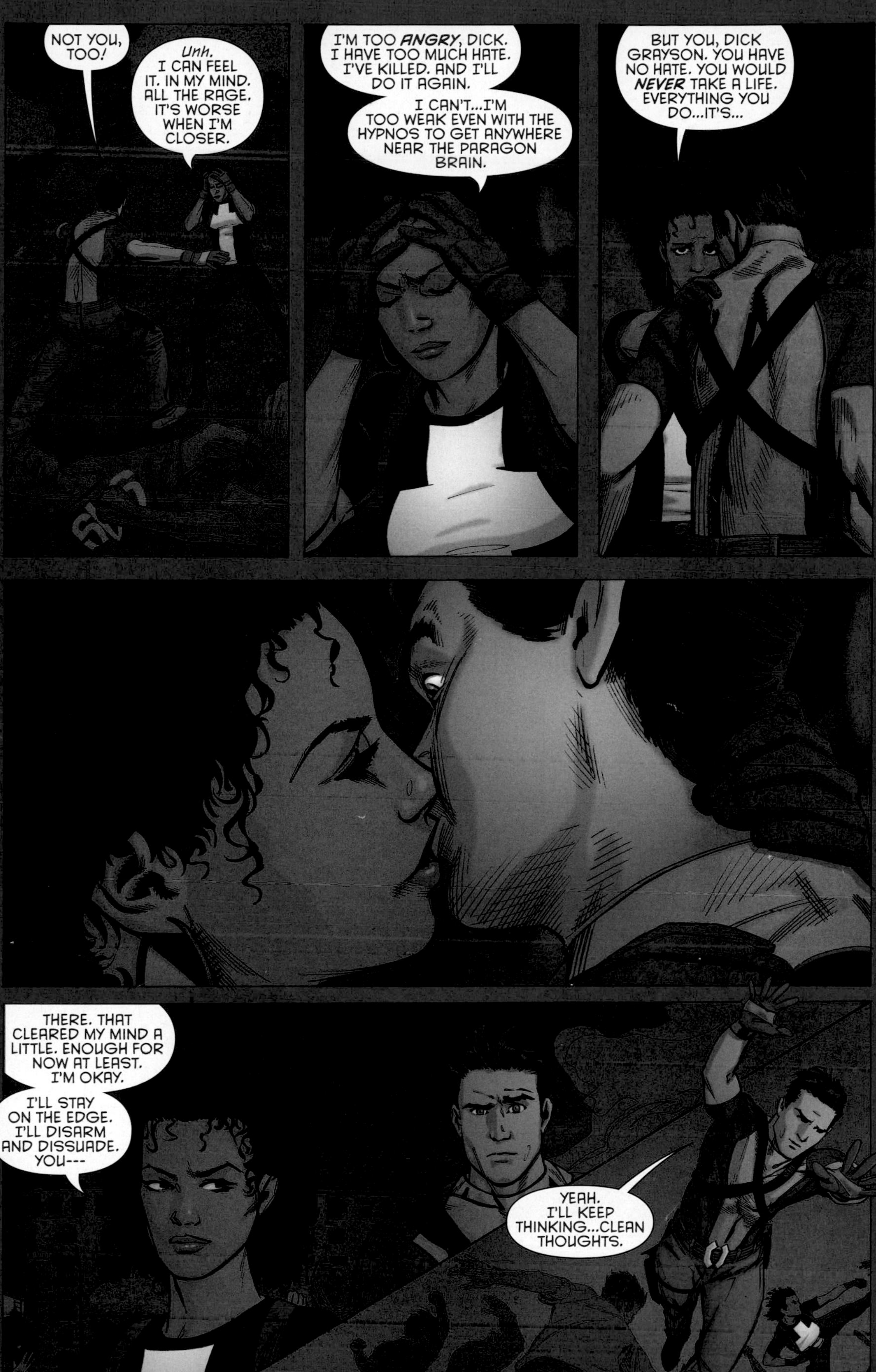
NOT YOU, TOO!
Unh. I CAN FEEL IT. IN MY MIND. ALL THE RAGE. IT'S WORSE WHEN I'M CLOSER.
I'M TOO ANGRY, DICK. I HAVE TOO MUCH HATE. I'VE KILLED. AND I'LL DO IT AGAIN.
I CAN'T...I'M TOO WEAK EVEN WITH THE HYPNOS TO GET ANYWHERE NEAR THE PARAGON BRAIN.
BUT YOU, DICK GRAYSON. YOU HAVE NO HATE. YOU WOULD NEVER TAKE A LIFE. EVERYTHING YOU DO...IT'S...
THERE. THAT CLEARED MY MIND A LITTLE. ENOUGH FOR NOW AT LEAST. I'M OKAY.
I'LL STAY ON THE EDGE. I'LL DISARM AND DISSUADE. YOU---
YEAH. I'LL KEEP THINKING...CLEAN THOUGHTS.

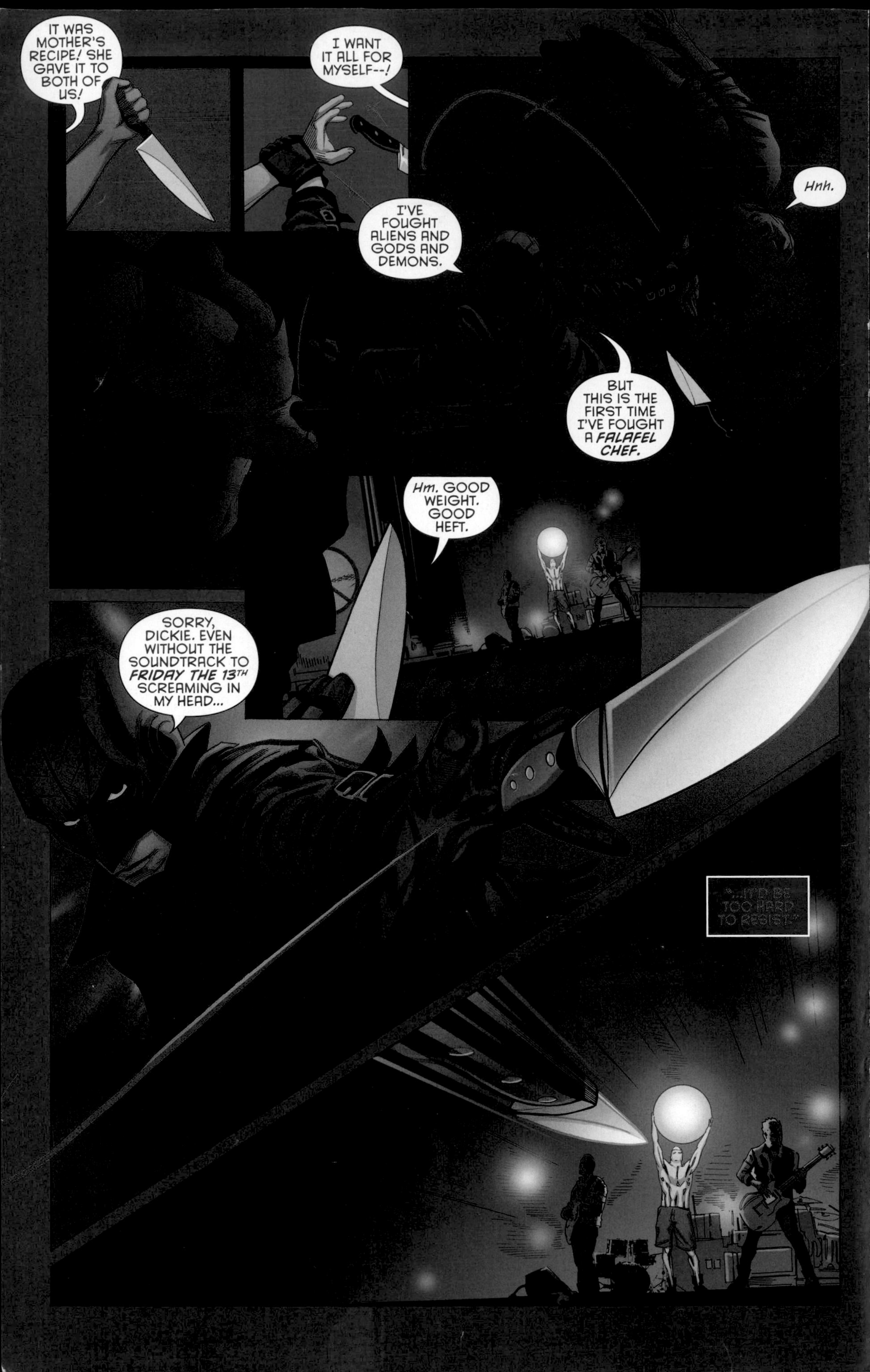

IT WAS MOTHER'S RECIPE! SHE GAVE IT TO BOTH OF US!
I WANT IT ALL FOR MYSELF--!
Hnh.
I'VE FOUGHT ALIENS AND GODS AND DEMONS.
BUT THIS IS THE FIRST TIME I'VE FOUGHT A FALAFEL CHEF.
Hm. GOOD WEIGHT. GOOD HEFT.
SORRY, DICKIE. EVEN WITHOUT THE SOUNDTRACK TO FRIDAY THE 13TH SCREAMING IN MY HEAD...
"...IT'D BE TOO HARD TO RESIST."

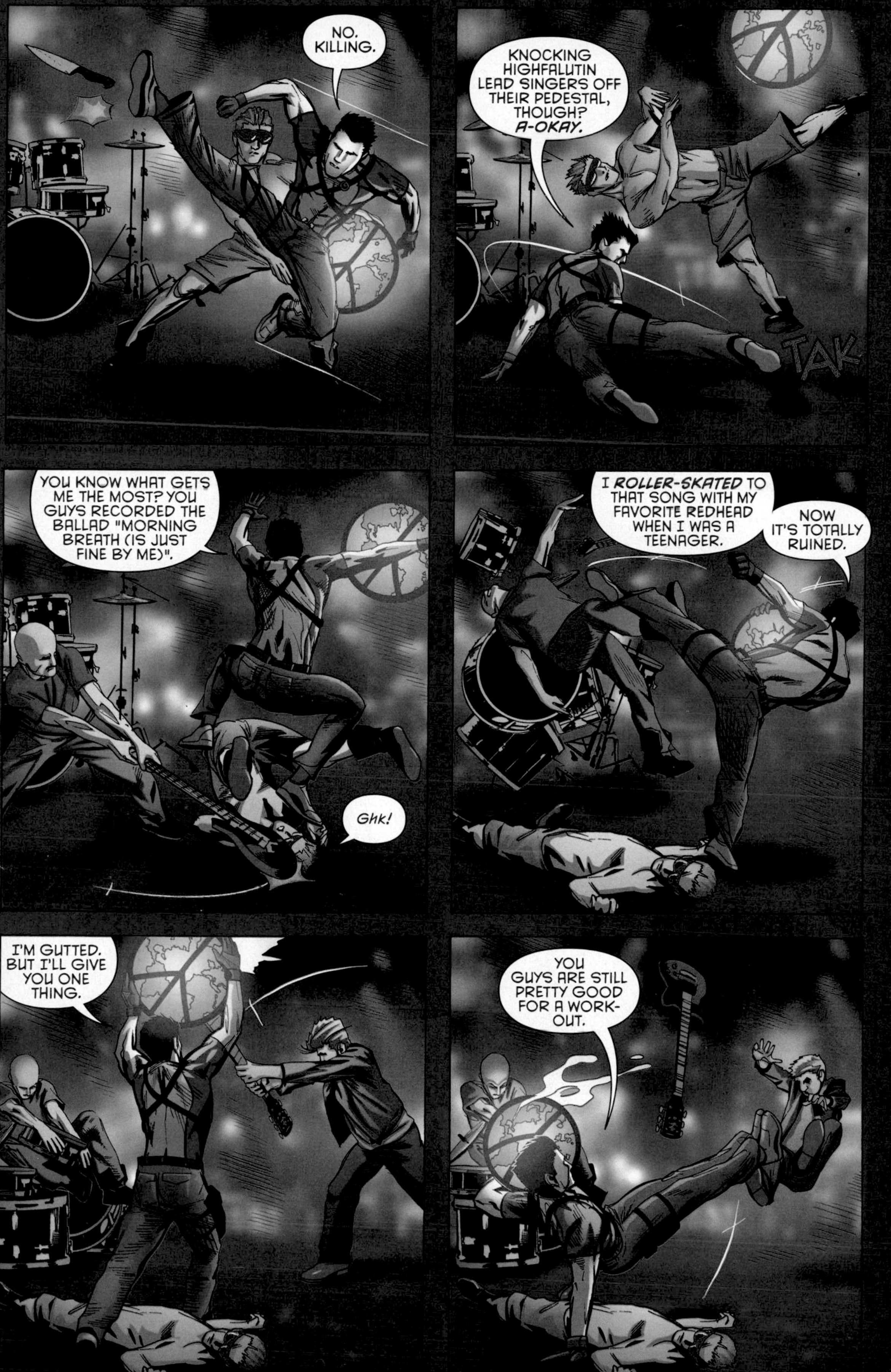
NO. KILLING.
KNOCKING HIGHFALUTIN LEAD SINGERS OFF THEIR PEDESTAL, THOUGH? A-OKAY.
TAK
YOU KNOW WHAT GETS ME THE MOST? YOU GUYS RECORDED THE BALLAD "MORNING BREATH (IS JUST FINE BY ME)".
Ghk!
I ROLLER-SKATED TO THAT SONG WITH MY FAVORITE REDHEAD WHEN I WAS A TEENAGER.
NOW IT'S TOTALLY RUINED.
I'M GUTTED. BUT I'LL GIVE YOU ONE THING.
YOU GUYS ARE STILL PRETTY GOOD FOR A WORK-OUT.

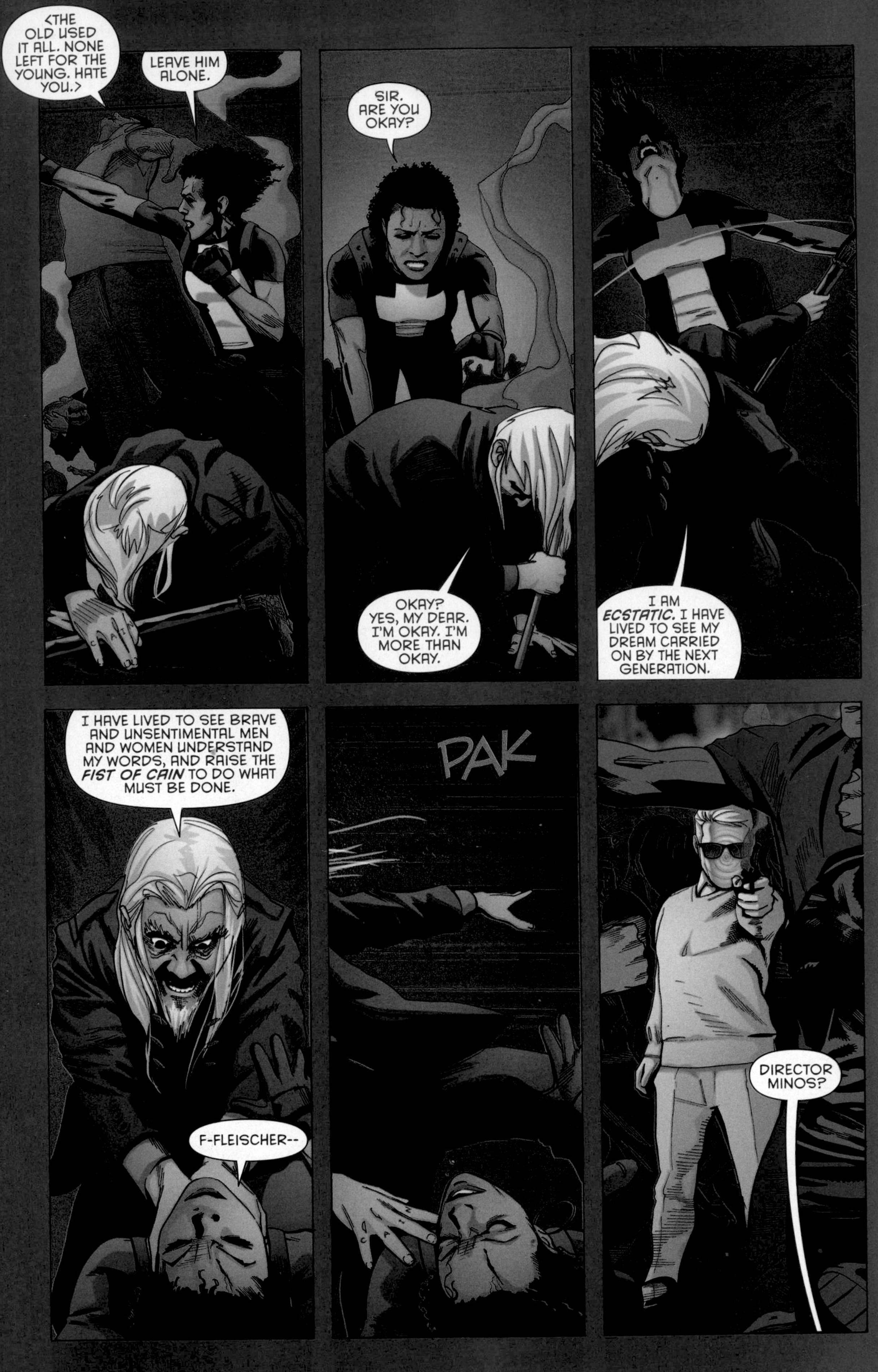
<THE OLD USED IT ALL. NONE LEFT FOR THE YOUNG. HATE YOU.>
LEAVE HIM ALONE.
SIR. ARE YOU OKAY?
OKAY? YES, MY DEAR. I'M OKAY. I'M MORE THAN OKAY.
I AM *ECSTATIC.* I HAVE LIVED TO SEE MY DREAM CARRIED ON BY THE NEXT GENERATION.
I HAVE LIVED TO SEE BRAVE AND UNSENTIMENTAL MEN AND WOMEN UNDERSTAND MY WORDS, AND RAISE THE *FIST OF CAIN* TO DO WHAT MUST BE DONE.
F-FLEISCHER--
PAK
DIRECTOR MINOS?

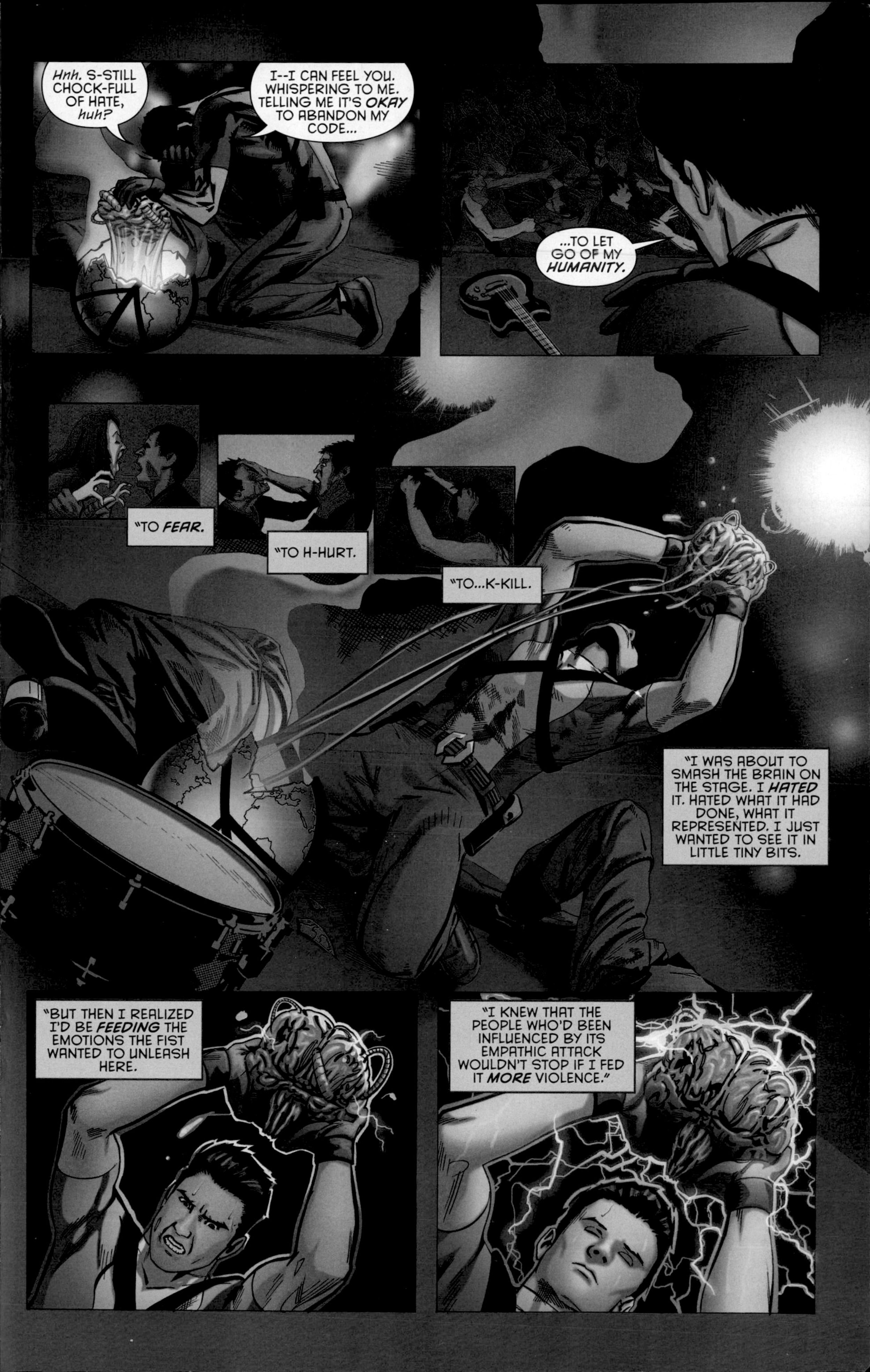

Hnh. S-STILL CHOCK-FULL OF HATE, huh?
I--I CAN FEEL YOU. WHISPERING TO ME. TELLING ME IT'S OKAY TO ABANDON MY CODE...
...TO LET GO OF MY HUMANITY.
"TO FEAR.
"TO H-HURT.
"TO...K-KILL.
"I WAS ABOUT TO SMASH THE BRAIN ON THE STAGE. I HATED IT. HATED WHAT IT HAD DONE, WHAT IT REPRESENTED. I JUST WANTED TO SEE IT IN LITTLE TINY BITS.
"BUT THEN I REALIZED I'D BE FEEDING THE EMOTIONS THE FIST WANTED TO UNLEASH HERE.
"I KNEW THAT THE PEOPLE WHO'D BEEN INFLUENCED BY ITS EMPATHIC ATTACK WOULDN'T STOP IF I FED IT MORE VIOLENCE."

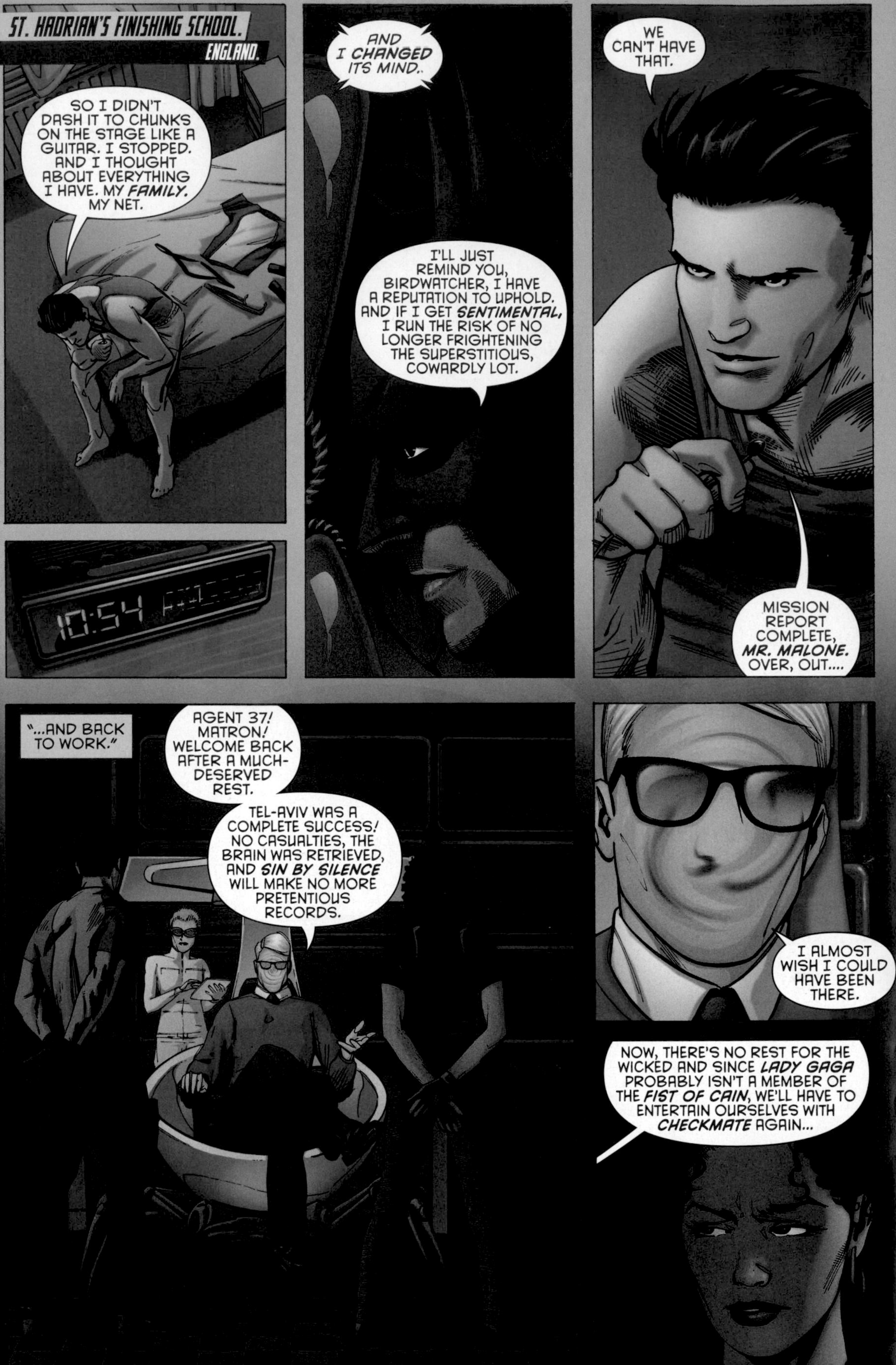

ST. HADRIAN'S FINISHING SCHOOL.
ENGLAND.
SO I DIDN'T DASH IT TO CHUNKS ON THE STAGE LIKE A GUITAR. I STOPPED. AND I THOUGHT ABOUT EVERYTHING I HAVE. MY FAMILY. MY NET.
10:54
AND I CHANGED ITS MIND..
I'LL JUST REMIND YOU, BIRDWATCHER, I HAVE A REPUTATION TO UPHOLD. AND IF I GET SENTIMENTAL, I RUN THE RISK OF NO LONGER FRIGHTENING THE SUPERSTITIOUS, COWARDLY LOT.
WE CAN'T HAVE THAT.
MISSION REPORT COMPLETE, MR. MALONE. OVER, OUT....
"...AND BACK TO WORK."
AGENT 37! MATRON! WELCOME BACK AFTER A MUCH-DESERVED REST.
TEL-AVIV WAS A COMPLETE SUCCESS! NO CASUALTIES, THE BRAIN WAS RETRIEVED, AND SIN BY SILENCE WILL MAKE NO MORE PRETENTIOUS RECORDS.
I ALMOST WISH I COULD HAVE BEEN THERE.
NOW, THERE'S NO REST FOR THE WICKED AND SINCE LADY GAGA PROBABLY ISN'T A MEMBER OF THE FIST OF CAIN, WE'LL HAVE TO ENTERTAIN OURSELVES WITH CHECKMATE AGAIN...

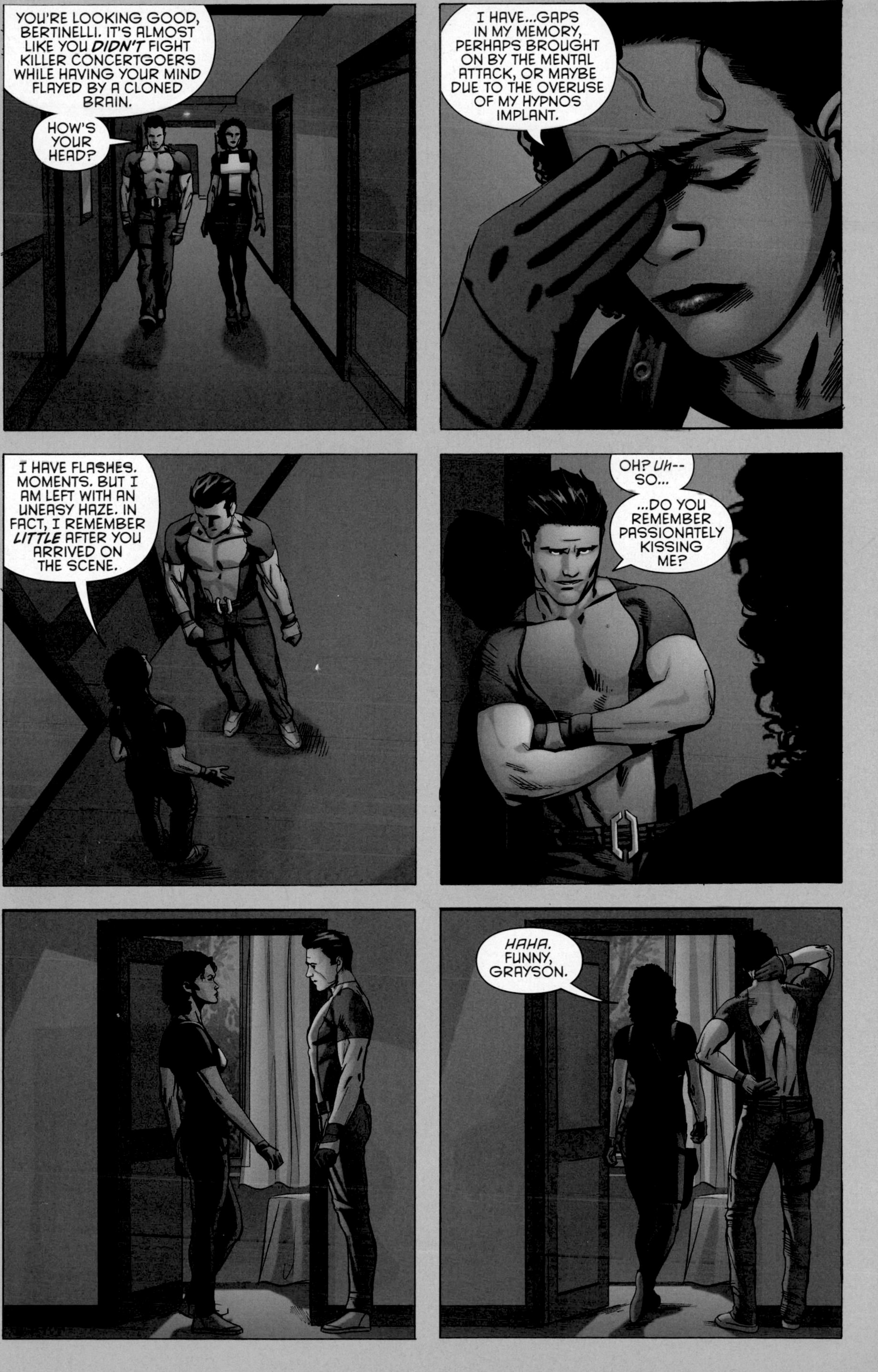
YOU'RE LOOKING GOOD, BERTINELLI. IT'S ALMOST LIKE YOU DIDN'T FIGHT KILLER CONCERTGOERS WHILE HAVING YOUR MIND FLAYED BY A CLONED BRAIN.
HOW'S YOUR HEAD?
I HAVE...GAPS IN MY MEMORY, PERHAPS BROUGHT ON BY THE MENTAL ATTACK, OR MAYBE DUE TO THE OVERUSE OF MY HYPNOS IMPLANT.
I HAVE FLASHES. MOMENTS. BUT I AM LEFT WITH AN UNEASY HAZE. IN FACT, I REMEMBER LITTLE AFTER YOU ARRIVED ON THE SCENE.
OH? UH-- SO...
...DO YOU REMEMBER PASSIONATELY KISSING ME?
HAHA. FUNNY, GRAYSON.

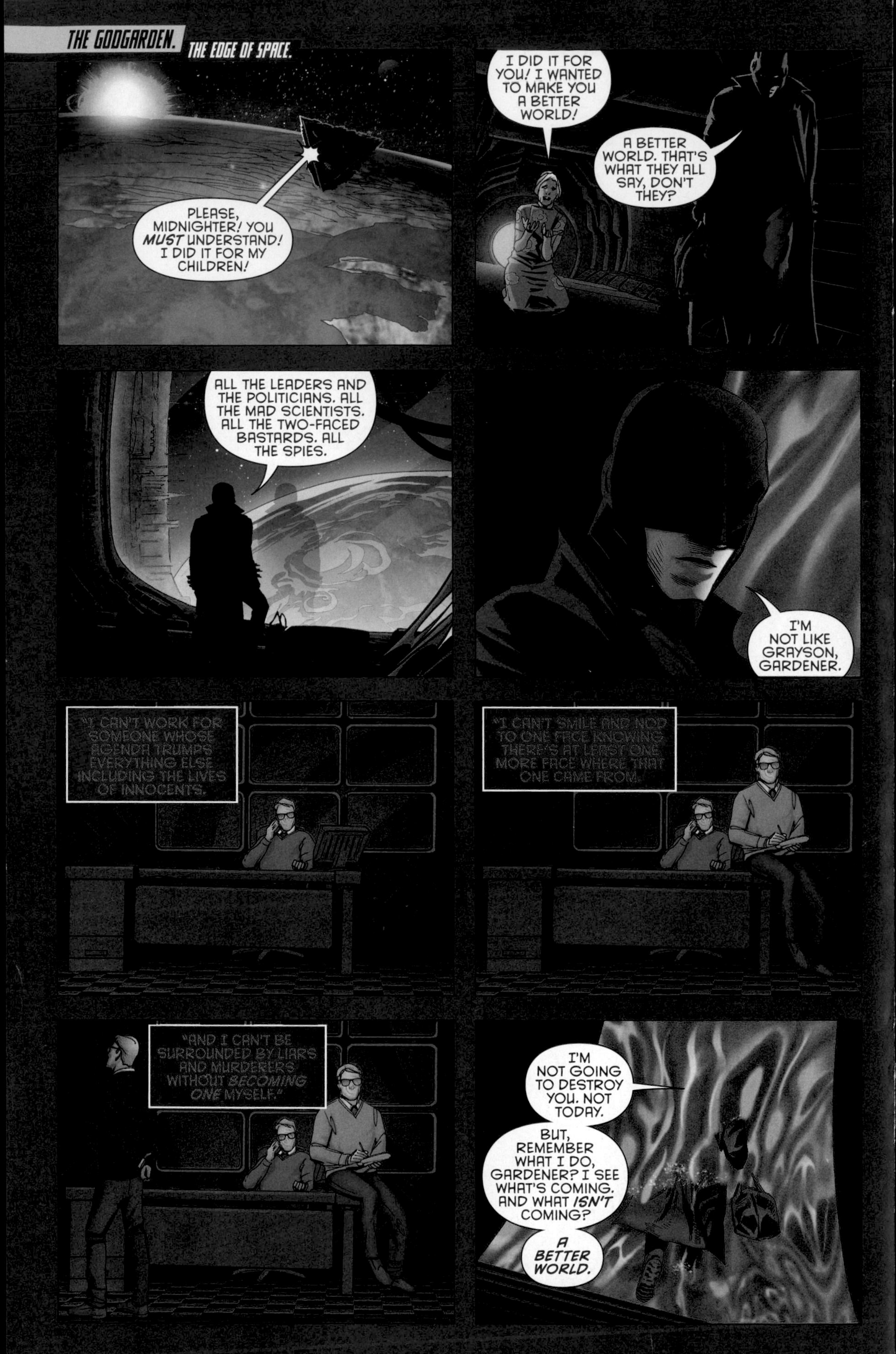
THE GODGARDEN. THE EDGE OF SPACE.
PLEASE, MIDNIGHTER! YOU *MUST* UNDERSTAND! I DID IT FOR MY CHILDREN!
I DID IT FOR YOU! I WANTED TO MAKE YOU A BETTER WORLD!
A BETTER WORLD. THAT'S WHAT THEY ALL SAY, DON'T THEY?
ALL THE LEADERS AND THE POLITICIANS. ALL THE MAD SCIENTISTS. ALL THE TWO-FACED BASTARDS. ALL THE SPIES.
I'M NOT LIKE GRAYSON, GARDENER.
"I CAN'T WORK FOR SOMEONE WHOSE AGENDA TRUMPS EVERYTHING ELSE INCLUDING THE LIVES OF INNOCENTS.
"I CAN'T SMILE AND NOD TO ONE FACE KNOWING THERE'S AT LEAST ONE MORE FACE WHERE THAT ONE CAME FROM.
"AND I CAN'T BE SURROUNDED BY LIARS AND MURDERERS WITHOUT *BECOMING ONE* MYSELF."
I'M NOT GOING TO DESTROY YOU. NOT TODAY.
BUT, REMEMBER WHAT I DO, GARDENER? I SEE WHAT'S COMING. AND WHAT *ISN'T* COMING?
A BETTER WORLD.

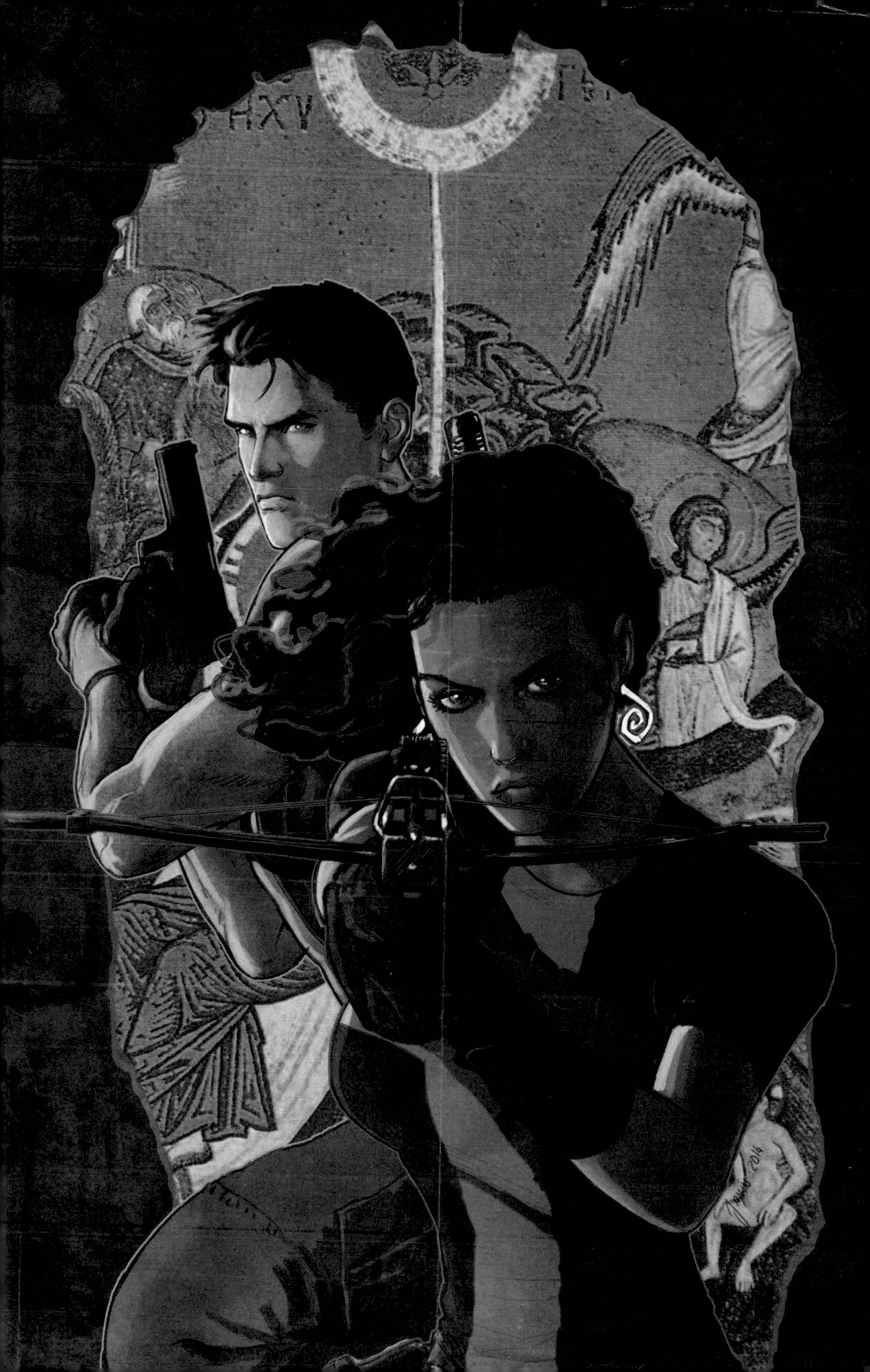

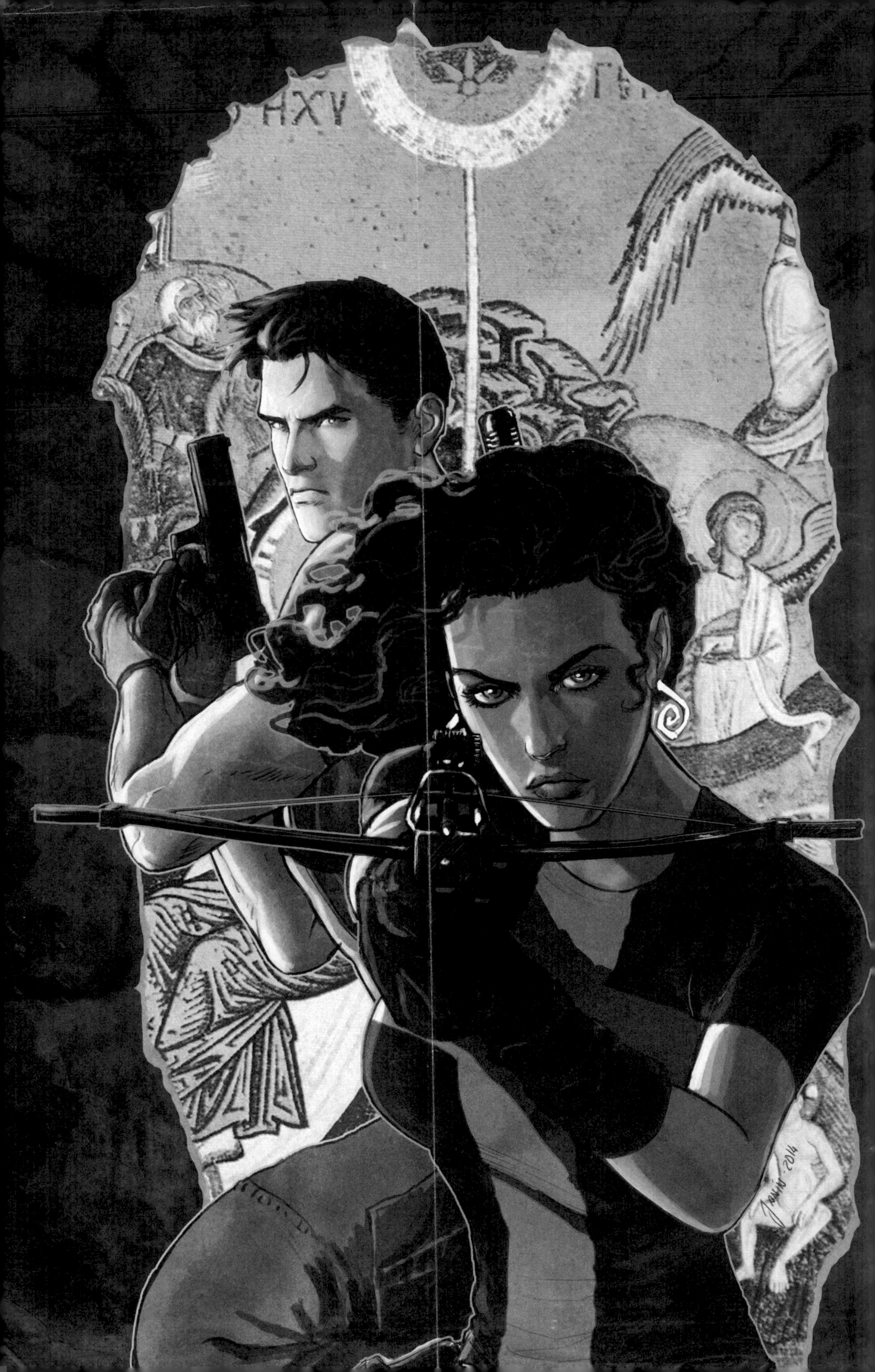

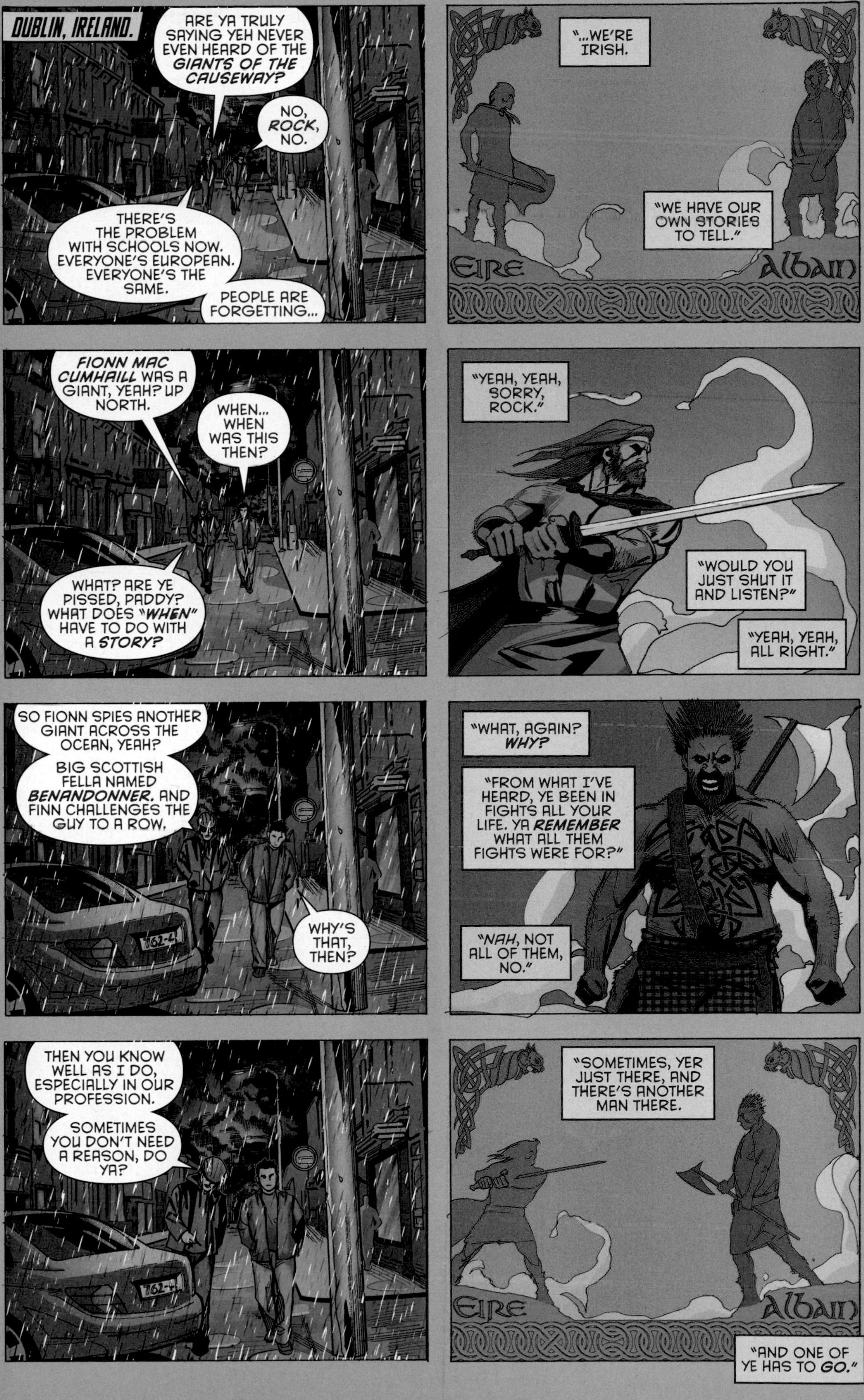
DUBLIN, IRELAND.
ARE YA TRULY SAYING YEH NEVER EVEN HEARD OF THE GIANTS OF THE CAUSEWAY?
NO, ROCK, NO.
THERE'S THE PROBLEM WITH SCHOOLS NOW. EVERYONE'S EUROPEAN. EVERYONE'S THE SAME.
PEOPLE ARE FORGETTING...
"...WE'RE IRISH.
"WE HAVE OUR OWN STORIES TO TELL."
EIRE
ALBAN
FIONN MAC CUMHAILL WAS A GIANT, YEAH? UP NORTH.
WHEN... WHEN WAS THIS THEN?
WHAT? ARE YE PISSED, PADDY? WHAT DOES "WHEN" HAVE TO DO WITH A STORY?
"YEAH, YEAH, SORRY, ROCK."
"WOULD YOU JUST SHUT IT AND LISTEN?"
"YEAH, YEAH, ALL RIGHT."
SO FIONN SPIES ANOTHER GIANT ACROSS THE OCEAN, YEAH?
BIG SCOTTISH FELLA NAMED BENANDONNER. AND FINN CHALLENGES THE GUY TO A ROW.
WHY'S THAT, THEN?
"WHAT, AGAIN? WHY?
"FROM WHAT I'VE HEARD, YE BEEN IN FIGHTS ALL YOUR LIFE. YA REMEMBER WHAT ALL THEM FIGHTS WERE FOR?"
"NAH, NOT ALL OF THEM, NO."
THEN YOU KNOW WELL AS I DO, ESPECIALLY IN OUR PROFESSION.
SOMETIMES YOU DON'T NEED A REASON, DO YA?
"SOMETIMES, YER JUST THERE, AND THERE'S ANOTHER MAN THERE.
EIRE
ALBAN
"AND ONE OF YE HAS TO GO."

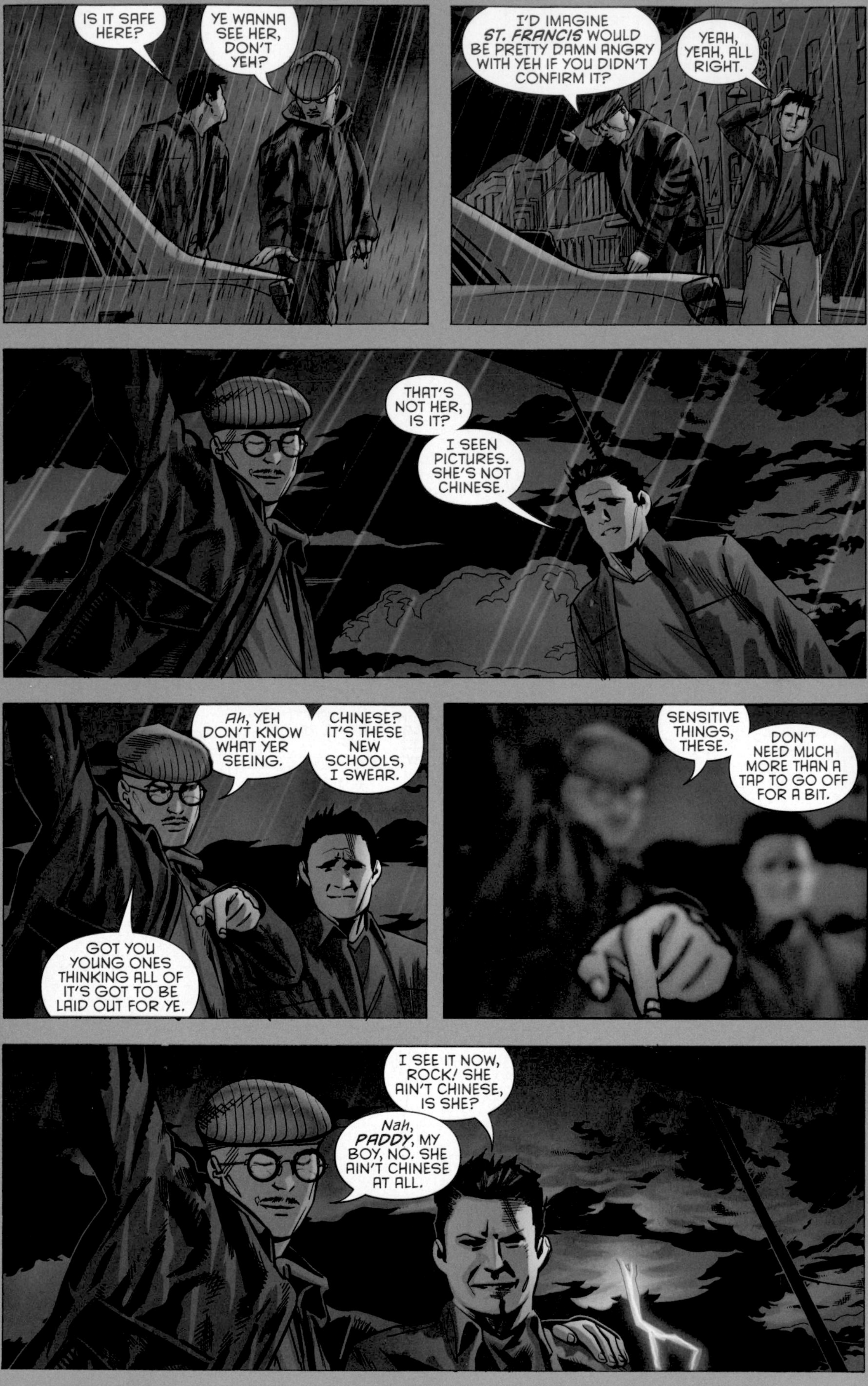

IS IT SAFE HERE?
YE WANNA SEE HER, DON'T YEH?
I'D IMAGINE ST. FRANCIS WOULD BE PRETTY DAMN ANGRY WITH YEH IF YOU DIDN'T CONFIRM IT?
YEAH, YEAH, ALL RIGHT.
THAT'S NOT HER, IS IT?
I SEEN PICTURES. SHE'S NOT CHINESE.
Ah, YEH DON'T KNOW WHAT YER SEEING.
CHINESE? IT'S THESE NEW SCHOOLS, I SWEAR.
GOT YOU YOUNG ONES THINKING ALL OF IT'S GOT TO BE LAID OUT FOR YE.
SENSITIVE THINGS, THESE.
DON'T NEED MUCH MORE THAN A TAP TO GO OFF FOR A BIT.
I SEE IT NOW, ROCK! SHE AIN'T CHINESE, IS SHE?
Nah, PADDY, MY BOY, NO. SHE AIN'T CHINESE AT ALL.

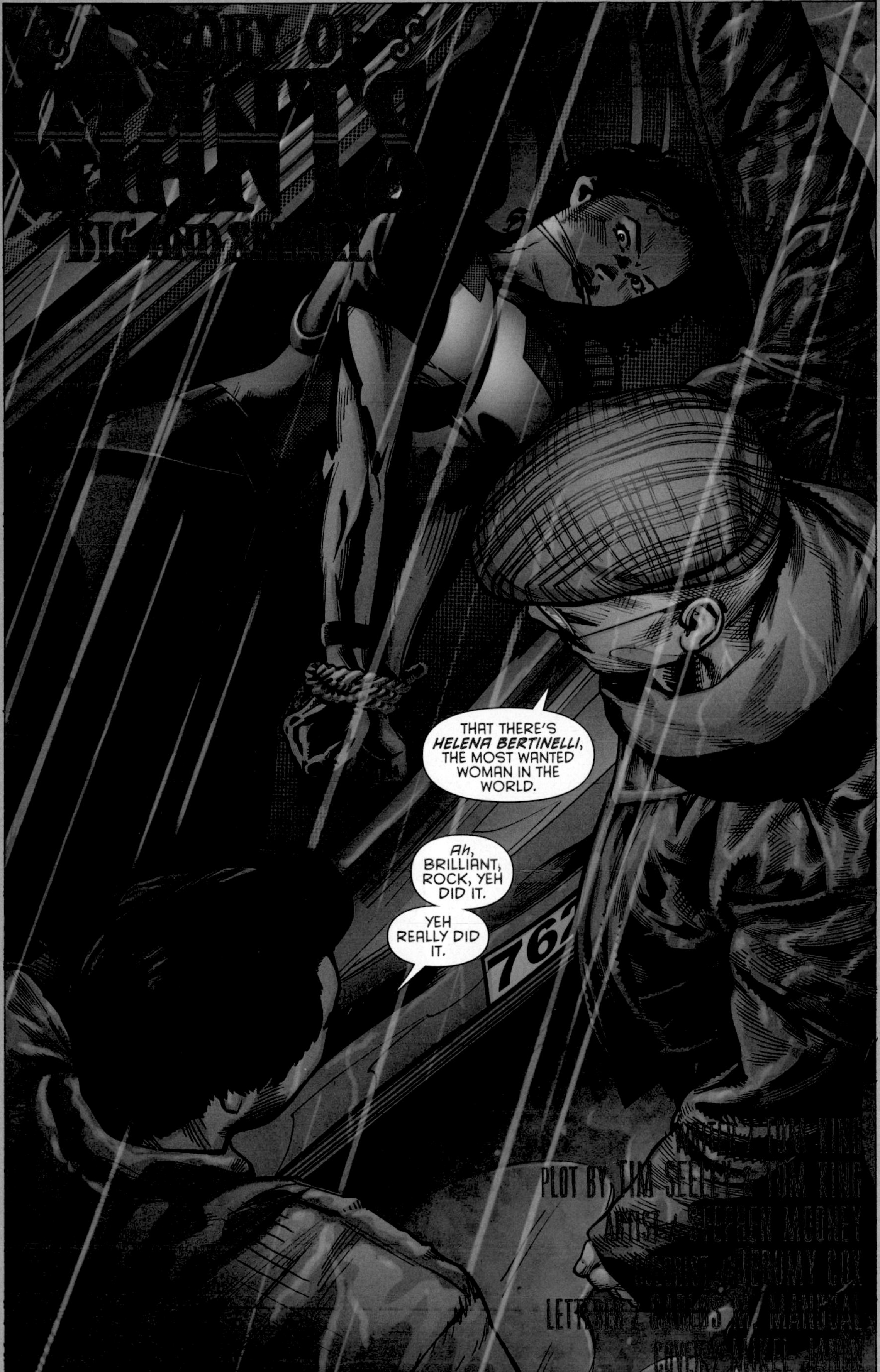
THAT THERE'S *HELENA BERTINELLI,* THE MOST WANTED WOMAN IN THE WORLD.
Ah, BRILLIANT, ROCK, YEH DID IT.
YEH REALLY DID IT.
PLOT BY TIM SEELEY & TOM KING
ARTIST / STEPHEN MOONEY
LETTERER / CARLOS M. MANGUAL
COVER / MIKEL JANIN

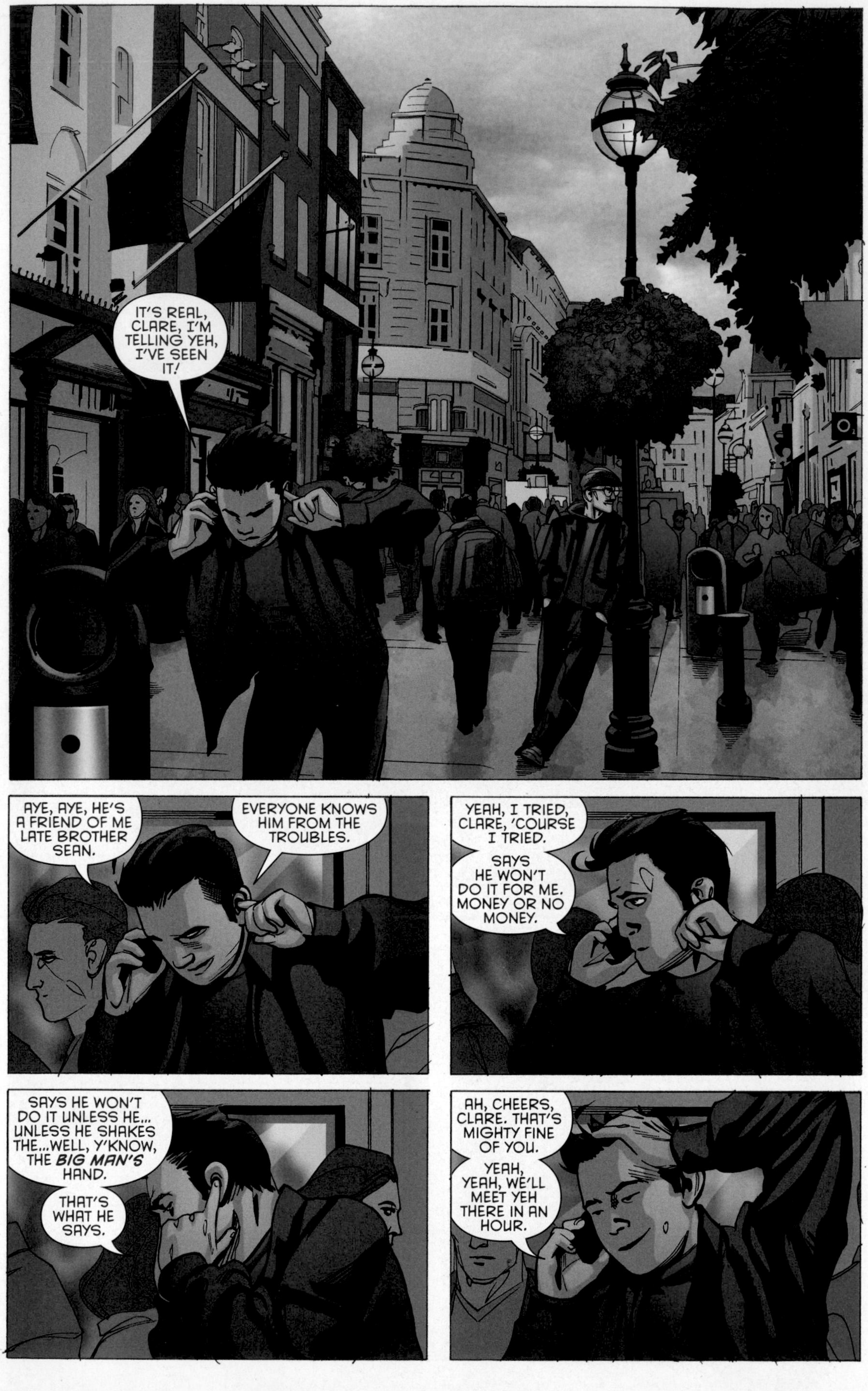
IT'S REAL, CLARE, I'M TELLING YEH, I'VE SEEN IT!
AYE, AYE, HE'S A FRIEND OF ME LATE BROTHER SEAN.
EVERYONE KNOWS HIM FROM THE TROUBLES.
YEAH, I TRIED, CLARE, 'COURSE I TRIED.
SAYS HE WON'T DO IT FOR ME. MONEY OR NO MONEY.
SAYS HE WON'T DO IT UNLESS HE... UNLESS HE SHAKES THE...WELL, Y'KNOW, THE BIG MAN'S HAND.
THAT'S WHAT HE SAYS.
AH, CHEERS, CLARE. THAT'S MIGHTY FINE OF YOU.
YEAH, YEAH, WE'LL MEET YEH THERE IN AN HOUR.

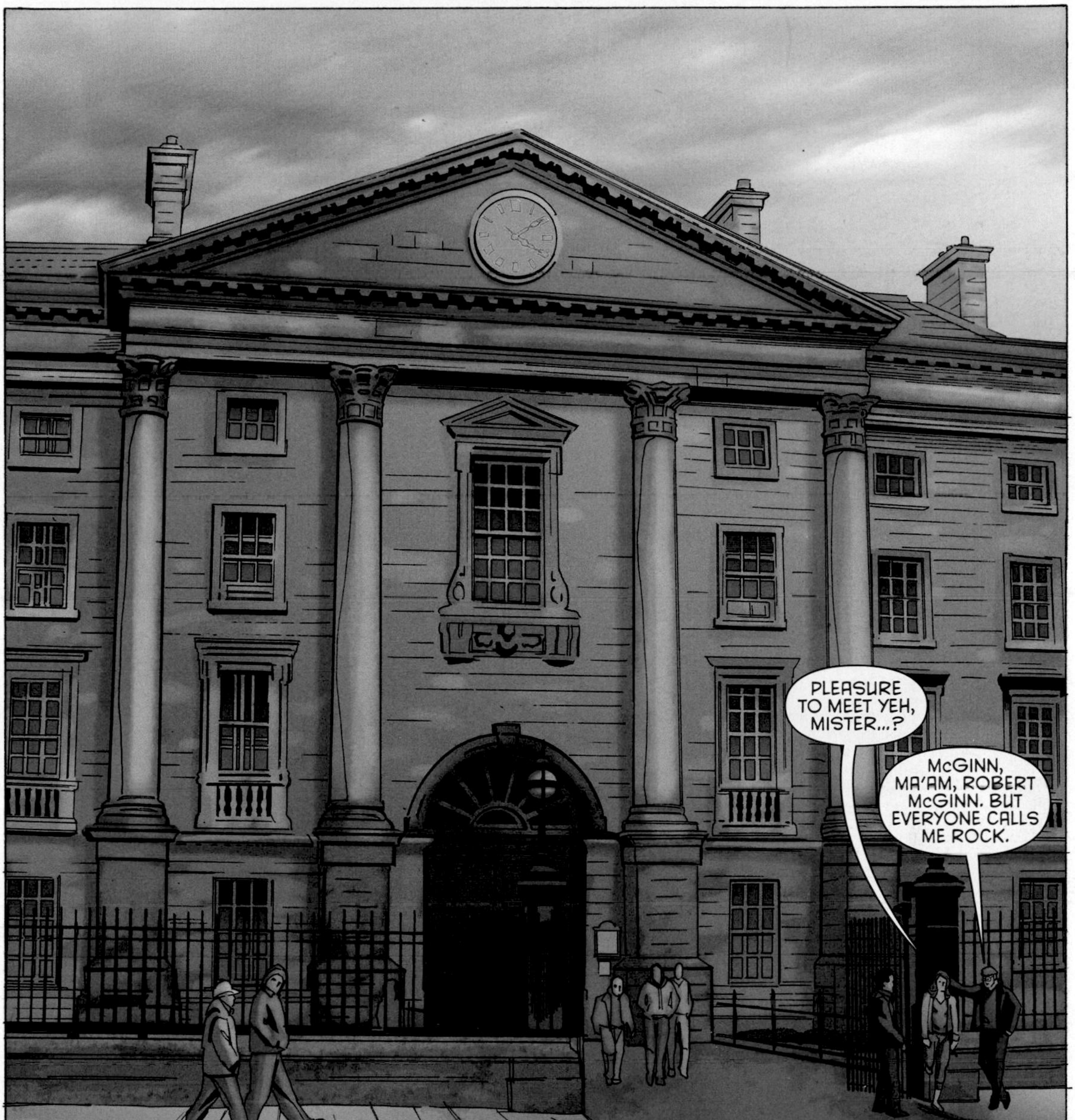
PLEASURE TO MEET YEH, MISTER...?
McGINN, MA'AM, ROBERT McGINN. BUT EVERYONE CALLS ME ROCK.

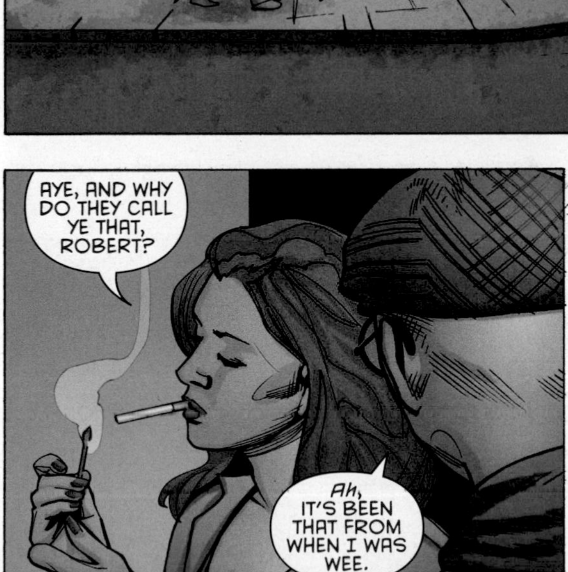
AYE, AND WHY DO THEY CALL YE THAT, ROBERT?
Ah, IT'S BEEN THAT FROM WHEN I WAS WEE.

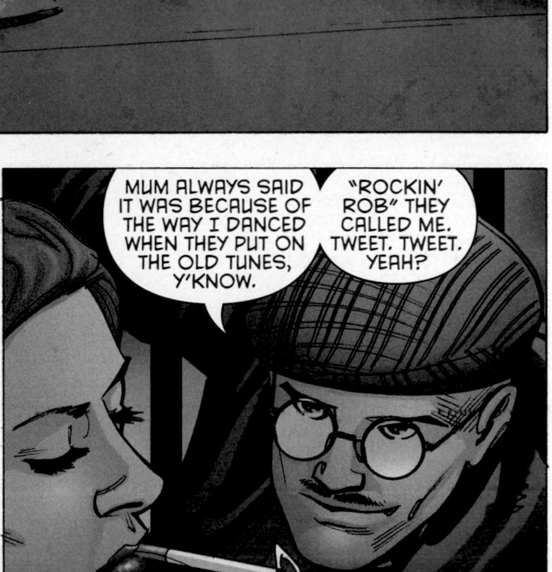
MUM ALWAYS SAID IT WAS BECAUSE OF THE WAY I DANCED WHEN THEY PUT ON THE OLD TUNES, Y'KNOW.
"ROCKIN' ROB" THEY CALLED ME. TWEET. TWEET. YEAH?

TWEET?

TWEET?

AND HOW, MAY I ASK, DID WEE ROCKIN' ROB COME BY THIS PARTICULAR PACKAGE?

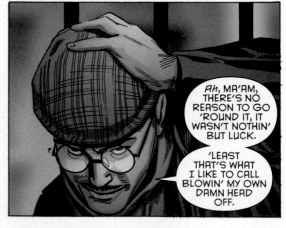

AH, MA'AM, THERE'S NO REASON TO GO 'ROUND IT, IT WASN'T NOTHIN' BUT LUCK.

'LEAST THAT'S WHAT I LIKE TO CALL BLOWIN' MY OWN DAMN HEAD OFF.

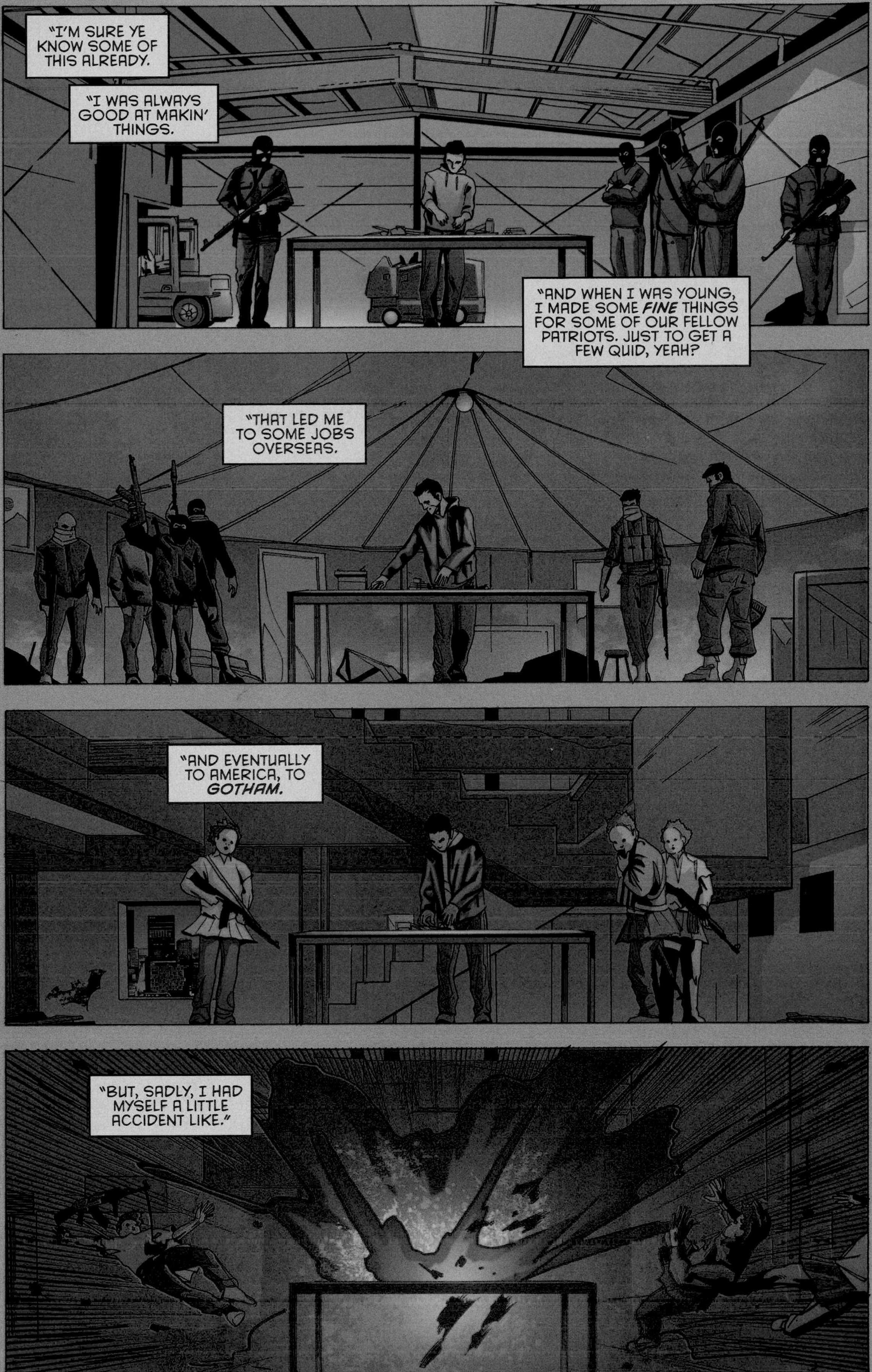
"I'M SURE YE KNOW SOME OF THIS ALREADY.
"I WAS ALWAYS GOOD AT MAKIN' THINGS.
"AND WHEN I WAS YOUNG, I MADE SOME *FINE* THINGS FOR SOME OF OUR FELLOW PATRIOTS. JUST TO GET A FEW QUID, YEAH?
"THAT LED ME TO SOME JOBS OVERSEAS.
"AND EVENTUALLY TO AMERICA, TO *GOTHAM*.
"BUT, SADLY, I HAD MYSELF A LITTLE ACCIDENT LIKE."

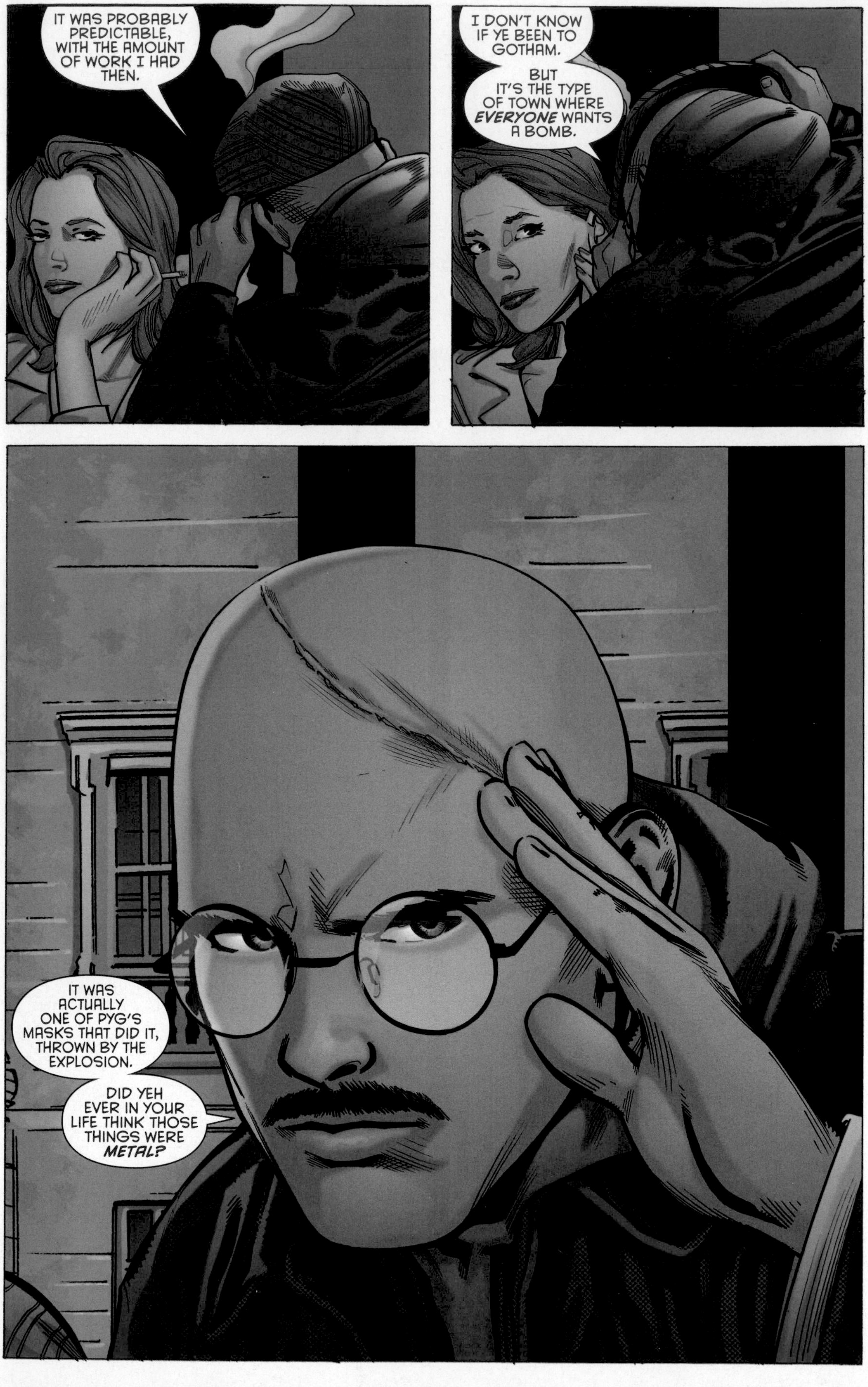
IT WAS PROBABLY PREDICTABLE, WITH THE AMOUNT OF WORK I HAD THEN.
I DON'T KNOW IF YE BEEN TO GOTHAM.
BUT IT'S THE TYPE OF TOWN WHERE *EVERYONE* WANTS A BOMB.
IT WAS ACTUALLY ONE OF PYG'S MASKS THAT DID IT, THROWN BY THE EXPLOSION.
DID YEH EVER IN YOUR LIFE THINK THOSE THINGS WERE *METAL?*

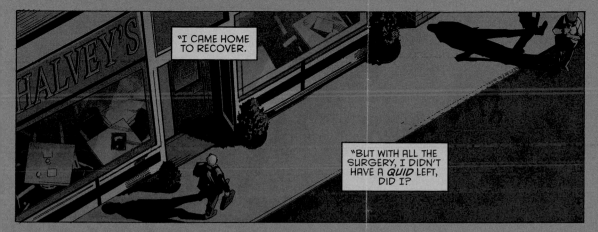

"I CAME HOME TO RECOVER.

"BUT WITH ALL THE SURGERY, I DIDN'T HAVE A *QUID* LEFT, DID I?

"SO, I FOUND SOME OLD FRIENDS HERE WHO NEEDED A BIT OF WORK.

"IT WAS ABOUT A WEEK AGO THEN.

"I WAS PUTTIN' IN A TIMER, AND I JUST LOOKED UP AT THE USUAL CROWD.

"IT WAS ALL WHAT I'D SEEN BEFORE. WHAT I'D BEEN SEEIN' FOR DECADES.

"AND THEN THERE SHE WAS.

"LOOKING LIKE A *MILLION.*"

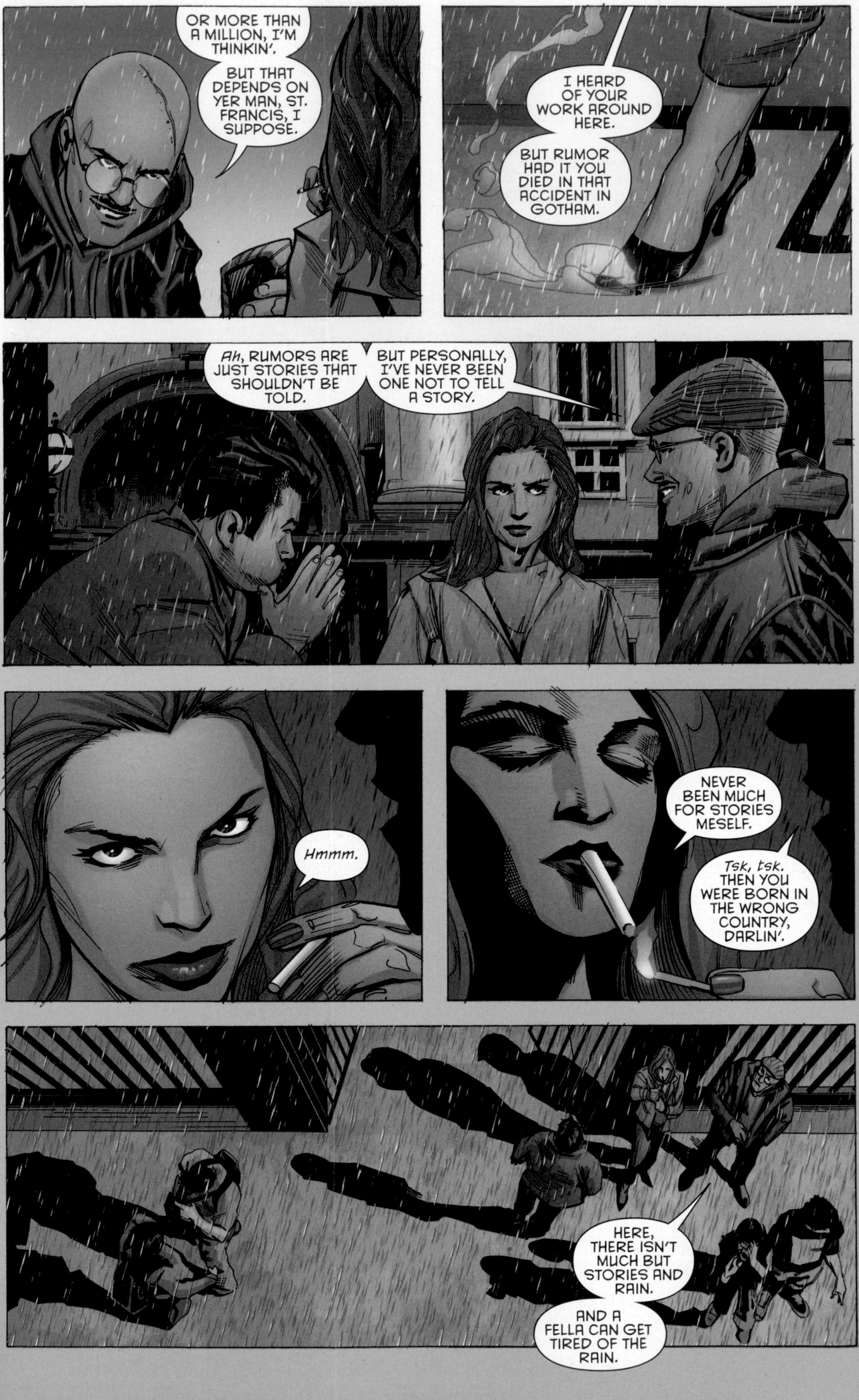
OR MORE THAN A MILLION, I'M THINKIN'.
BUT THAT DEPENDS ON YER MAN, ST. FRANCIS, I SUPPOSE.
I HEARD OF YOUR WORK AROUND HERE.
BUT RUMOR HAD IT YOU DIED IN THAT ACCIDENT IN GOTHAM.
Ah, RUMORS ARE JUST STORIES THAT SHOULDN'T BE TOLD.
BUT PERSONALLY, I'VE NEVER BEEN ONE NOT TO TELL A STORY.
Hmmm.
NEVER BEEN MUCH FOR STORIES MESELF.
Tsk, tsk. THEN YOU WERE BORN IN THE WRONG COUNTRY, DARLIN'.
HERE, THERE ISN'T MUCH BUT STORIES AND RAIN.
AND A FELLA CAN GET TIRED OF THE RAIN.

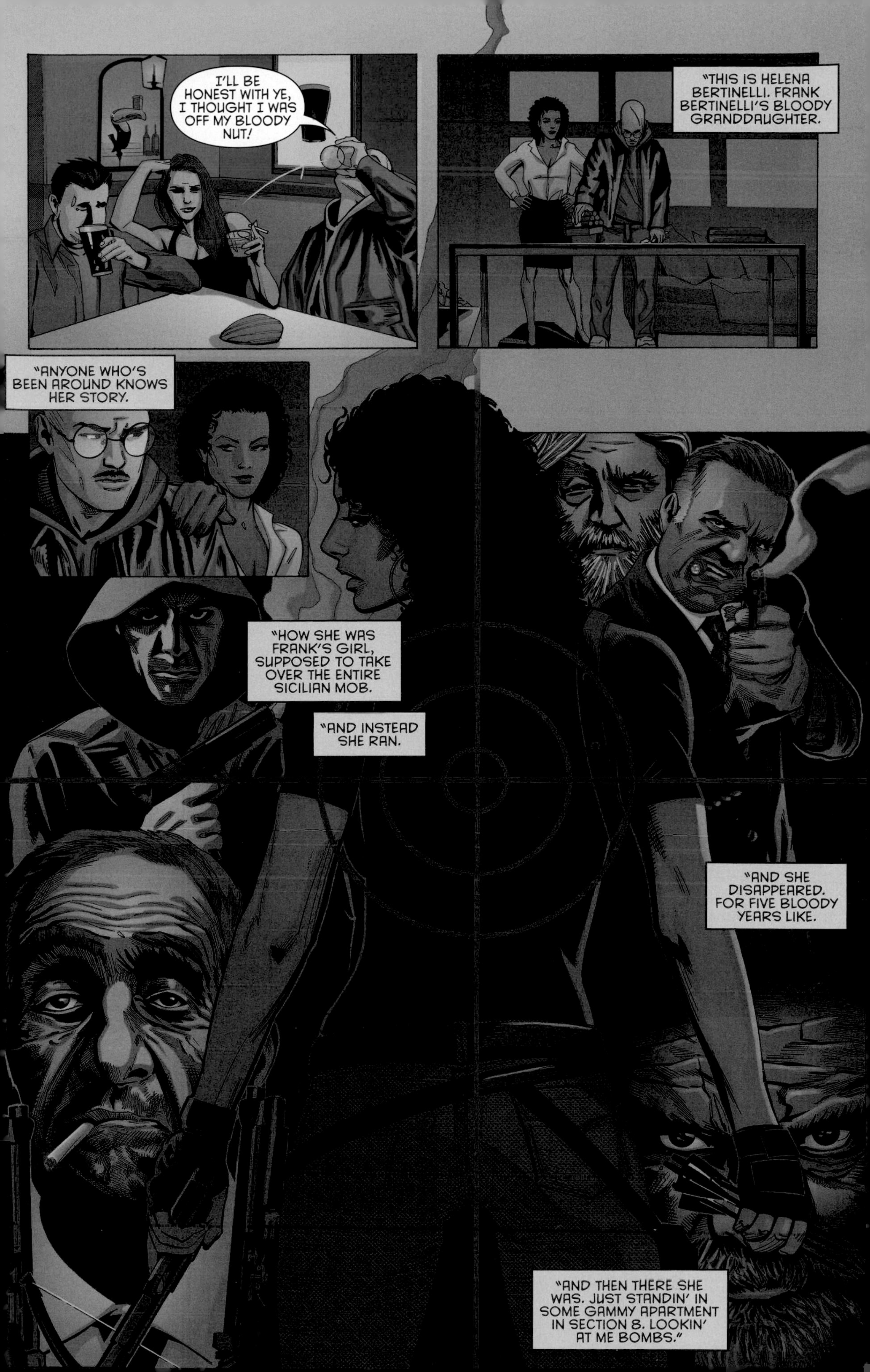
I'LL BE HONEST WITH YE, I THOUGHT I WAS OFF MY BLOODY NUT!
"THIS IS HELENA BERTINELLI. FRANK BERTINELLI'S BLOODY GRANDDAUGHTER.
"ANYONE WHO'S BEEN AROUND KNOWS HER STORY.
"HOW SHE WAS FRANK'S GIRL, SUPPOSED TO TAKE OVER THE ENTIRE SICILIAN MOB.
"AND INSTEAD SHE RAN.
"AND SHE DISAPPEARED. FOR FIVE BLOODY YEARS LIKE.
"AND THEN THERE SHE WAS. JUST STANDIN' IN SOME GAMMY APARTMENT IN SECTION 8. LOOKIN' AT ME BOMBS."

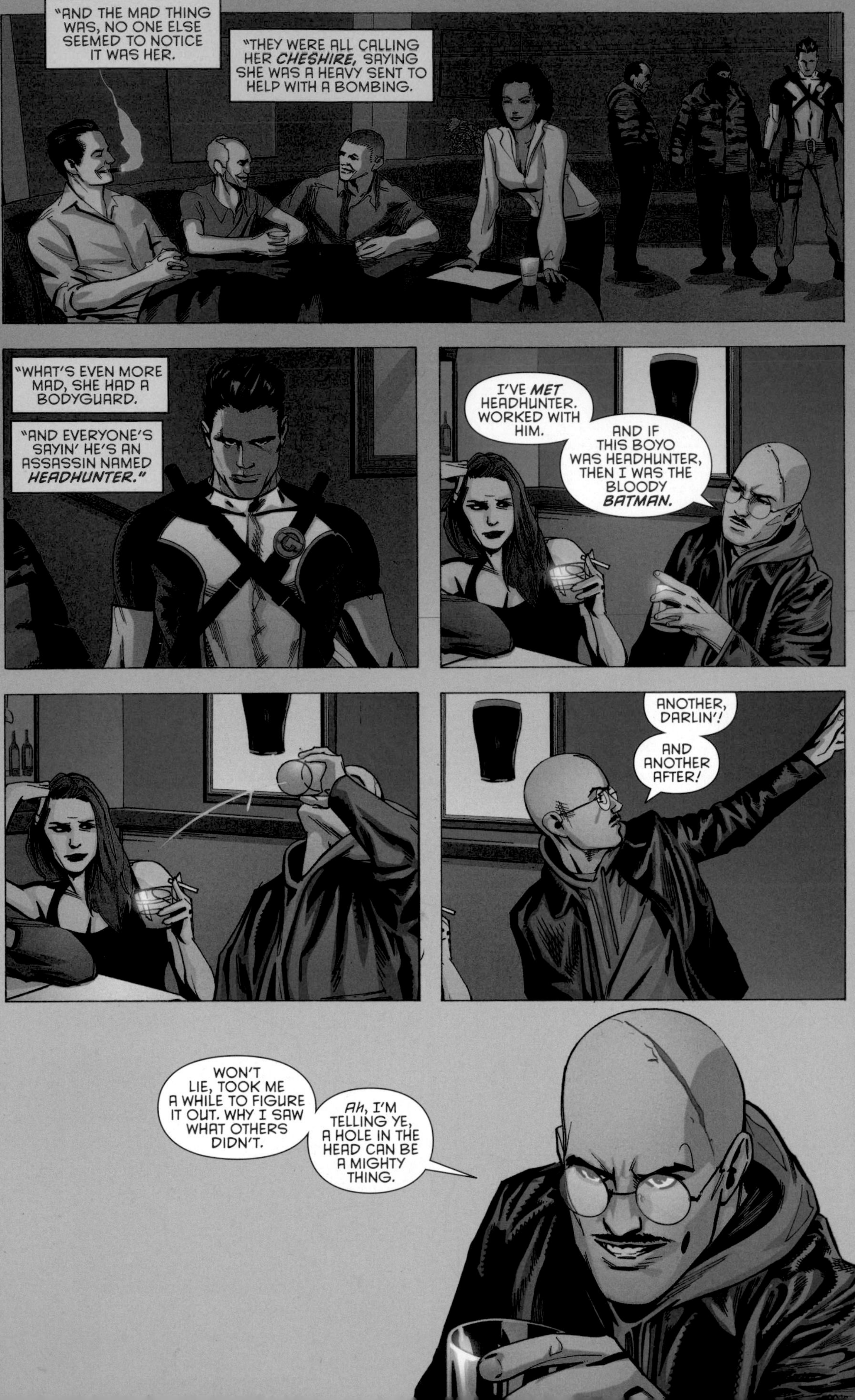
"AND THE MAD THING WAS, NO ONE ELSE SEEMED TO NOTICE IT WAS HER.
"THEY WERE ALL CALLING HER CHESHIRE, SAYING SHE WAS A HEAVY SENT TO HELP WITH A BOMBING.
"WHAT'S EVEN MORE MAD, SHE HAD A BODYGUARD.
"AND EVERYONE'S SAYIN' HE'S AN ASSASSIN NAMED HEADHUNTER."
I'VE MET HEADHUNTER. WORKED WITH HIM.
AND IF THIS BOYO WAS HEADHUNTER, THEN I WAS THE BLOODY BATMAN.
ANOTHER, DARLIN'!
AND ANOTHER AFTER!
WON'T LIE, TOOK ME A WHILE TO FIGURE IT OUT. WHY I SAW WHAT OTHERS DIDN'T.
Ah, I'M TELLING YE, A HOLE IN THE HEAD CAN BE A MIGHTY THING.

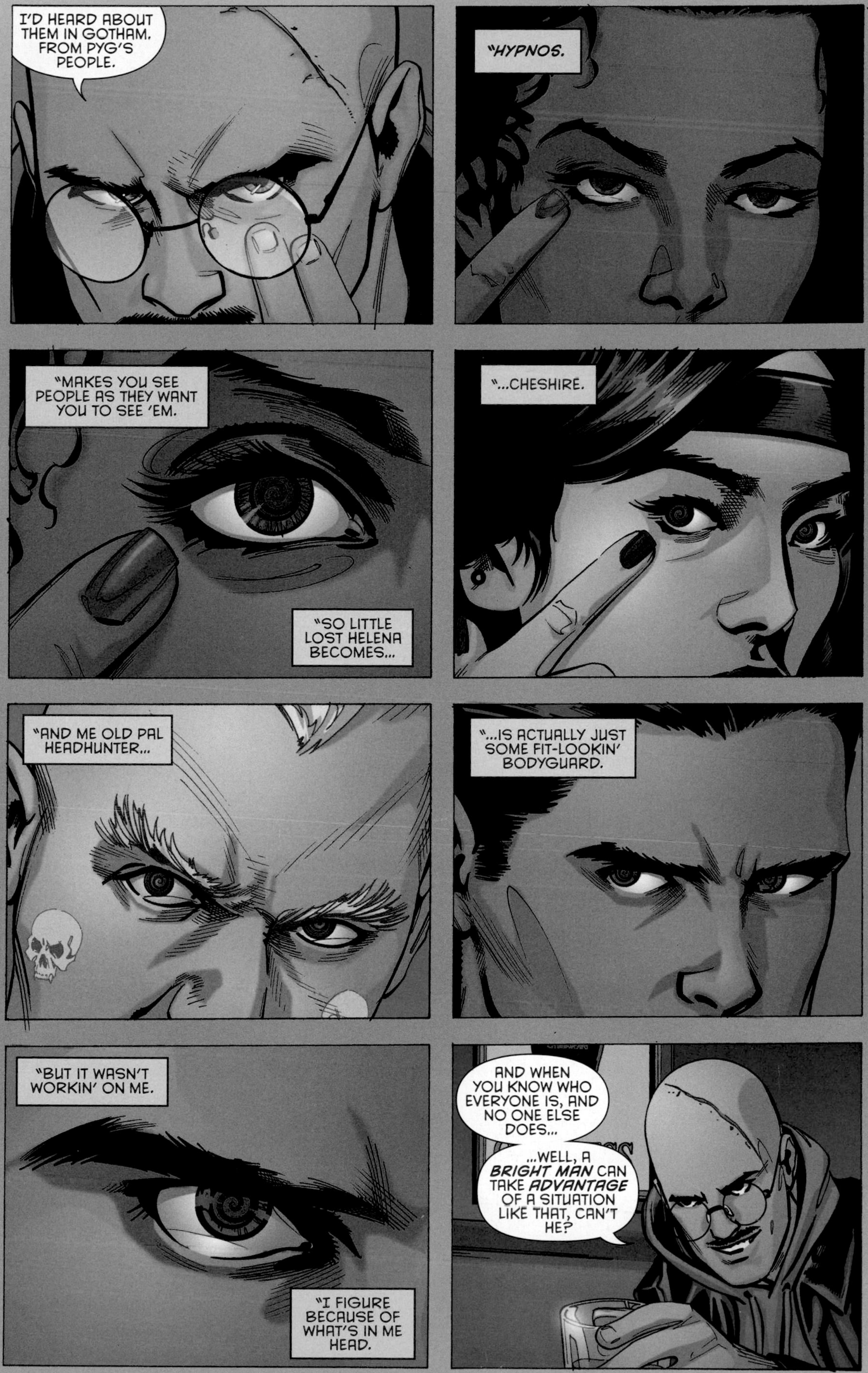
I'D HEARD ABOUT THEM IN GOTHAM. FROM PYG'S PEOPLE.
"HYPNOS.
"MAKES YOU SEE PEOPLE AS THEY WANT YOU TO SEE 'EM.
"SO LITTLE LOST HELENA BECOMES...
"...CHESHIRE.
"AND ME OLD PAL HEADHUNTER...
"...IS ACTUALLY JUST SOME FIT-LOOKIN' BODYGUARD.
"BUT IT WASN'T WORKIN' ON ME.
"I FIGURE BECAUSE OF WHAT'S IN ME HEAD.
AND WHEN YOU KNOW WHO EVERYONE IS, AND NO ONE ELSE DOES...
...WELL, A BRIGHT MAN CAN TAKE ADVANTAGE OF A SITUATION LIKE THAT, CAN'T HE?

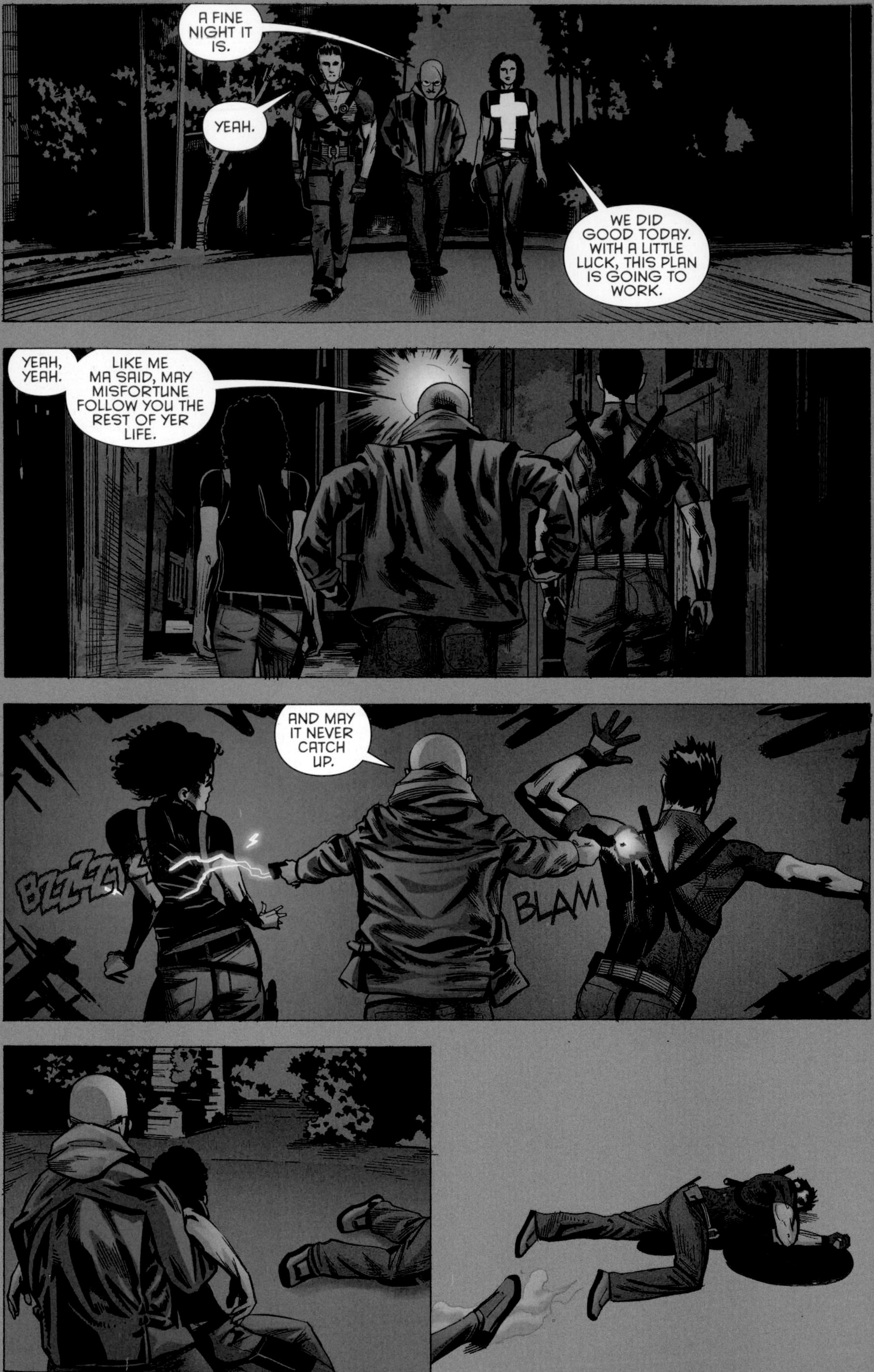
A FINE NIGHT IT IS.
YEAH.
WE DID GOOD TODAY. WITH A LITTLE LUCK, THIS PLAN IS GOING TO WORK.
YEAH, YEAH.
LIKE ME MA SAID, MAY MISFORTUNE FOLLOW YOU THE REST OF YER LIFE.
AND MAY IT NEVER CATCH UP.
BZZZZT
BLAM

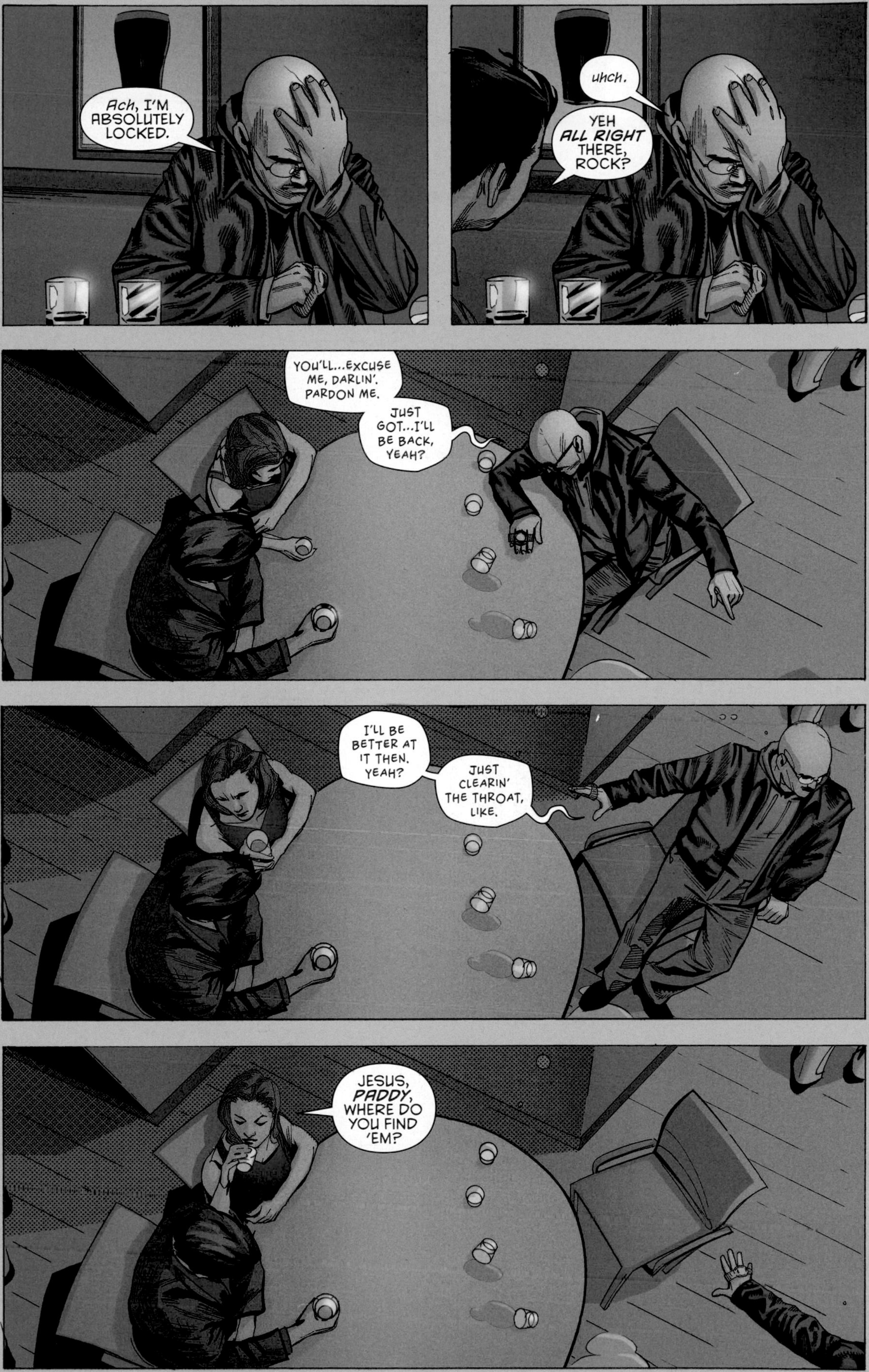
Ach, I'M ABSOLUTELY LOCKED.
uhch.
YEH ALL RIGHT THERE, ROCK?
YOU'LL...EXCUSE ME, DARLIN'. PARDON ME.
JUST GOT...I'LL BE BACK, YEAH?
I'LL BE BETTER AT IT THEN. YEAH?
JUST CLEARIN' THE THROAT, LIKE.
JESUS, PADDY, WHERE DO YOU FIND 'EM?

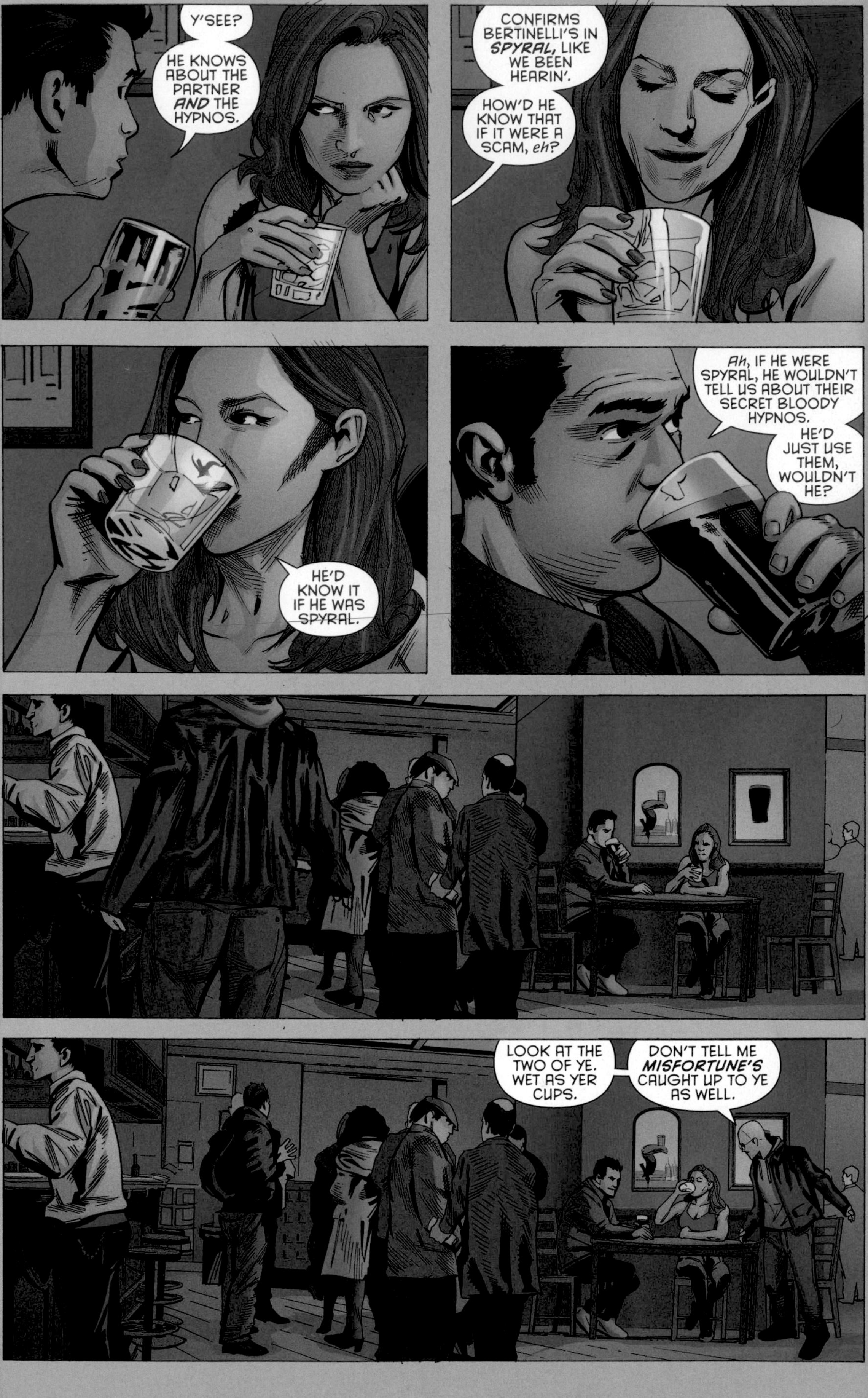

Y'SEE?
HE KNOWS ABOUT THE PARTNER *AND* THE HYPNOS.
CONFIRMS BERTINELLI'S IN *SPYRAL,* LIKE WE BEEN HEARIN'.
HOW'D HE KNOW THAT IF IT WERE A SCAM, *eh?*
HE'D KNOW IT IF HE WAS SPYRAL.
Ah, IF HE WERE SPYRAL, HE WOULDN'T TELL US ABOUT THEIR SECRET BLOODY HYPNOS.
HE'D JUST USE THEM, WOULDN'T HE?
LOOK AT THE TWO OF YE. WET AS YER CUPS.
DON'T TELL ME *MISFORTUNE'S* CAUGHT UP TO YE AS WELL.

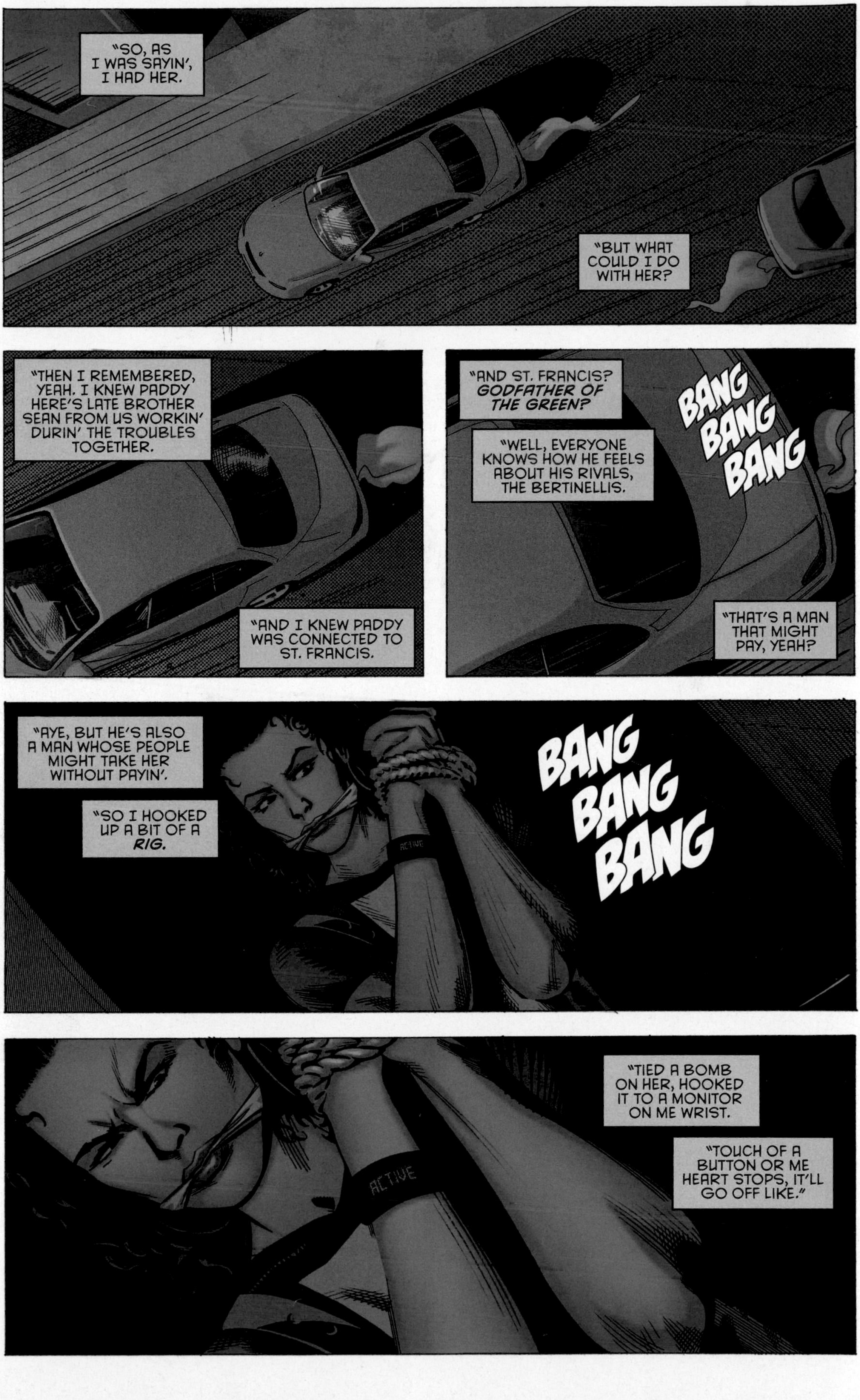
"SO, AS I WAS SAYIN', I HAD HER.
"BUT WHAT COULD I DO WITH HER?
"THEN I REMEMBERED, YEAH. I KNEW PADDY HERE'S LATE BROTHER SEAN FROM US WORKIN' DURIN' THE TROUBLES TOGETHER.
"AND I KNEW PADDY WAS CONNECTED TO ST. FRANCIS.
"AND ST. FRANCIS? *GODFATHER OF THE GREEN?*
BANG BANG BANG
"WELL, EVERYONE KNOWS HOW HE FEELS ABOUT HIS RIVALS, THE BERTINELLIS.
"THAT'S A MAN THAT MIGHT PAY, YEAH?
"AYE, BUT HE'S ALSO A MAN WHOSE PEOPLE MIGHT TAKE HER WITHOUT PAYIN'.
"SO I HOOKED UP A BIT OF A *RIG.*
ACTIVE
BANG BANG BANG
"TIED A BOMB ON HER, HOOKED IT TO A MONITOR ON ME WRIST.
"TOUCH OF A BUTTON OR ME HEART STOPS, IT'LL GO OFF LIKE."
ACTIVE

BOOM.

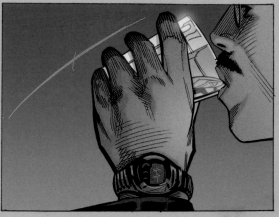

THEN I MET PADDY, AND HE BROUGHT YOU. AND YOU'LL MAYBE BRING ST. FRANCIS.

ST. FRANCIS'LL BRING THE *MONEY*. I'LL TURN OFF THE BOMB.

I KNOW, I KNOW. I'M STILL SMALL. COMPARED TO HIM, I MEAN.

HE COULD STILL DO ANYTHIN', ONCE HE HAD HER, COULDN'T HE?

BUT I'VE HEARD IF YEH SHAKE HIS HAND, THAT'S IT.

YOU CAN TRUST IN HIM LIKE YOU CAN TRUST IN THE LORD.

AND AFTER WHAT'S HAPPENED. WHAT I HAVE NOW. WHAT'S IN THAT TRUNK.

DON'T HAVE MUCH CHOICE BUT TO TRUST IN THE LORD, DO I?

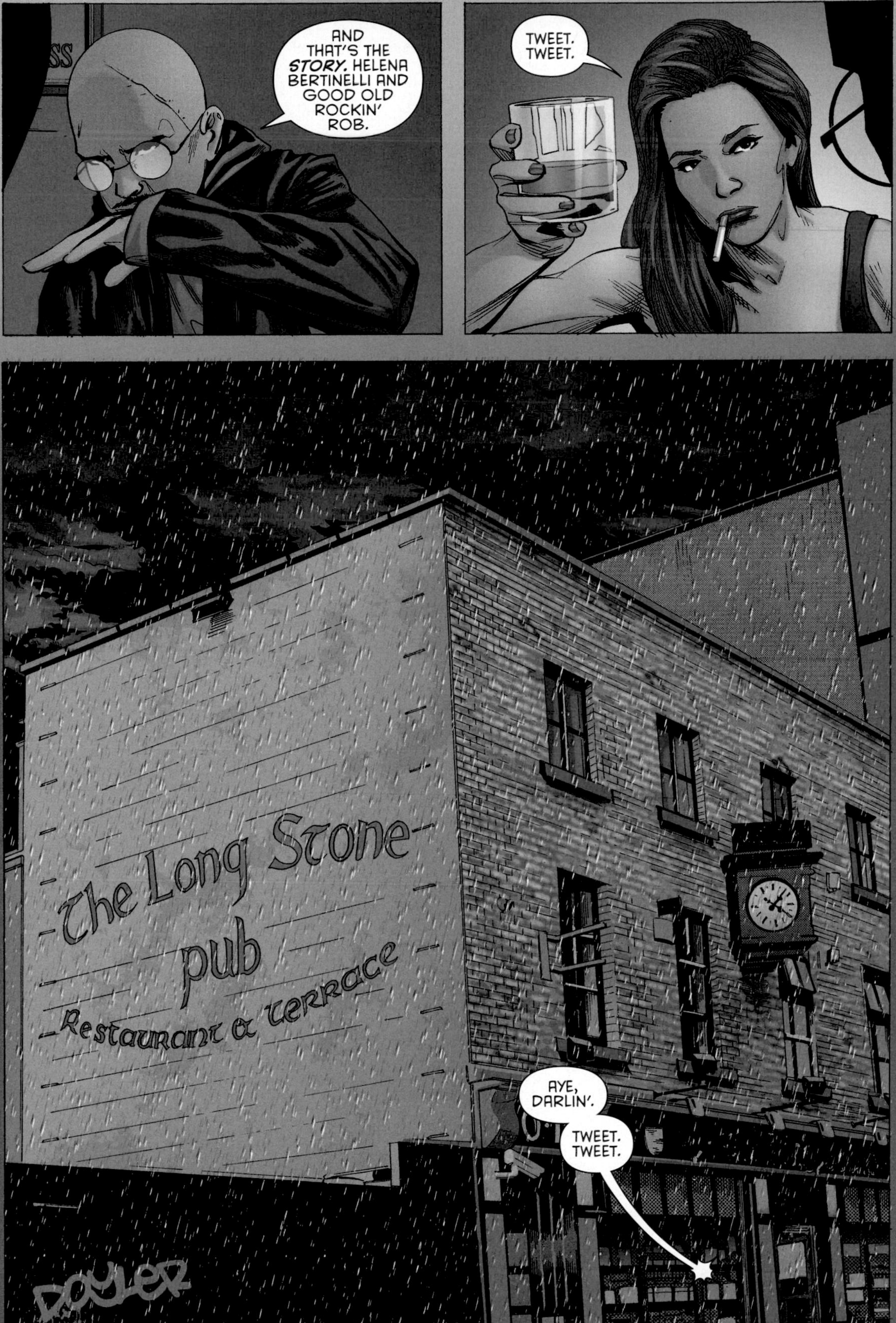
AND THAT'S THE STORY. HELENA BERTINELLI AND GOOD OLD ROCKIN' ROB.
TWEET. TWEET.
The Long Stone pub
Restaurant & Terrace
DOYLER
TEEHANWOLF
AYE, DARLIN'.
TWEET. TWEET.

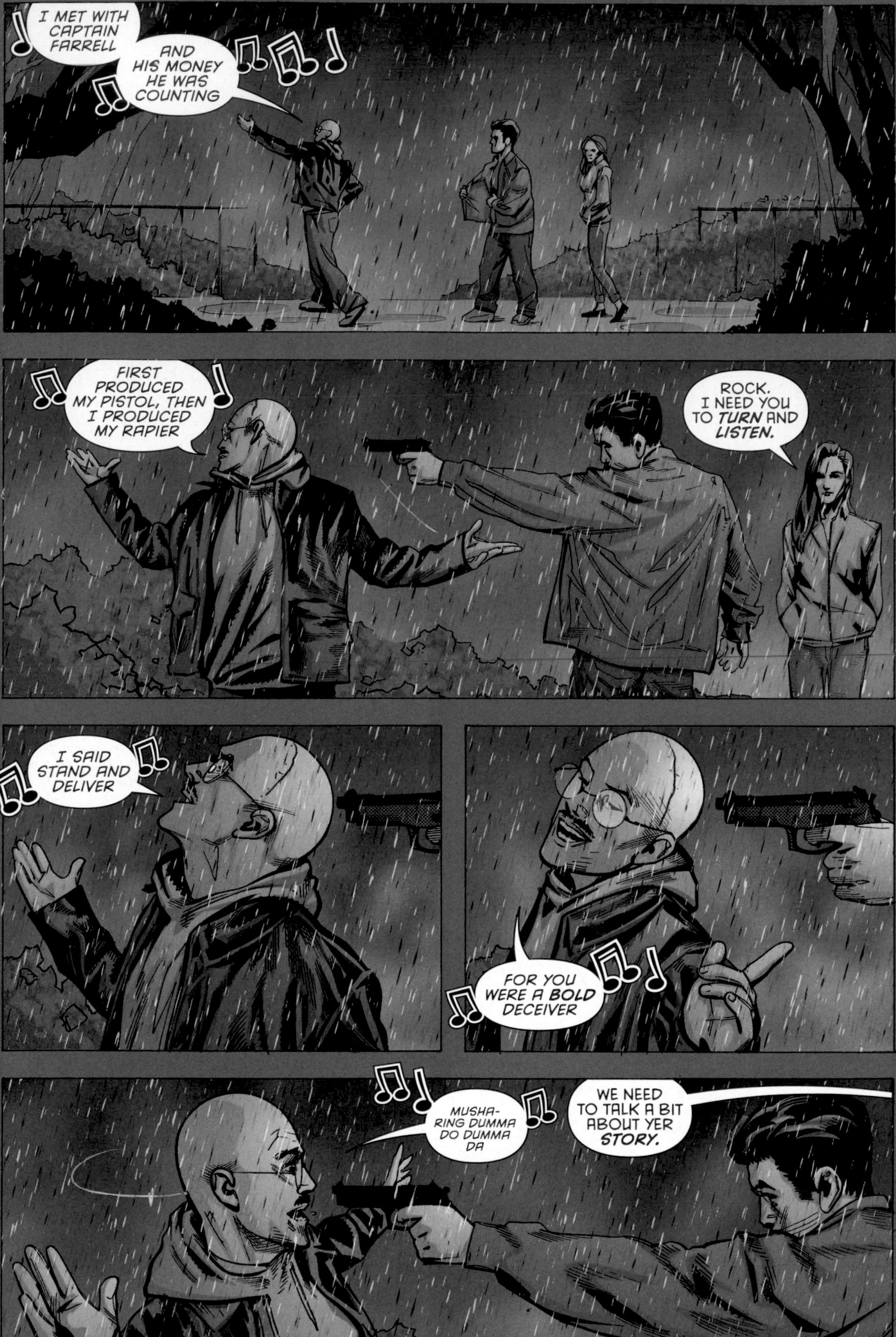
I MET WITH CAPTAIN FARRELL
AND HIS MONEY HE WAS COUNTING
FIRST PRODUCED MY PISTOL, THEN I PRODUCED MY RAPIER
ROCK. I NEED YOU TO *TURN* AND *LISTEN.*
I SAID STAND AND DELIVER
FOR YOU WERE A *BOLD* DECEIVER
MUSHA-RING DUMMA DO DUMMA DA
WE NEED TO TALK A BIT ABOUT YER *STORY.*

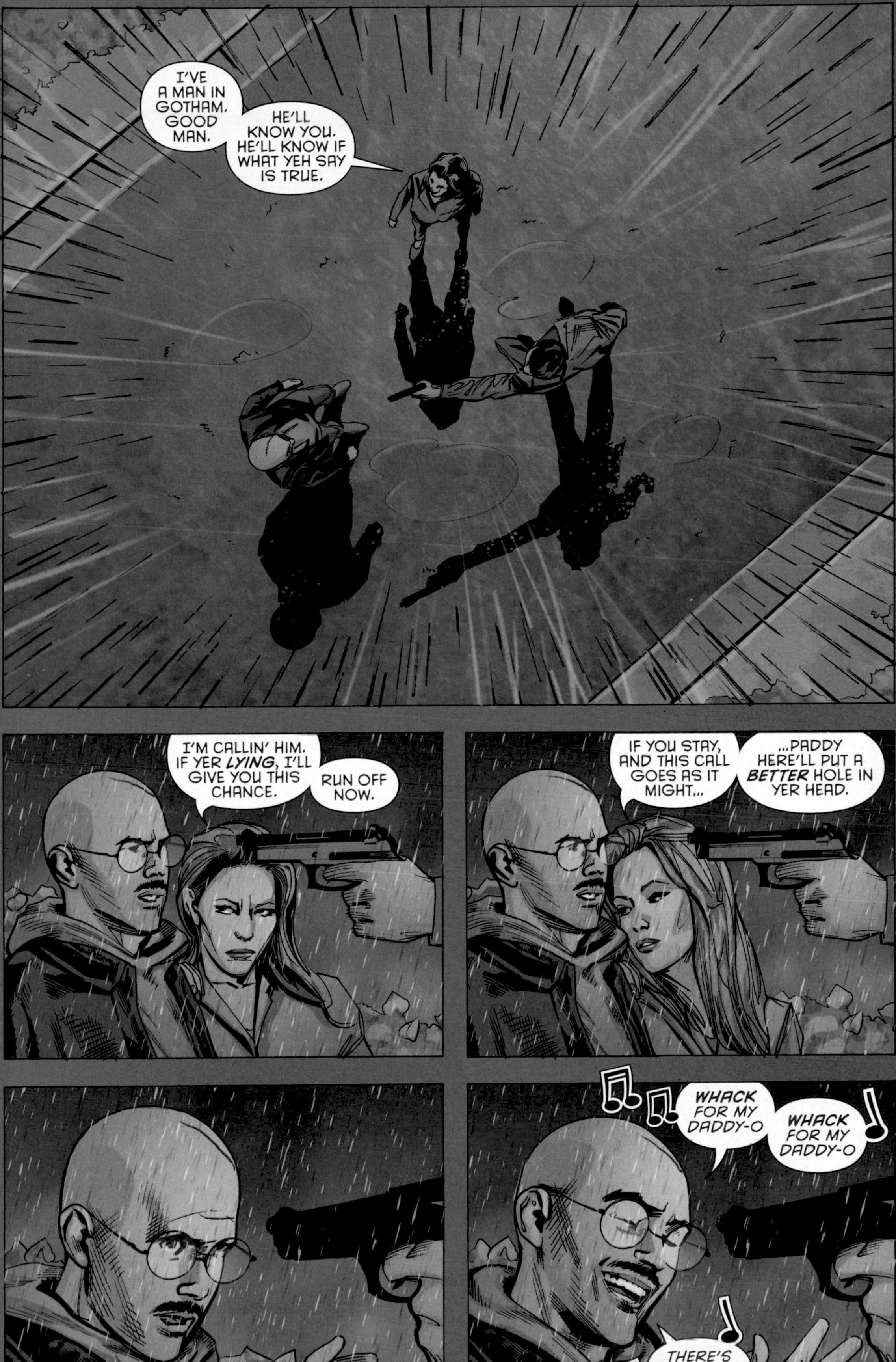
I'VE A MAN IN GOTHAM. GOOD MAN.
HE'LL KNOW YOU. HE'LL KNOW IF WHAT YEH SAY IS TRUE.
I'M CALLIN' HIM. IF YER *LYING*, I'LL GIVE YOU THIS CHANCE.
RUN OFF NOW.
IF YOU STAY, AND THIS CALL GOES AS IT MIGHT...
...PADDY HERE'LL PUT A *BETTER* HOLE IN YER HEAD.
WHACK FOR MY DADDY-O
WHACK FOR MY DADDY-O
THERE'S WHISKEY IN THE JAR!

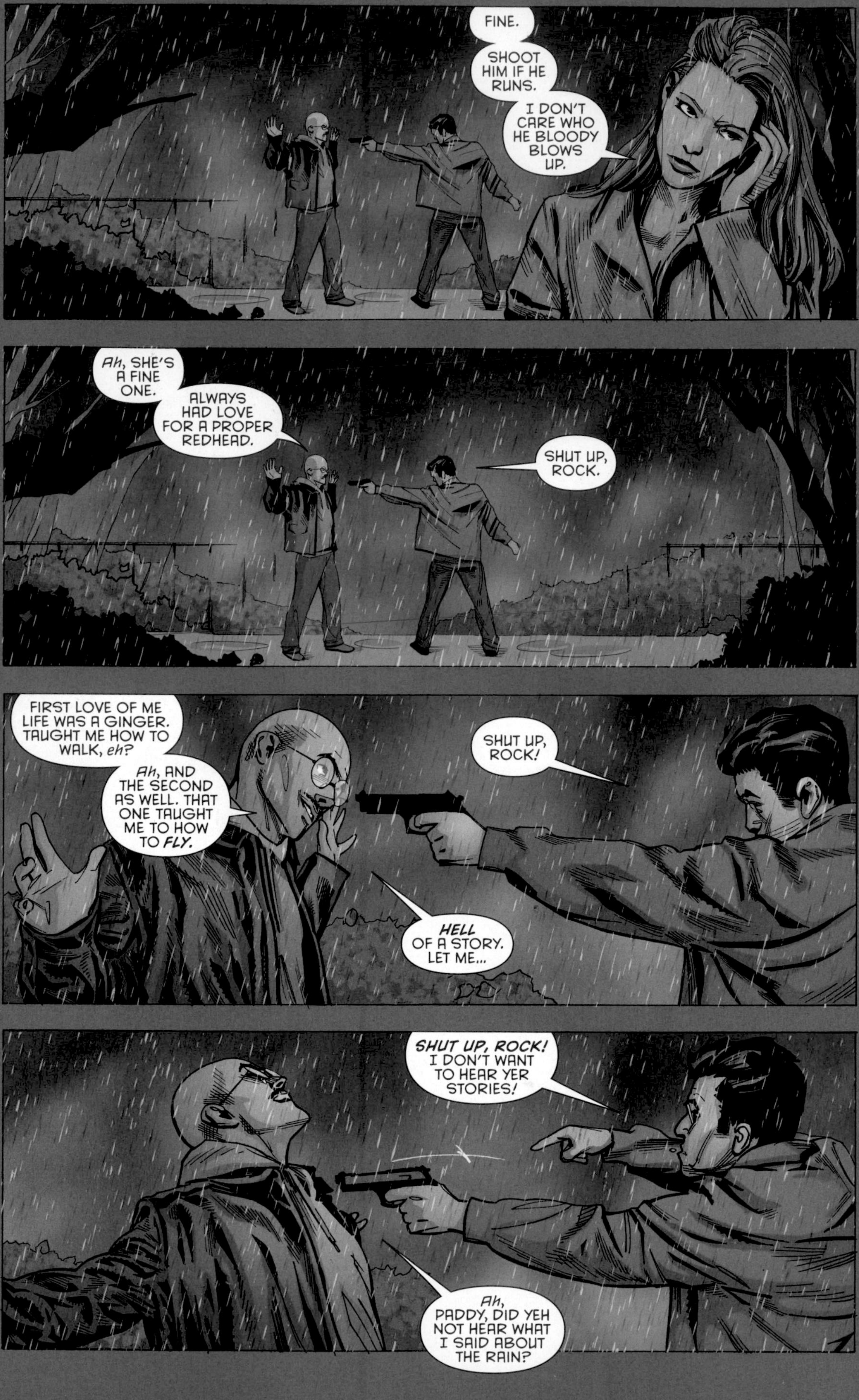
FINE.
SHOOT HIM IF HE RUNS.
I DON'T CARE WHO HE BLOODY BLOWS UP.
Ah, SHE'S A FINE ONE.
ALWAYS HAD LOVE FOR A PROPER REDHEAD.
SHUT UP, ROCK.
FIRST LOVE OF ME LIFE WAS A GINGER. TAUGHT ME HOW TO WALK, *eh*?
Ah, AND THE SECOND AS WELL. THAT ONE TAUGHT ME TO HOW TO ***FLY.***
SHUT UP, ROCK!
HELL OF A STORY. LET ME...
SHUT UP, ROCK! I DON'T WANT TO HEAR YER STORIES!
Ah, PADDY, DID YEH NOT HEAR WHAT I SAID ABOUT THE RAIN?

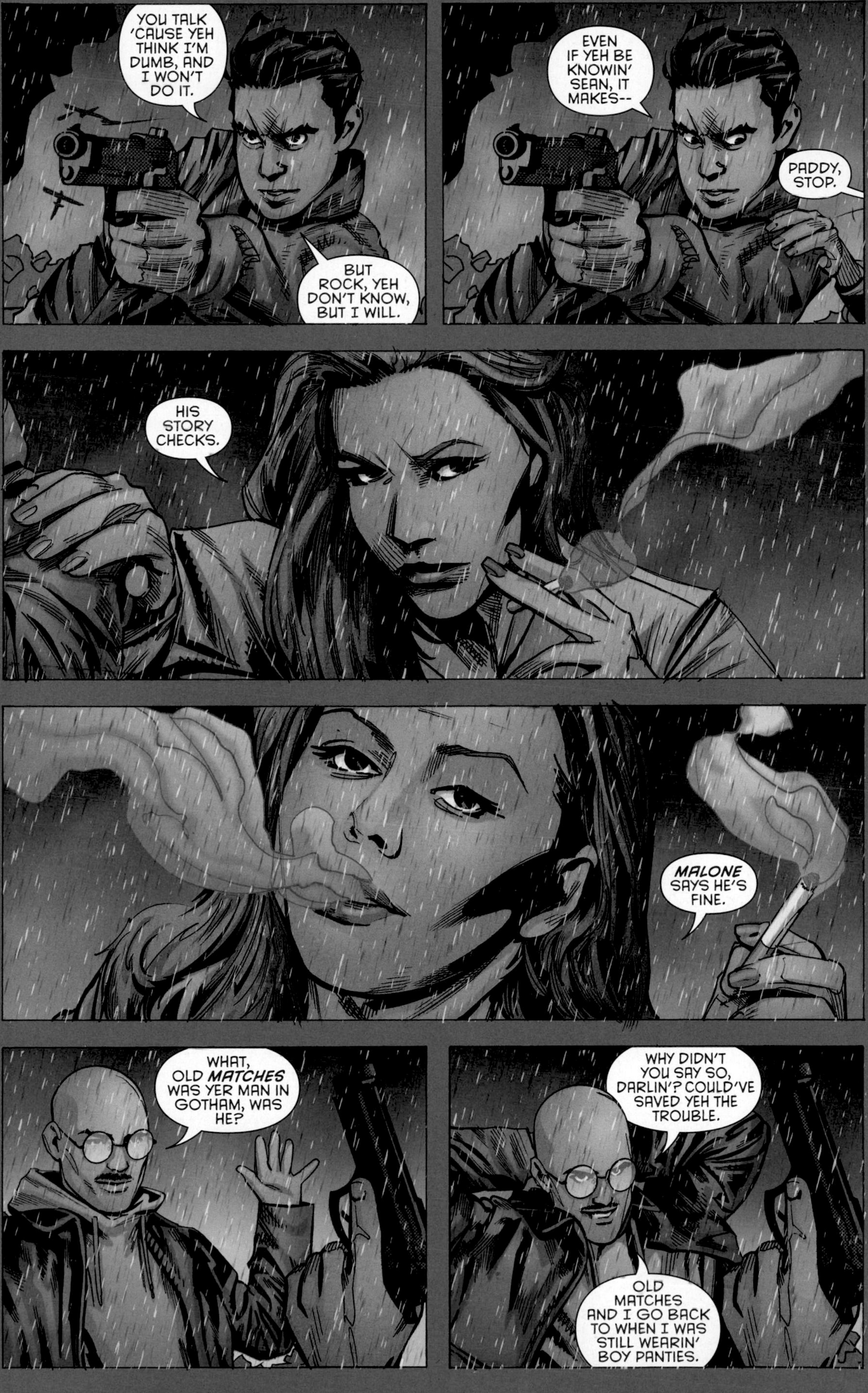
YOU TALK 'CAUSE YEH THINK I'M DUMB, AND I WON'T DO IT.
BUT ROCK, YEH DON'T KNOW, BUT I WILL.
EVEN IF YEH BE KNOWIN' SEAN, IT MAKES--
PADDY, STOP.
HIS STORY CHECKS.
MALONE SAYS HE'S FINE.
WHAT, OLD MATCHES WAS YER MAN IN GOTHAM, WAS HE?
WHY DIDN'T YOU SAY SO, DARLIN'? COULD'VE SAVED YEH THE TROUBLE.
OLD MATCHES AND I GO BACK TO WHEN I WAS STILL WEARIN' BOY PANTIES.

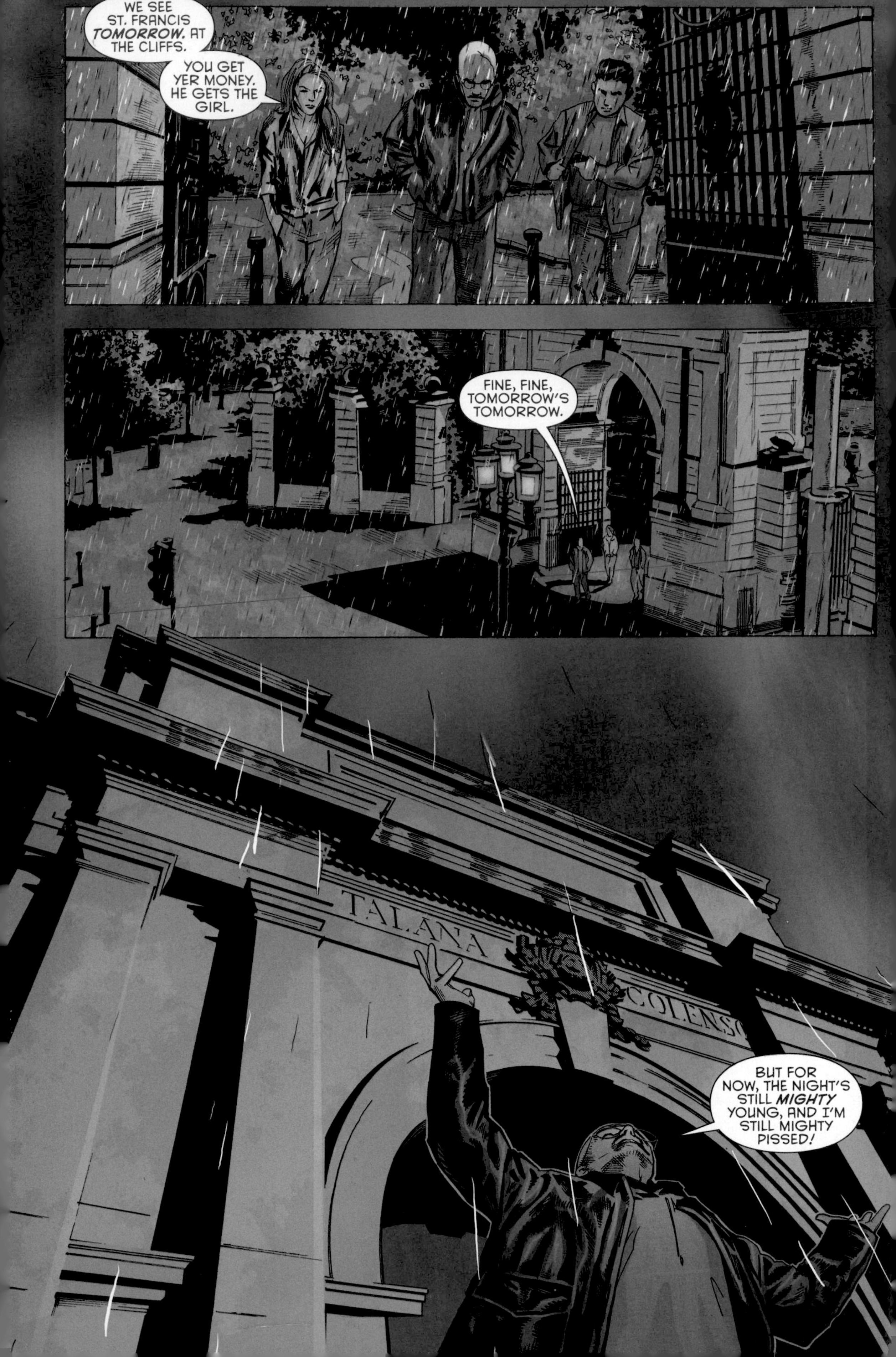
WE SEE ST. FRANCIS TOMORROW. AT THE CLIFFS.
YOU GET YER MONEY. HE GETS THE GIRL.
FINE, FINE, TOMORROW'S TOMORROW.
TALANA
COLENSO
BUT FOR NOW, THE NIGHT'S STILL MIGHTY YOUNG, AND I'M STILL MIGHTY PISSED!

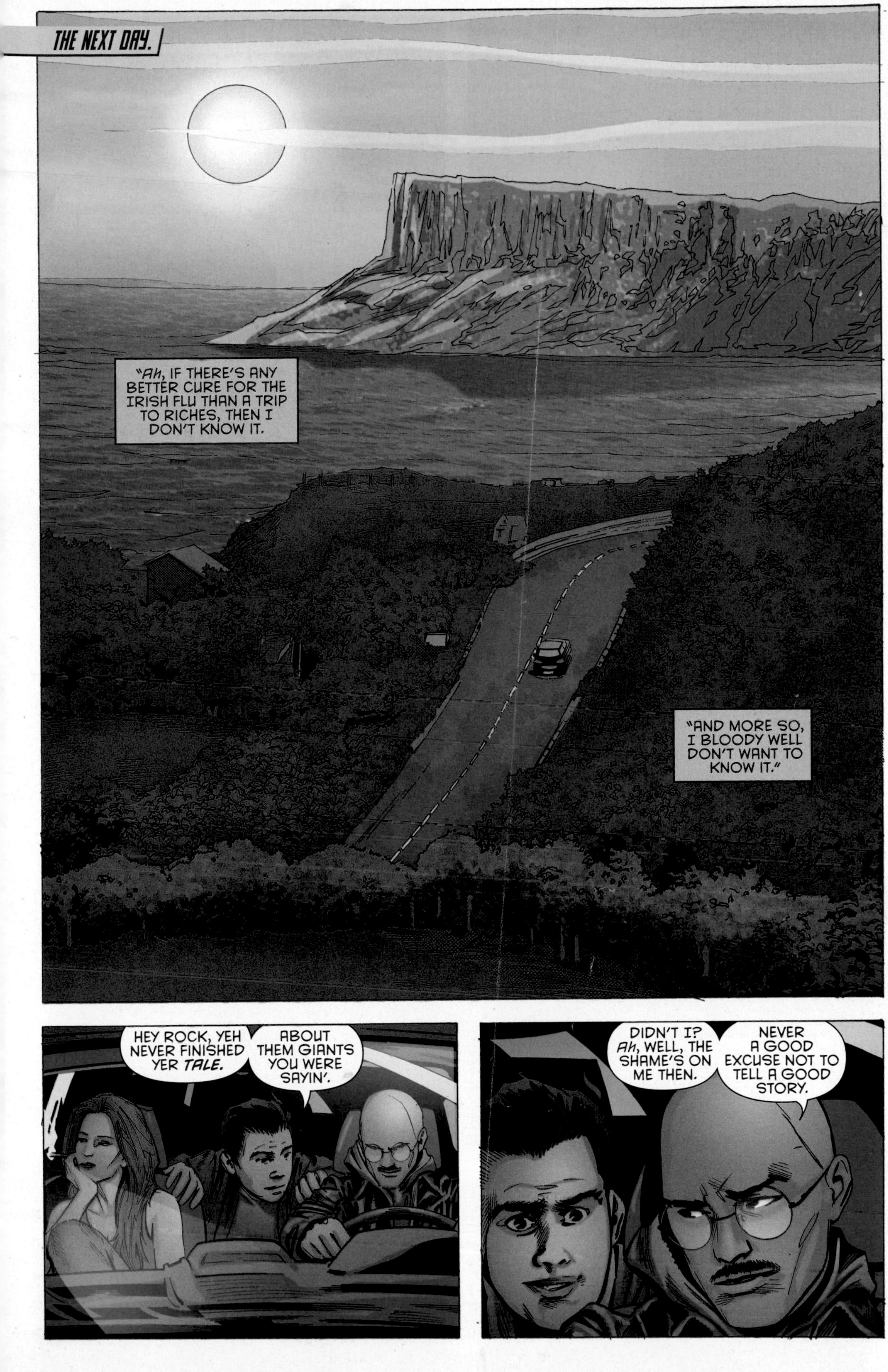
THE NEXT DAY.
"Ah, IF THERE'S ANY BETTER CURE FOR THE IRISH FLU THAN A TRIP TO RICHES, THEN I DON'T KNOW IT.
"AND MORE SO, I BLOODY WELL DON'T WANT TO KNOW IT."
HEY ROCK, YEH NEVER FINISHED YER TALE.
ABOUT THEM GIANTS YOU WERE SAYIN'.
DIDN'T I? Ah, WELL, THE SHAME'S ON ME THEN.
NEVER A GOOD EXCUSE NOT TO TELL A GOOD STORY.

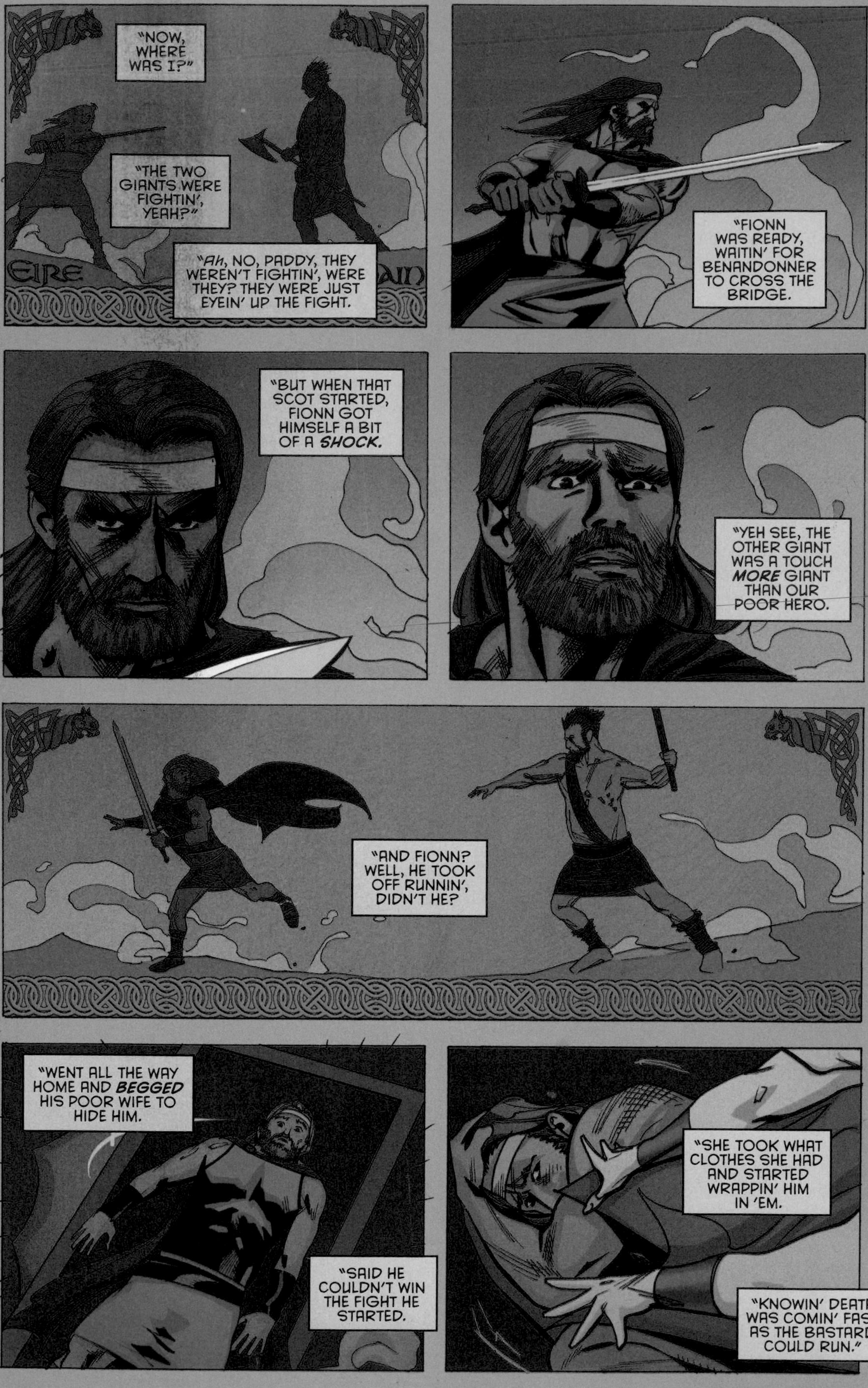
"NOW, WHERE WAS I?"
"THE TWO GIANTS WERE FIGHTIN', YEAH?"
"AH, NO, PADDY, THEY WEREN'T FIGHTIN', WERE THEY? THEY WERE JUST EYEIN' UP THE FIGHT.
EIRE
"FIONN WAS READY, WAITIN' FOR BENANDONNER TO CROSS THE BRIDGE.
"BUT WHEN THAT SCOT STARTED, FIONN GOT HIMSELF A BIT OF A SHOCK.
"YEH SEE, THE OTHER GIANT WAS A TOUCH MORE GIANT THAN OUR POOR HERO.
"AND FIONN? WELL, HE TOOK OFF RUNNIN', DIDN'T HE?
"WENT ALL THE WAY HOME AND BEGGED HIS POOR WIFE TO HIDE HIM.
"SAID HE COULDN'T WIN THE FIGHT HE STARTED.
"SHE TOOK WHAT CLOTHES SHE HAD AND STARTED WRAPPIN' HIM IN 'EM.
"KNOWIN' DEATH WAS COMIN' FAST AS THE BASTARD COULD RUN."

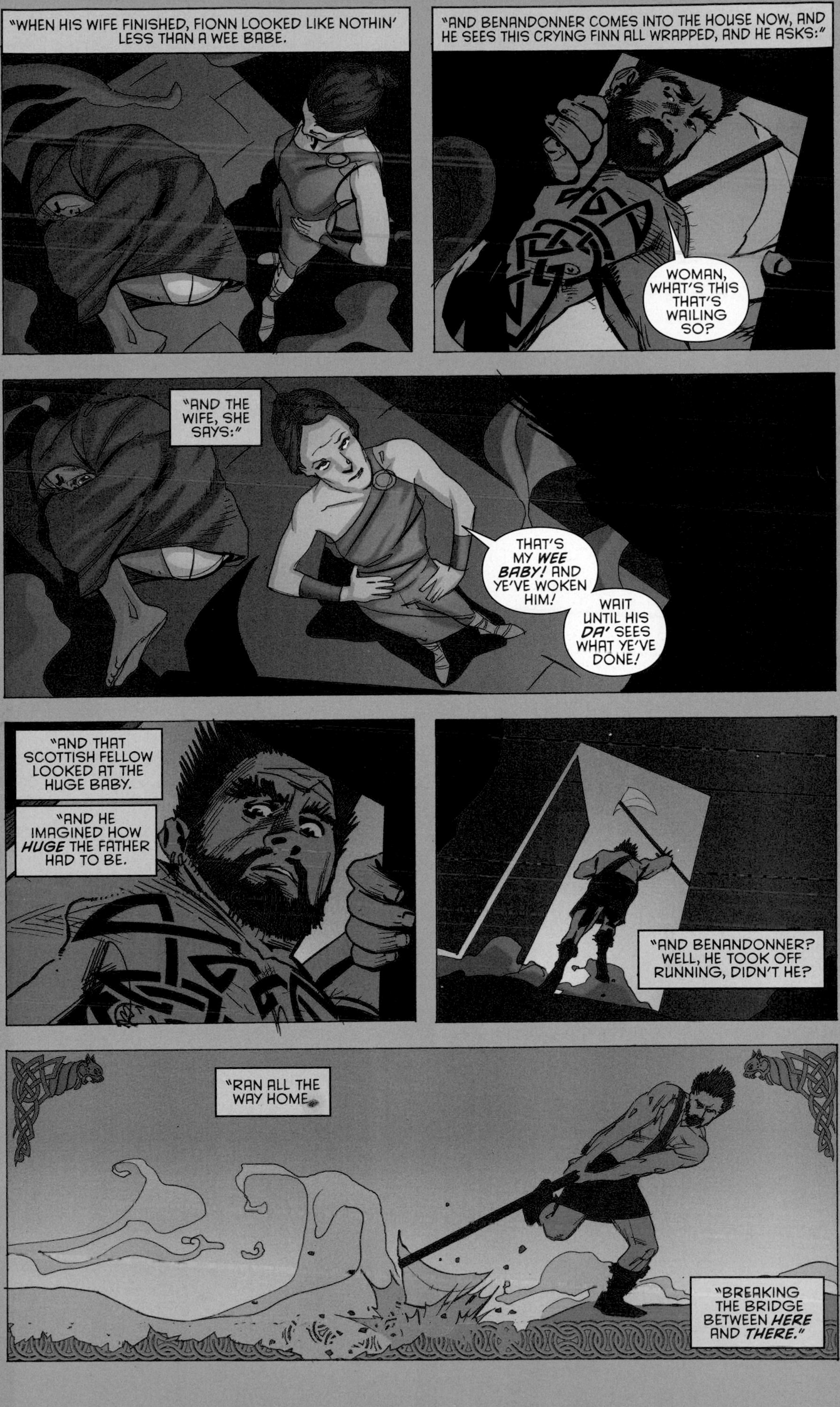
"WHEN HIS WIFE FINISHED, FIONN LOOKED LIKE NOTHIN' LESS THAN A WEE BABE.
"AND BENANDONNER COMES INTO THE HOUSE NOW, AND HE SEES THIS CRYING FINN ALL WRAPPED, AND HE ASKS:"
WOMAN, WHAT'S THIS THAT'S WAILING SO?
"AND THE WIFE, SHE SAYS:"
THAT'S MY WEE BABY! AND YE'VE WOKEN HIM!
WAIT UNTIL HIS DA' SEES WHAT YE'VE DONE!
"AND THAT SCOTTISH FELLOW LOOKED AT THE HUGE BABY.
"AND HE IMAGINED HOW HUGE THE FATHER HAD TO BE.
"AND BENANDONNER? WELL, HE TOOK OFF RUNNING, DIDN'T HE?
"RAN ALL THE WAY HOME.
"BREAKING THE BRIDGE BETWEEN HERE AND THERE."

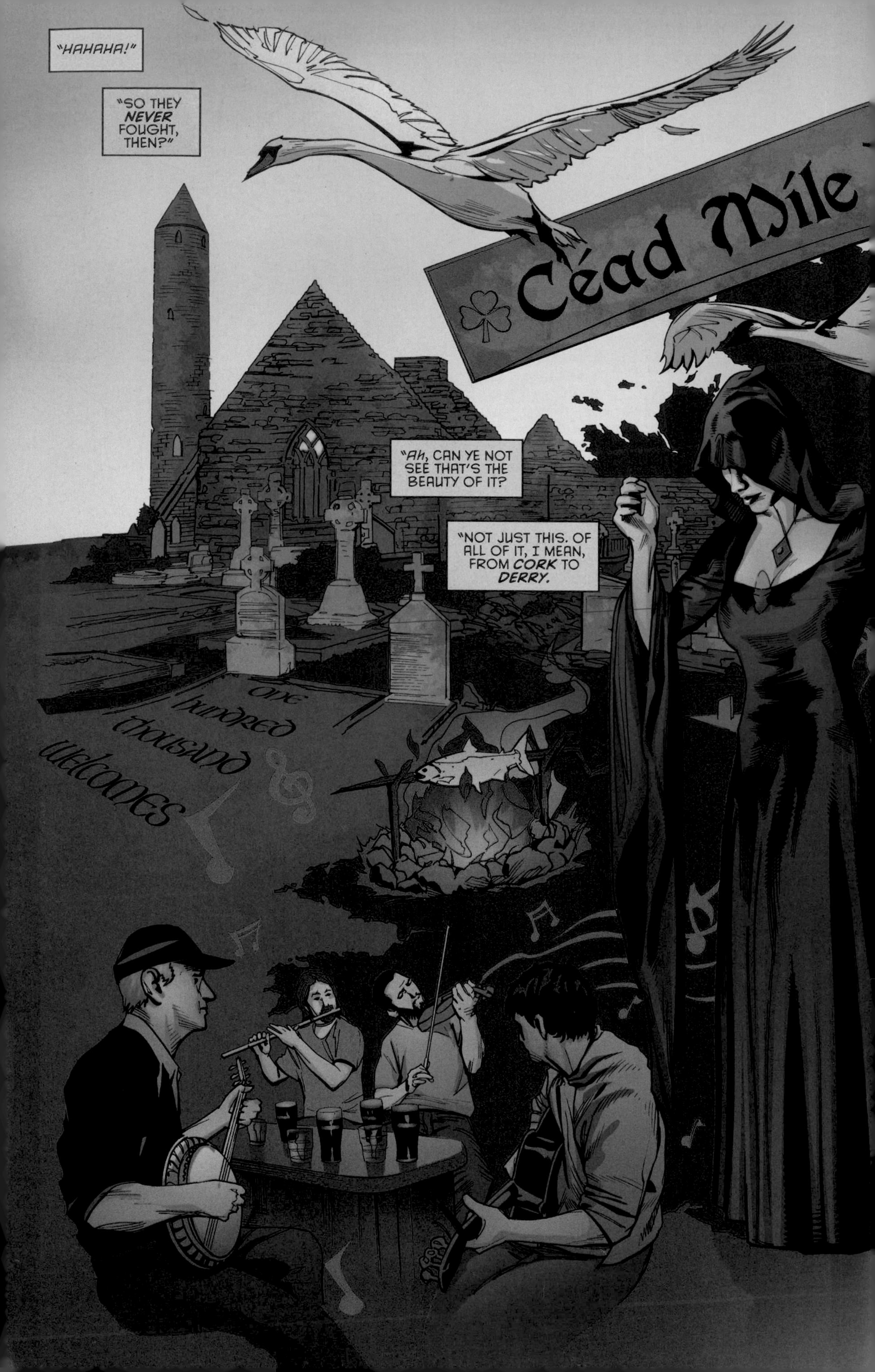

"HAHAHA!"
"SO THEY NEVER FOUGHT, THEN?"
Céad Míle
"Ah, CAN YE NOT SEE THAT'S THE BEAUTY OF IT?
"NOT JUST THIS. OF ALL OF IT, I MEAN, FROM CORK TO DERRY.
one hundred thousand welcomes

áilte
IRISH PUB
Cead Mile Fáilce
Storytelling and Singing
Dancing and Carrying On
"ANY SHEEP-RATTLER CAN WIN WITH A FIST, YEAH?
"ONLY *WE* CAN WIN WITH A *STORY.*"
TOMÁS AGUS STIOFÁN
"WE'RE HERE. PULL OVER."

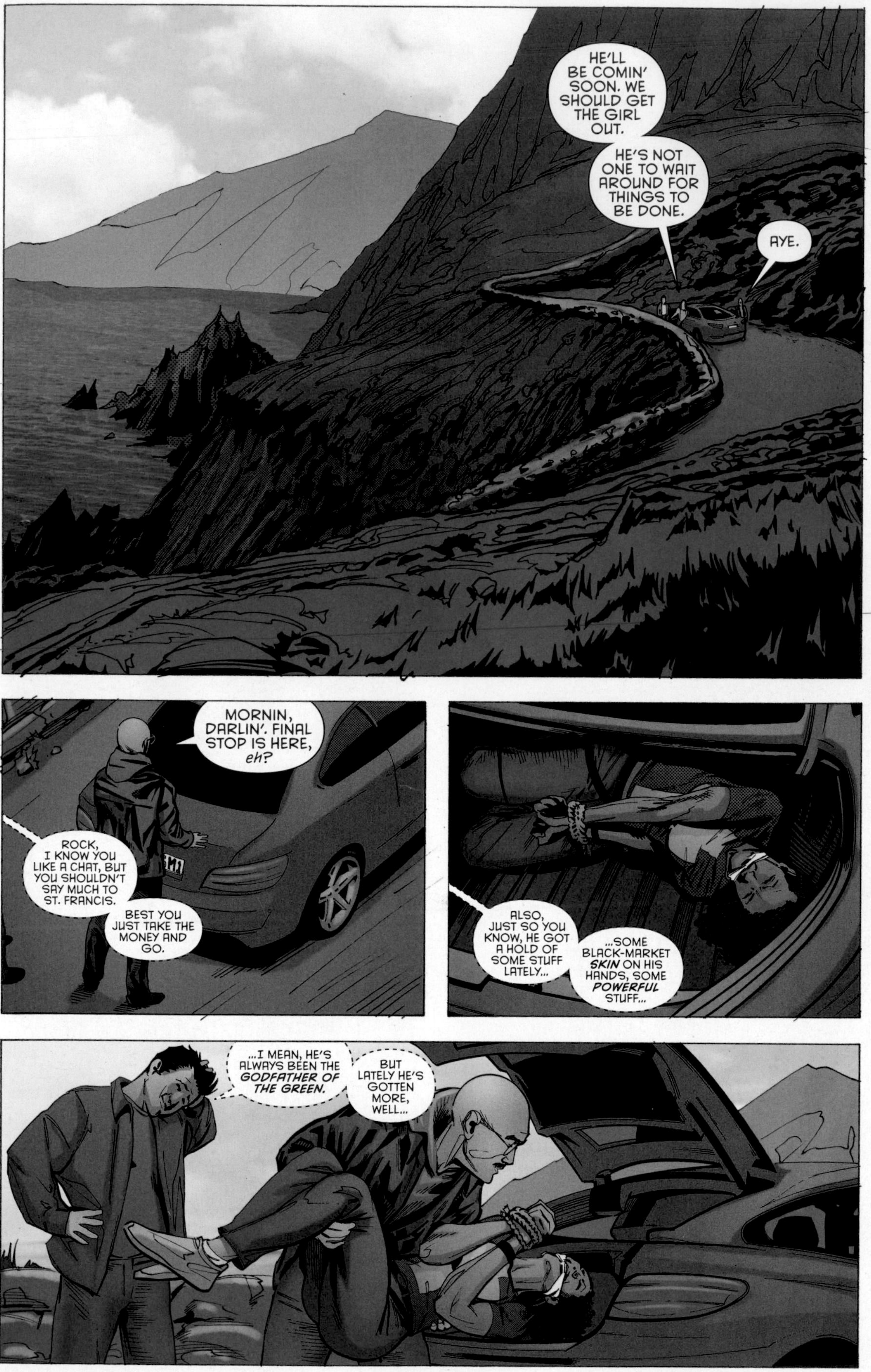
HE'LL BE COMIN' SOON. WE SHOULD GET THE GIRL OUT.
HE'S NOT ONE TO WAIT AROUND FOR THINGS TO BE DONE.
AYE.
MORNIN, DARLIN'. FINAL STOP IS HERE, *eh?*
ROCK, I KNOW YOU LIKE A CHAT, BUT YOU SHOULDN'T SAY MUCH TO ST. FRANCIS.
BEST YOU JUST TAKE THE MONEY AND GO.
ALSO, JUST SO YOU KNOW, HE GOT A HOLD OF SOME STUFF LATELY...
...SOME BLACK-MARKET ***SKIN*** ON HIS HANDS, SOME ***POWERFUL*** STUFF...
...I MEAN, HE'S ALWAYS BEEN THE ***GODFATHER OF THE GREEN.***
BUT LATELY HE'S GOTTEN MORE, WELL...

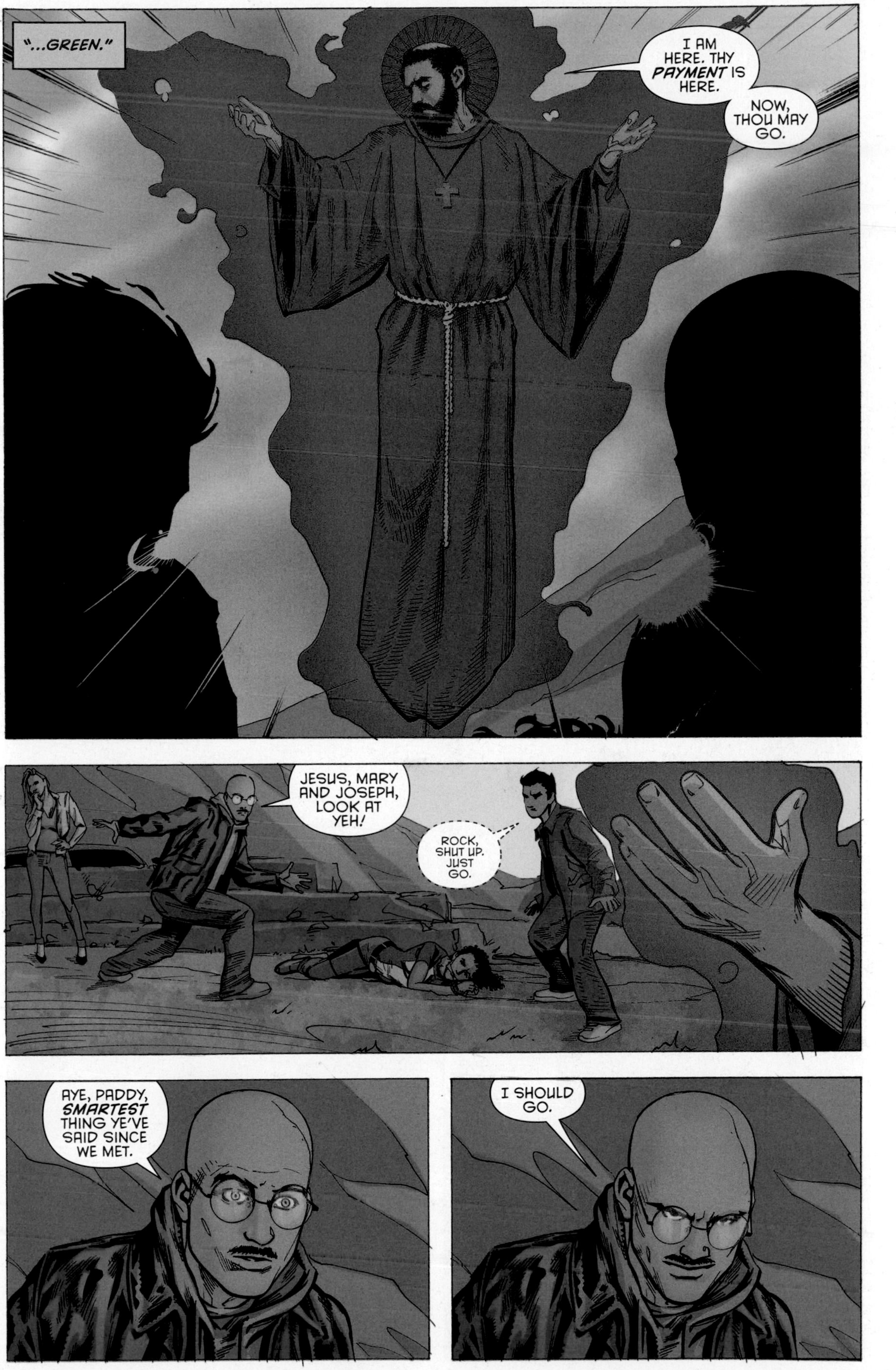
"...GREEN."
I AM HERE. THY PAYMENT IS HERE.
NOW, THOU MAY GO.
JESUS, MARY AND JOSEPH, LOOK AT YEH!
ROCK, SHUT UP. JUST GO.
AYE, PADDY, SMARTEST THING YE'VE SAID SINCE WE MET.
I SHOULD GO.

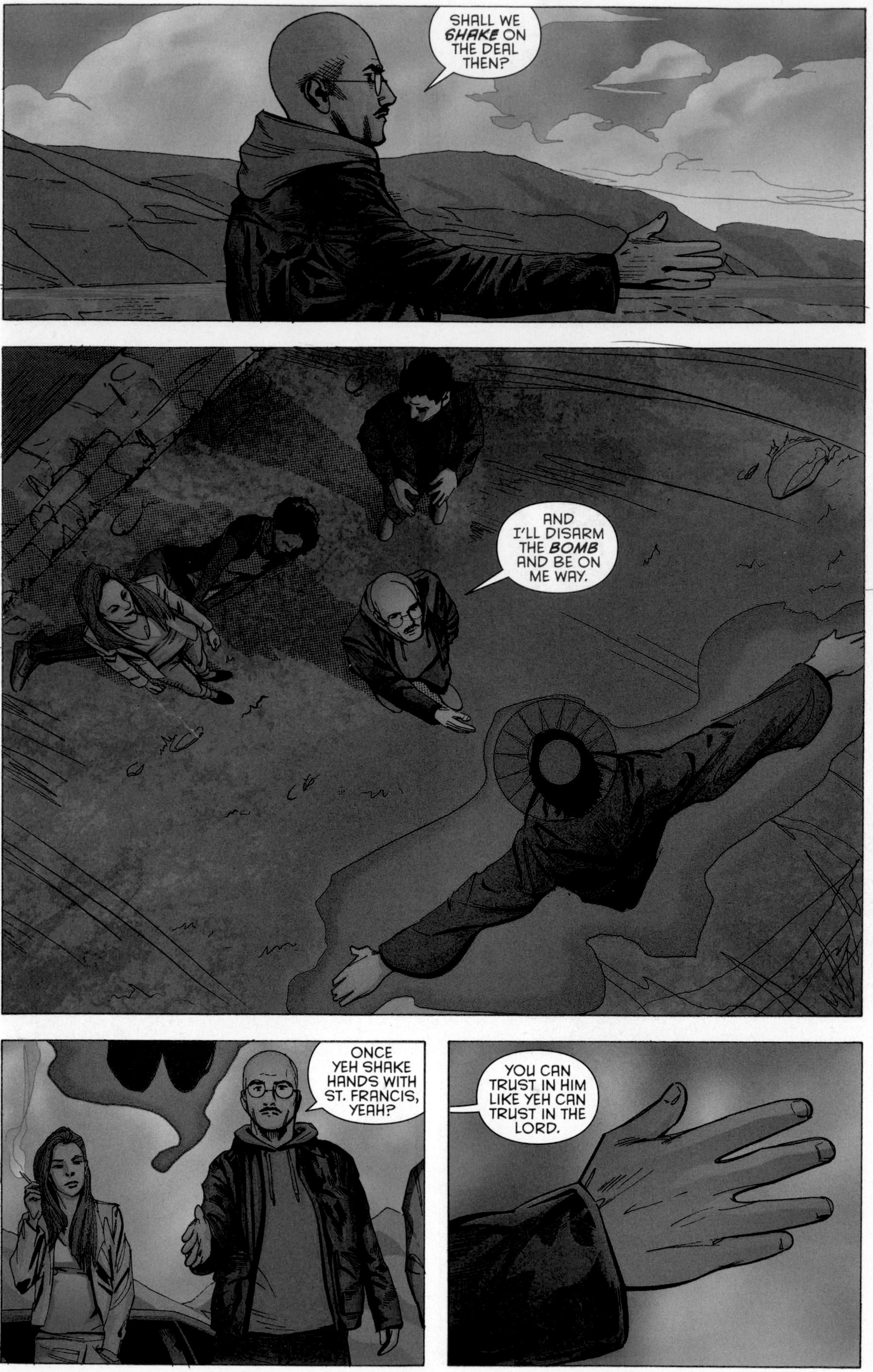
SHALL WE SHAKE ON THE DEAL THEN?
AND I'LL DISARM THE BOMB AND BE ON ME WAY.
ONCE YEH SHAKE HANDS WITH ST. FRANCIS, YEAH?
YOU CAN TRUST IN HIM LIKE YEH CAN TRUST IN THE LORD.

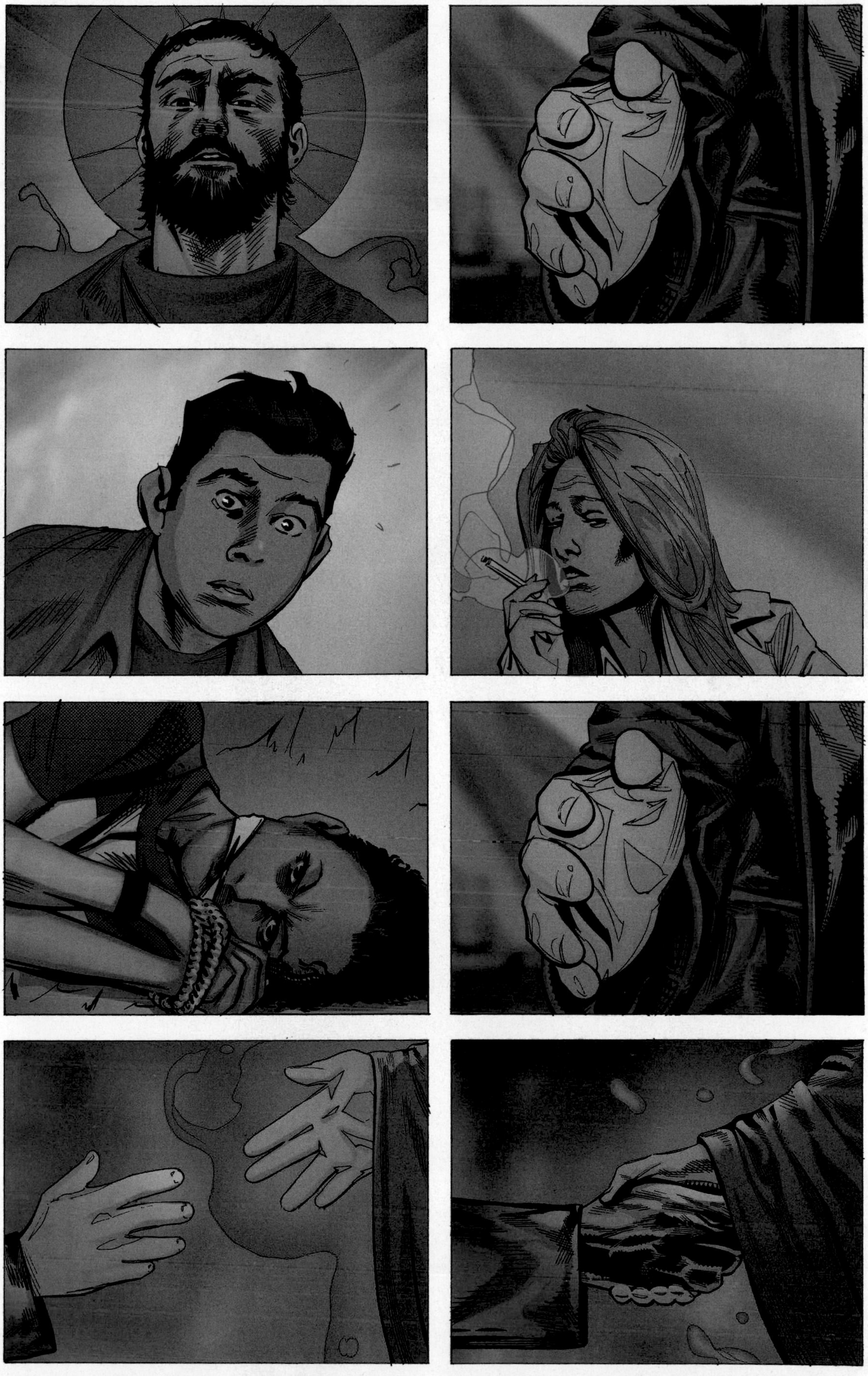

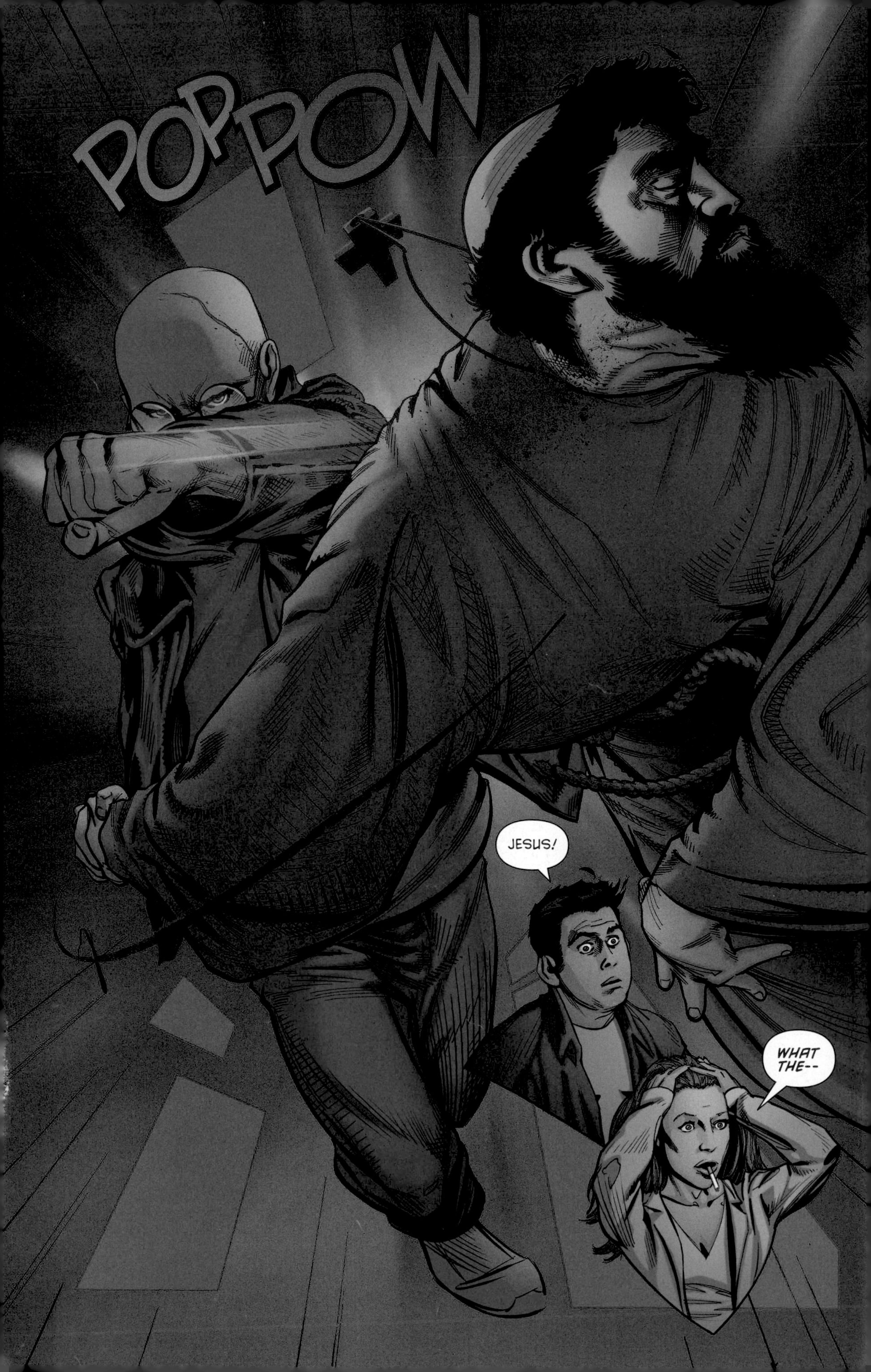
POP POW
JESUS!
WHAT THE--

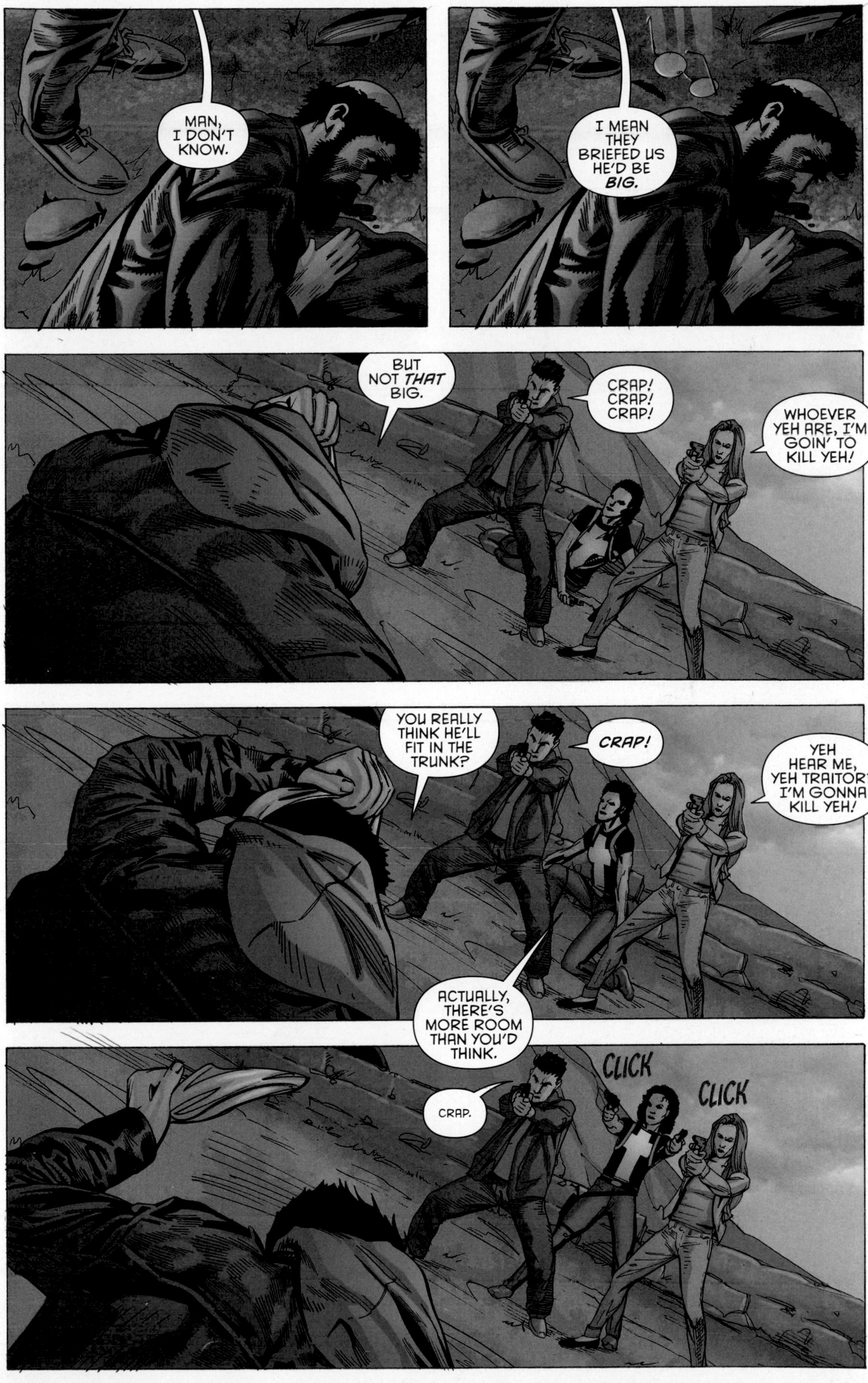
MAN, I DON'T KNOW.
I MEAN THEY BRIEFED US HE'D BE *BIG.*
BUT NOT *THAT* BIG.
CRAP! CRAP! CRAP!
WHOEVER YEH ARE, I'M GOIN' TO KILL YEH!
YOU REALLY THINK HE'LL FIT IN THE TRUNK?
CRAP!
YEH HEAR ME, YEH TRAITOR? I'M GONNA KILL YEH!
ACTUALLY, THERE'S MORE ROOM THAN YOU'D THINK.
CRAP.
CLICK
CLICK

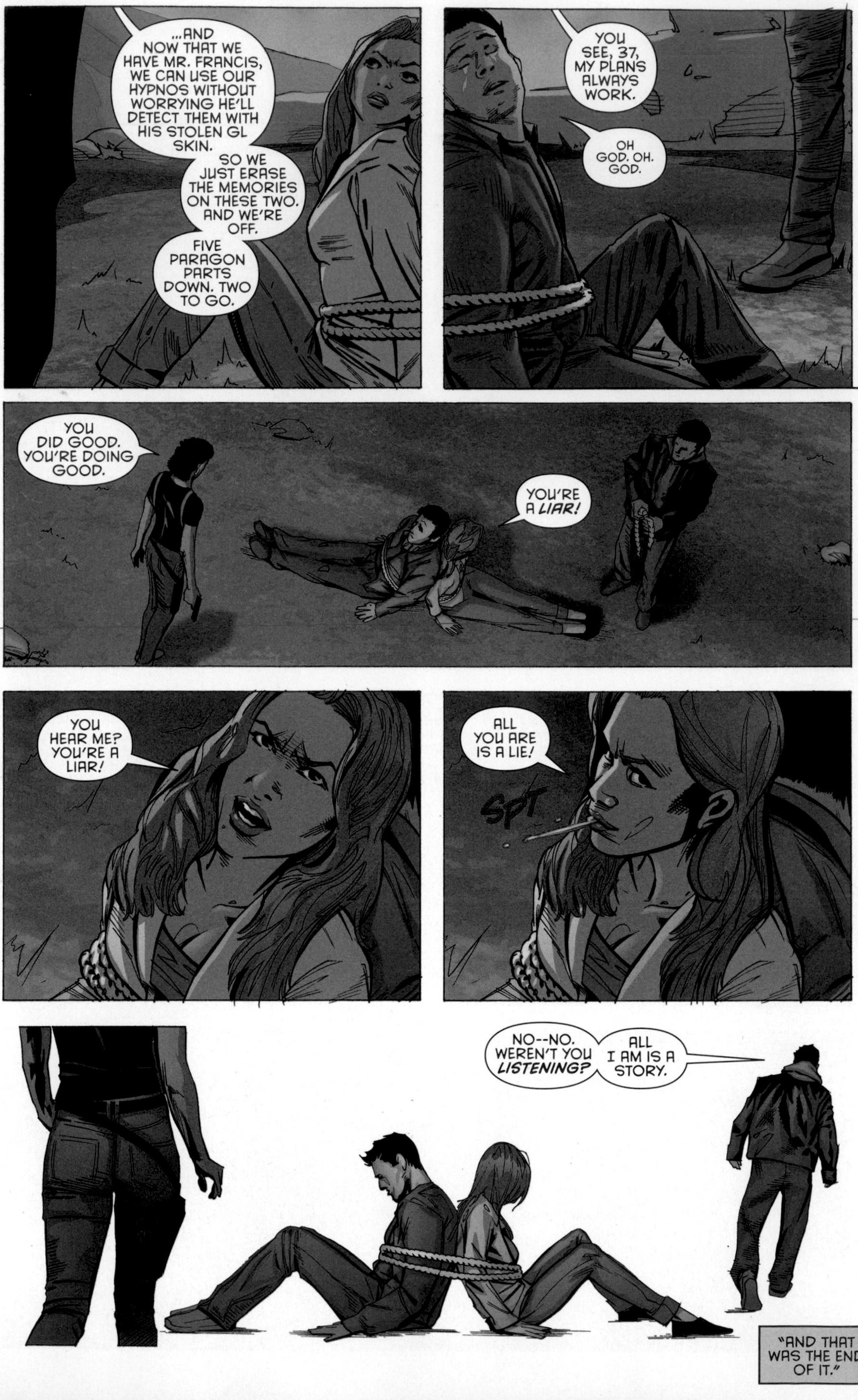
...AND NOW THAT WE HAVE MR. FRANCIS, WE CAN USE OUR HYPNOS WITHOUT WORRYING HE'LL DETECT THEM WITH HIS STOLEN GL SKIN.
SO WE JUST ERASE THE MEMORIES ON THESE TWO. AND WE'RE OFF.
FIVE PARAGON PARTS DOWN. TWO TO GO.
YOU SEE, 37, MY PLANS ALWAYS WORK.
OH GOD. OH. GOD.
YOU DID GOOD. YOU'RE DOING GOOD.
YOU'RE A *LIAR!*
YOU HEAR ME? YOU'RE A LIAR!
ALL YOU ARE IS A LIE!
SPT
NO--NO. WEREN'T YOU *LISTENING?*
ALL I AM IS A STORY.
"AND THAT WAS THE END OF IT."

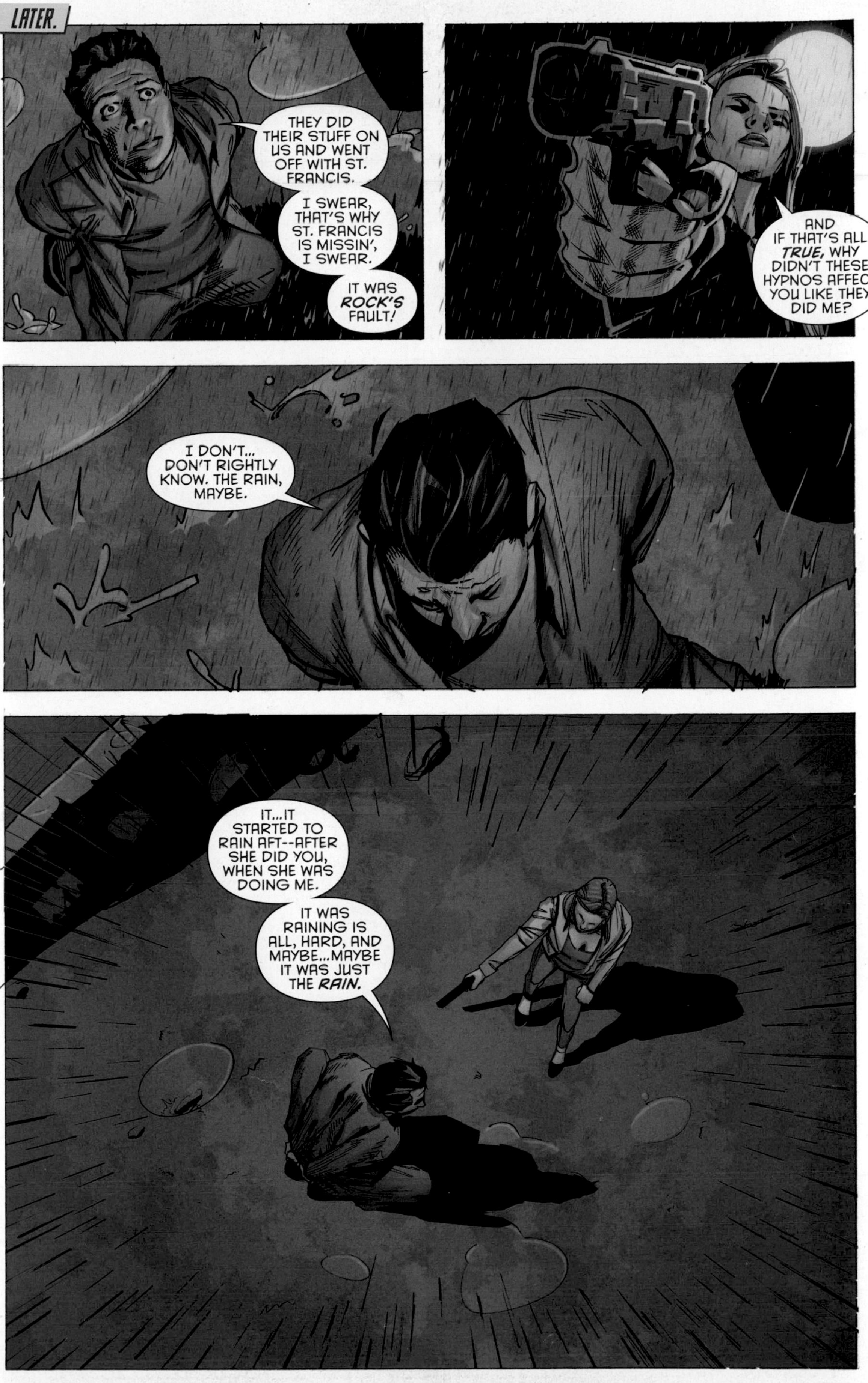
LATER.
THEY DID THEIR STUFF ON US AND WENT OFF WITH ST. FRANCIS.
I SWEAR, THAT'S WHY ST. FRANCIS IS MISSIN', I SWEAR.
IT WAS ROCK'S FAULT!
AND IF THAT'S ALL TRUE, WHY DIDN'T THESE HYPNOS AFFECT YOU LIKE THEY DID ME?
I DON'T... DON'T RIGHTLY KNOW. THE RAIN, MAYBE.
IT...IT STARTED TO RAIN AFT--AFTER SHE DID YOU, WHEN SHE WAS DOING ME.
IT WAS RAINING IS ALL, HARD, AND MAYBE...MAYBE IT WAS JUST THE RAIN.

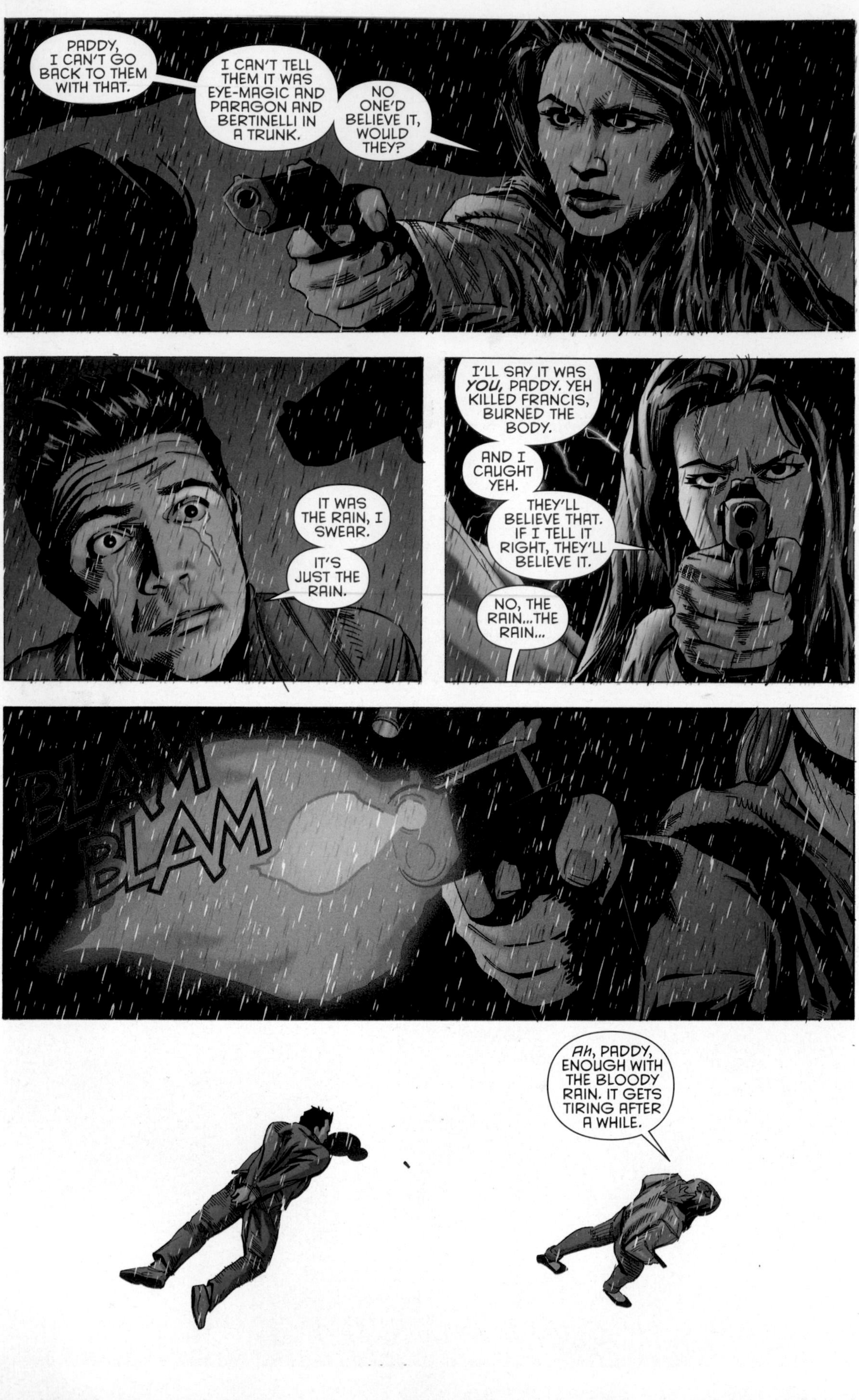
PADDY, I CAN'T GO BACK TO THEM WITH THAT.
I CAN'T TELL THEM IT WAS EYE-MAGIC AND PARAGON AND BERTINELLI IN A TRUNK.
NO ONE'D BELIEVE IT, WOULD THEY?
IT WAS THE RAIN, I SWEAR.
IT'S JUST THE RAIN.
I'LL SAY IT WAS *YOU,* PADDY. YEH KILLED FRANCIS, BURNED THE BODY.
AND I CAUGHT YEH.
THEY'LL BELIEVE THAT. IF I TELL IT RIGHT, THEY'LL BELIEVE IT.
NO, THE RAIN...THE RAIN...
BLAM BLAM
Ah, PADDY, ENOUGH WITH THE BLOODY RAIN. IT GETS TIRING AFTER A WHILE.

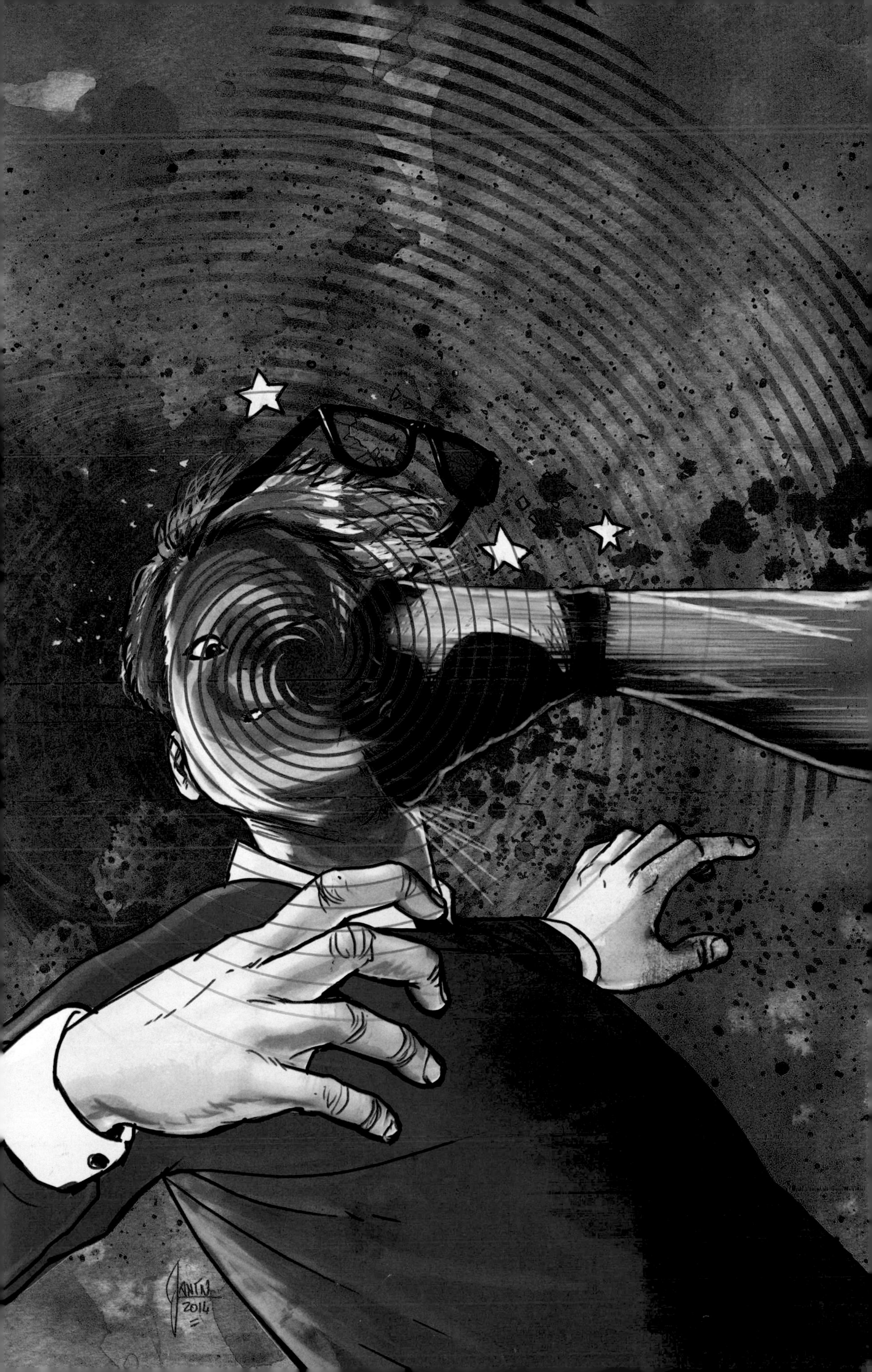
2014

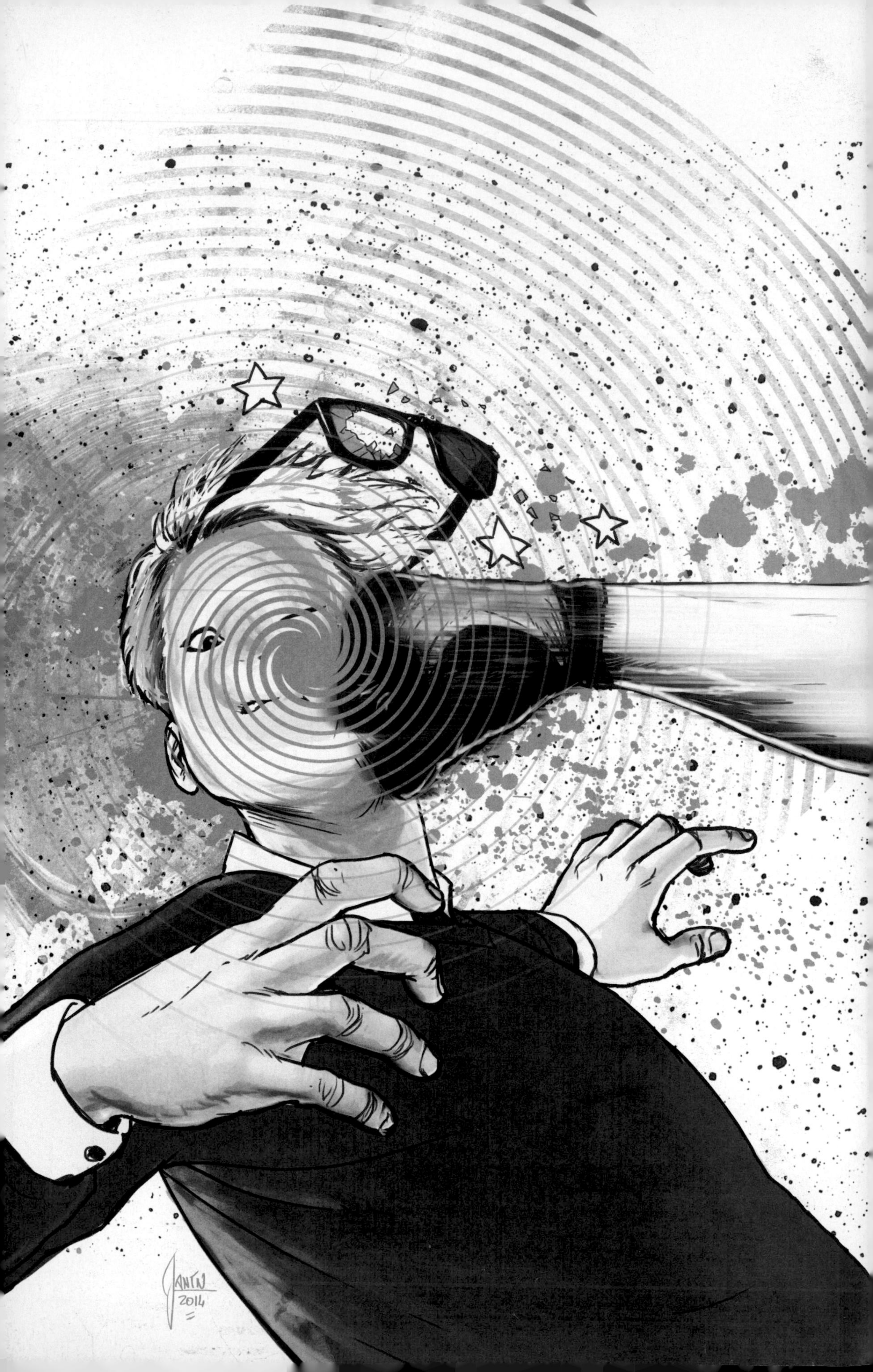

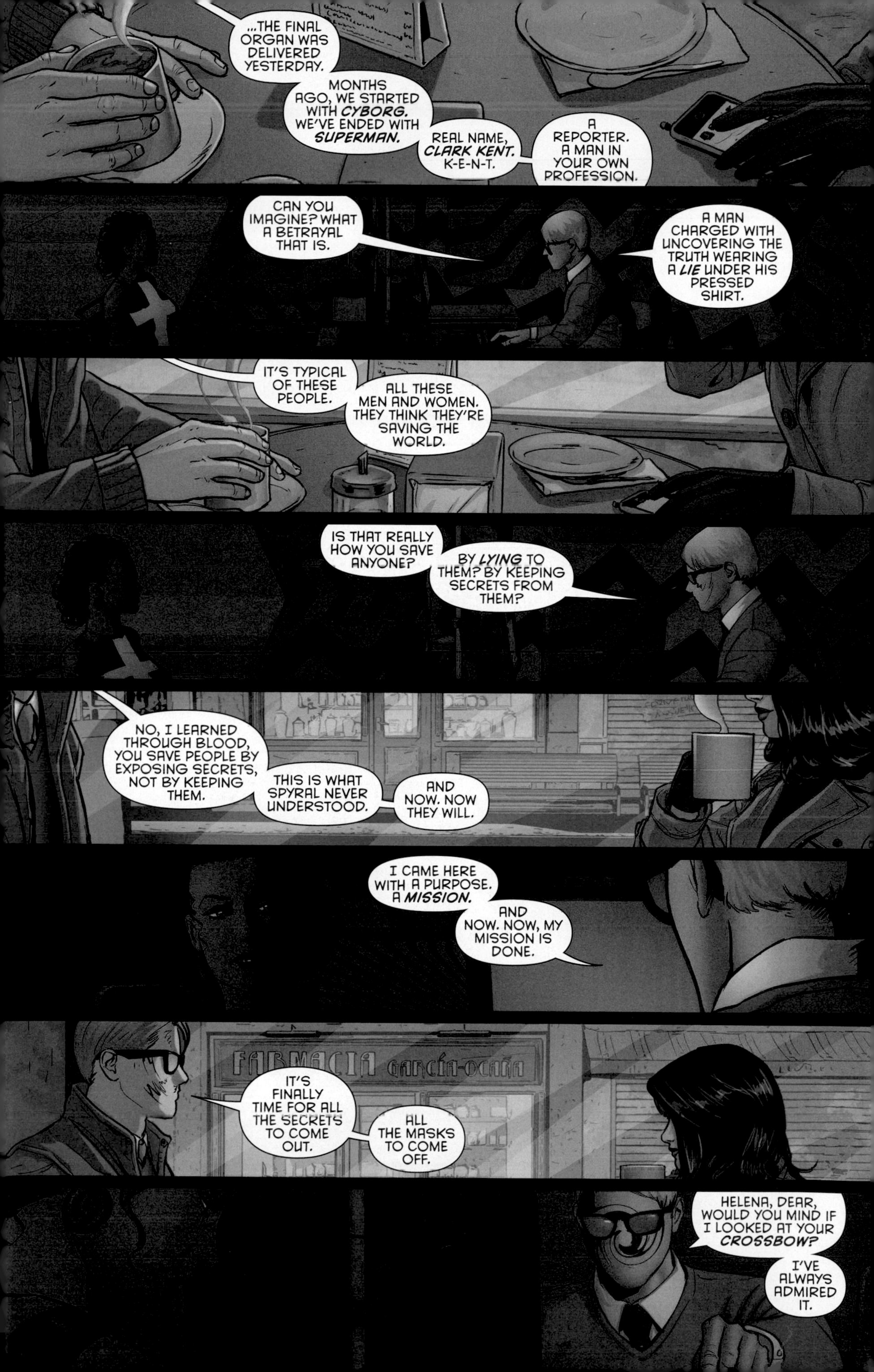
...THE FINAL ORGAN WAS DELIVERED YESTERDAY.
MONTHS AGO, WE STARTED WITH CYBORG. WE'VE ENDED WITH SUPERMAN.
REAL NAME, CLARK KENT. K-E-N-T.
A REPORTER. A MAN IN YOUR OWN PROFESSION.
CAN YOU IMAGINE? WHAT A BETRAYAL THAT IS.
A MAN CHARGED WITH UNCOVERING THE TRUTH WEARING A LIE UNDER HIS PRESSED SHIRT.
IT'S TYPICAL OF THESE PEOPLE.
ALL THESE MEN AND WOMEN. THEY THINK THEY'RE SAVING THE WORLD.
IS THAT REALLY HOW YOU SAVE ANYONE?
BY LYING TO THEM? BY KEEPING SECRETS FROM THEM?
NO, I LEARNED THROUGH BLOOD, YOU SAVE PEOPLE BY EXPOSING SECRETS, NOT BY KEEPING THEM.
THIS IS WHAT SPYRAL NEVER UNDERSTOOD.
AND NOW. NOW THEY WILL.
I CAME HERE WITH A PURPOSE. A MISSION.
AND NOW. NOW, MY MISSION IS DONE.
FARMACIA GARCÍA-OCAÑA
IT'S FINALLY TIME FOR ALL THE SECRETS TO COME OUT.
ALL THE MASKS TO COME OFF.
HELENA, DEAR, WOULD YOU MIND IF I LOOKED AT YOUR CROSSBOW?
I'VE ALWAYS ADMIRED IT.

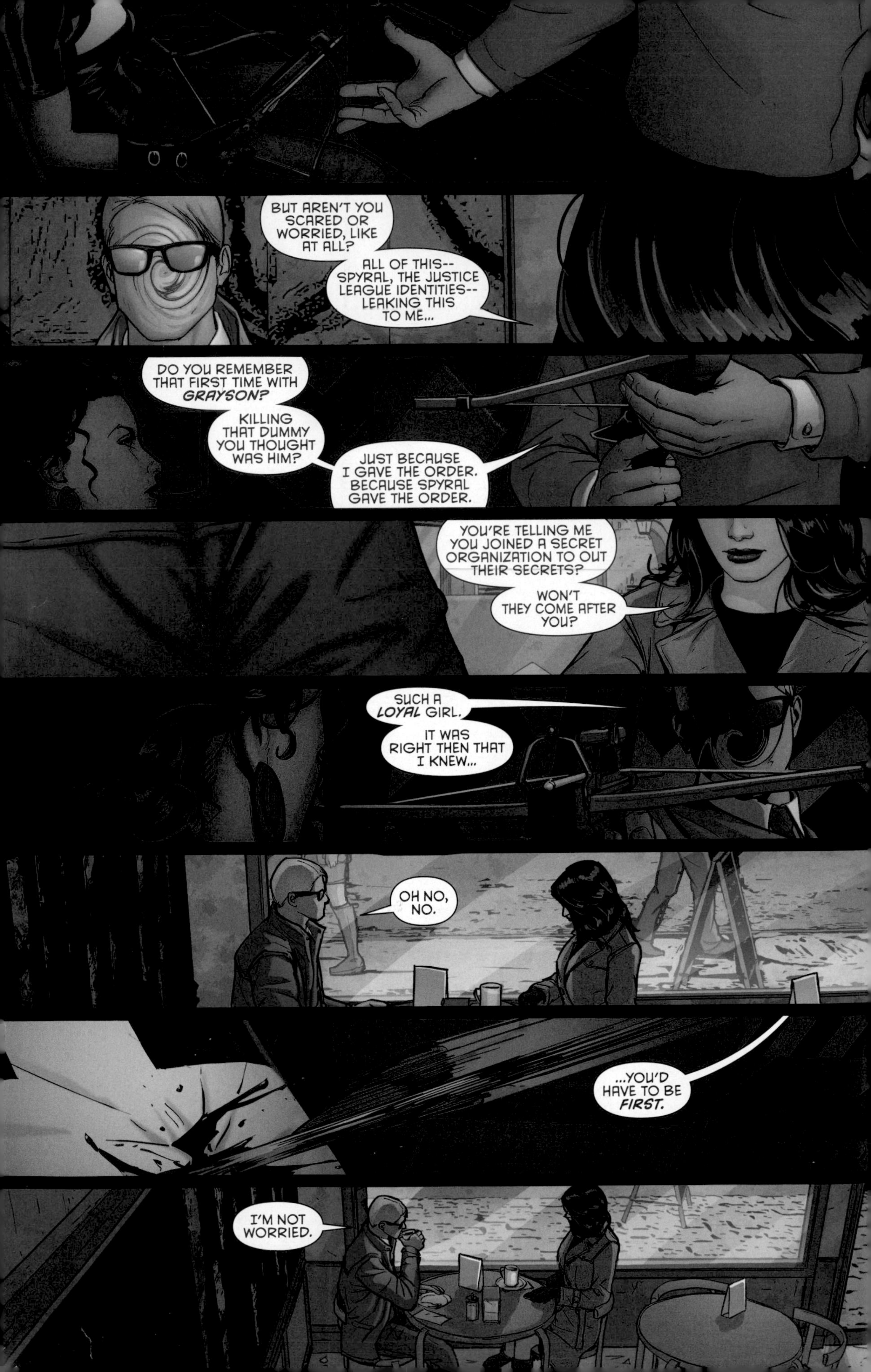
BUT AREN'T YOU SCARED OR WORRIED, LIKE AT ALL?
ALL OF THIS-- SPYRAL, THE JUSTICE LEAGUE IDENTITIES-- LEAKING THIS TO ME...
DO YOU REMEMBER THAT FIRST TIME WITH *GRAYSON?*
KILLING THAT DUMMY YOU THOUGHT WAS HIM?
JUST BECAUSE I GAVE THE ORDER. BECAUSE SPYRAL GAVE THE ORDER.
YOU'RE TELLING ME YOU JOINED A SECRET ORGANIZATION TO OUT THEIR SECRETS?
WON'T THEY COME AFTER YOU?
SUCH A *LOYAL* GIRL.
IT WAS RIGHT THEN THAT I KNEW...
OH NO, NO.
...YOU'D HAVE TO BE *FIRST.*
I'M NOT WORRIED.

I...I HAVE TO CONFESS IT. I. *LOVE*. GYM.

OH YEAH. BEST SUBJECT. BY FAR.

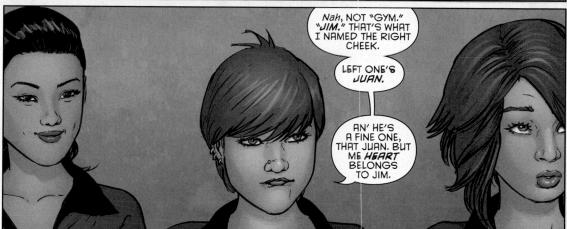

Nah, NOT "GYM." "*JIM.*" THAT'S WHAT I NAMED THE RIGHT CHEEK.

LEFT ONE'S *JUAN*.

AN' HE'S A FINE ONE, THAT JUAN. BUT ME *HEART* BELONGS TO JIM.

I CAN SEE THAT.

POOR JUAN THOUGH. ➛*sigh*➛ HE'S GOING TO NEED COMFORTING.

LOTS AND LOTS OF COMFORTING.

BUT IT'S ALL LIKE A WASTE THOUGH, RIGHT? I MEAN, HE'S GAY.

Ah, JANNI, DON'T YEH UNDER- STAND.

PARIS IS GAY...

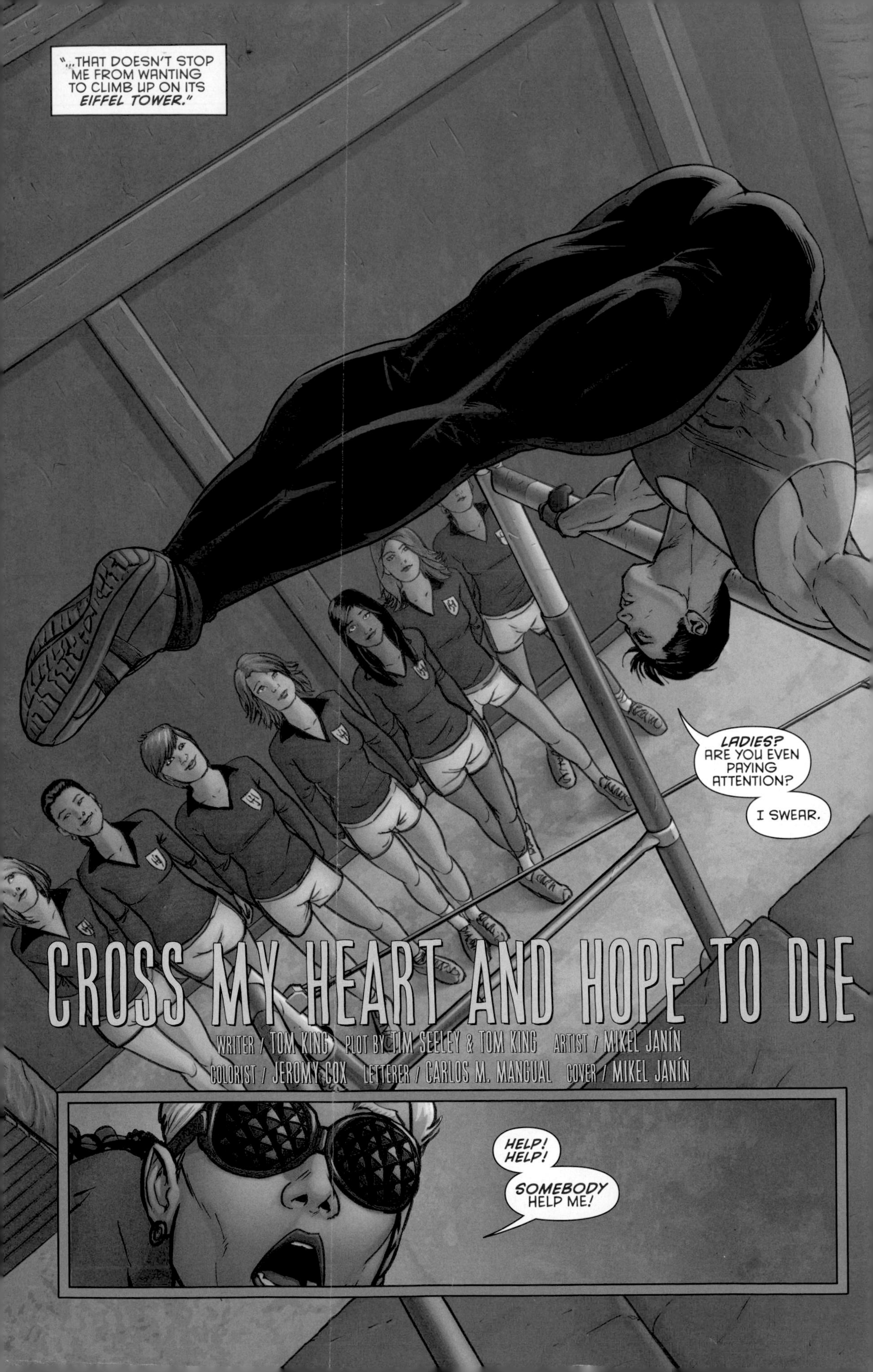
"...THAT DOESN'T STOP ME FROM WANTING TO CLIMB UP ON ITS EIFFEL TOWER."
LADIES? ARE YOU EVEN PAYING ATTENTION?
I SWEAR.
CROSS MY HEART AND HOPE TO DIE
WRITER / TOM KING PLOT BY TIM SEELEY & TOM KING ARTIST / MIKEL JANÍN
COLORIST / JEROMY COX LETTERER / CARLOS M. MANGUAL COVER / MIKEL JANÍN
HELP! HELP!
SOMEBODY HELP ME!

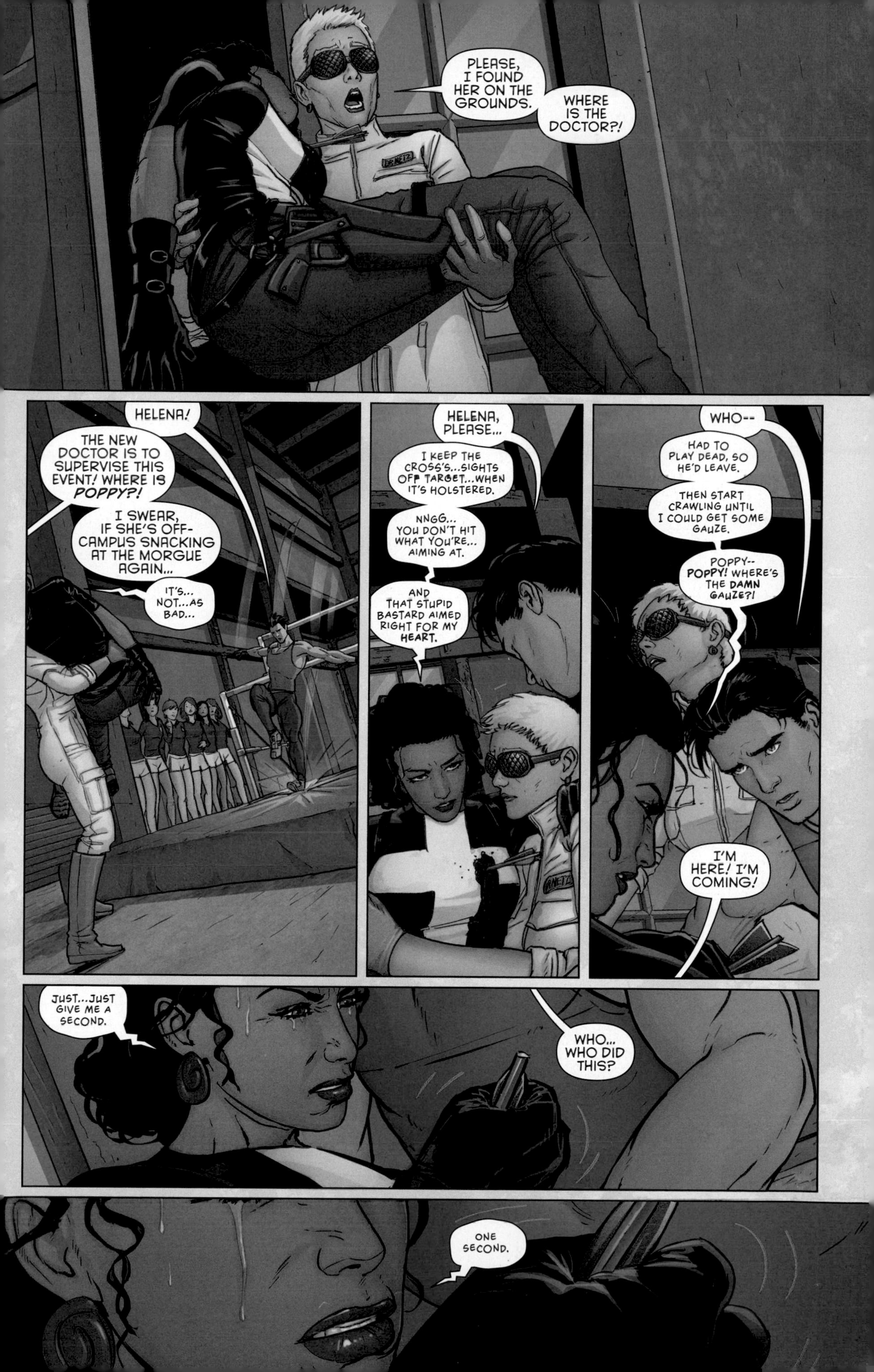

PLEASE, I FOUND HER ON THE GROUNDS.
WHERE IS THE DOCTOR?!
DR. NETZ
HELENA!
THE NEW DOCTOR IS TO SUPERVISE THIS EVENT! WHERE IS POPPY?!
I SWEAR, IF SHE'S OFF-CAMPUS SNACKING AT THE MORGUE AGAIN...
IT'S... NOT...AS BAD...
HELENA, PLEASE...
I KEEP THE CROSS'S...SIGHTS OFF TARGET...WHEN IT'S HOLSTERED.
NNGG... YOU DON'T HIT WHAT YOU'RE... AIMING AT.
AND THAT STUPID BASTARD AIMED RIGHT FOR MY HEART.
WHO--
HAD TO PLAY DEAD, SO HE'D LEAVE.
THEN START CRAWLING UNTIL I COULD GET SOME GAUZE.
POPPY-- POPPY! WHERE'S THE DAMN GAUZE?!
I'M HERE! I'M COMING!
JUST...JUST GIVE ME A SECOND.
WHO... WHO DID THIS?
ONE SECOND.

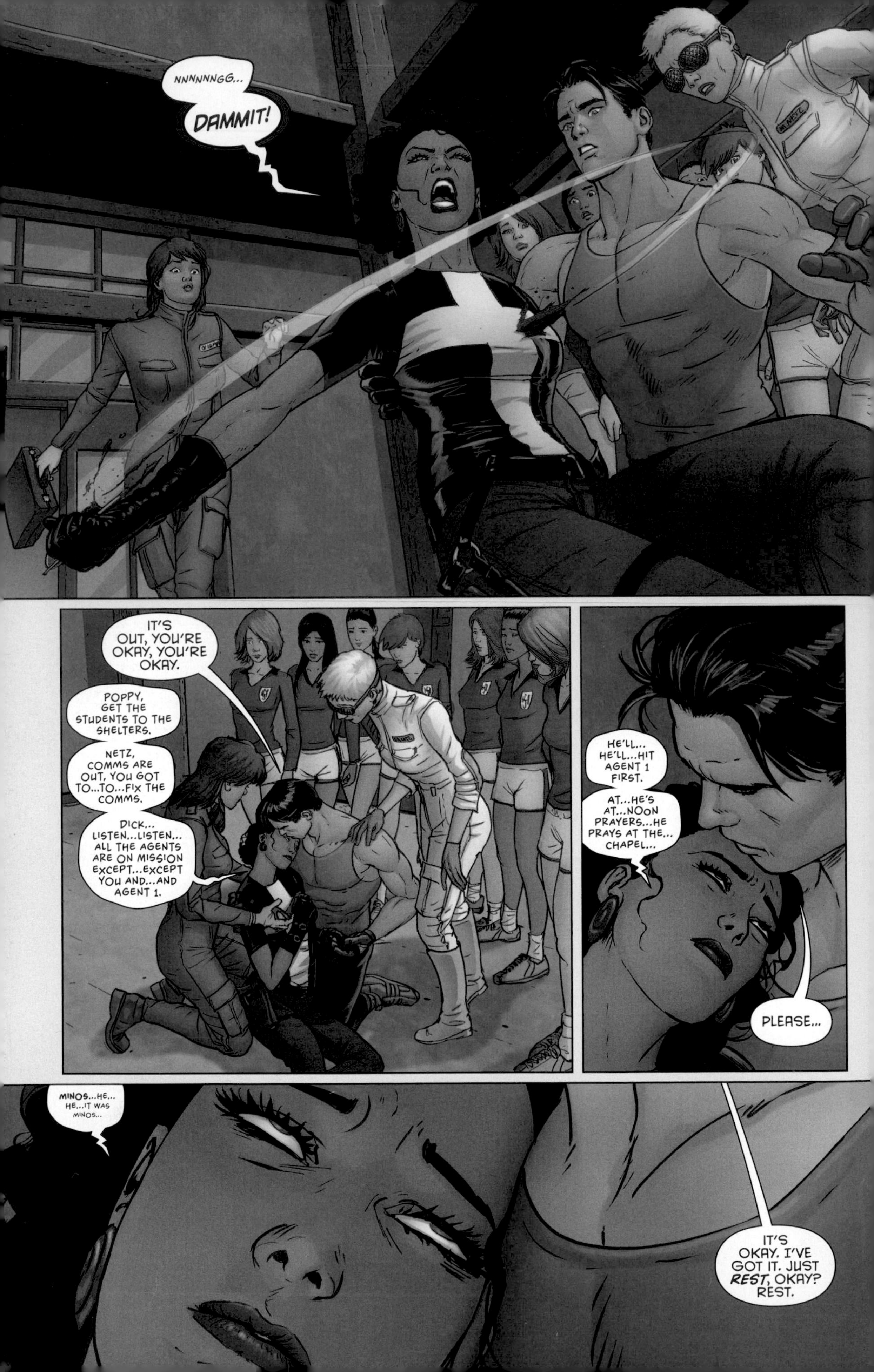
NNNNNNGG...
DAMMIT!
IT'S OUT, YOU'RE OKAY, YOU'RE OKAY.
POPPY, GET THE STUDENTS TO THE SHELTERS.
NETZ, COMMS ARE OUT, YOU GOT TO...TO...FIX THE COMMS.
DICK... LISTEN...LISTEN... ALL THE AGENTS ARE ON MISSION EXCEPT...EXCEPT YOU AND...AND AGENT 1.
HE'LL... HE'LL...HIT AGENT 1 FIRST.
AT...HE'S AT...NOON PRAYERS...HE PRAYS AT THE... CHAPEL...
PLEASE...
MINOS...HE... HE...IT WAS MINOS...
IT'S OKAY. I'VE GOT IT. JUST REST, OKAY? REST.

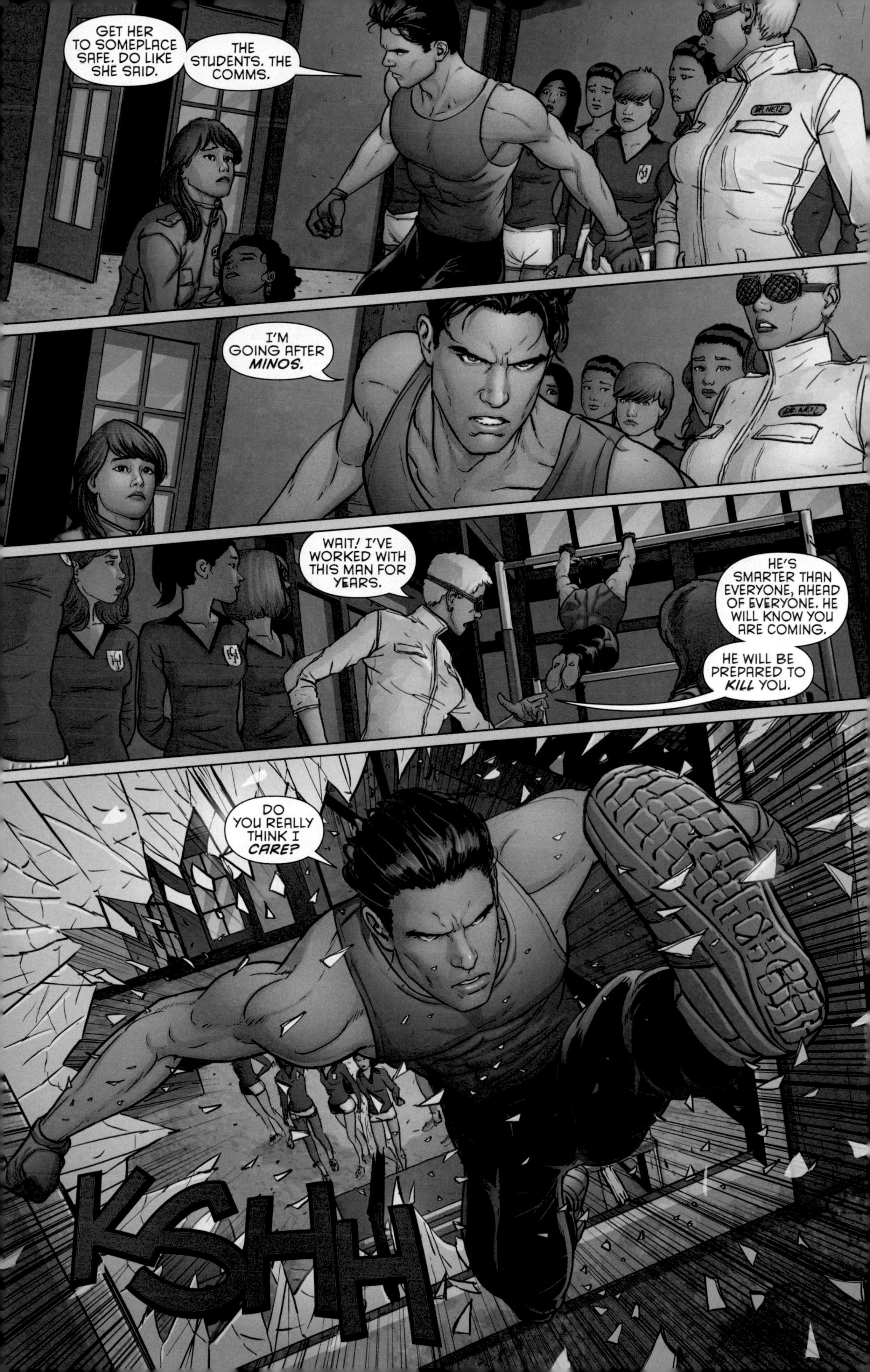
GET HER TO SOMEPLACE SAFE. DO LIKE SHE SAID.
THE STUDENTS. THE COMMS.
DR. NETZ
I'M GOING AFTER *MINOS.*
DR. NETZ
WAIT! I'VE WORKED WITH THIS MAN FOR *YEARS.*
HE'S SMARTER THAN EVERYONE, AHEAD OF EVERYONE. HE WILL KNOW YOU ARE COMING.
HE WILL BE PREPARED TO *KILL* YOU.
DO YOU REALLY THINK I *CARE?*
KSHH

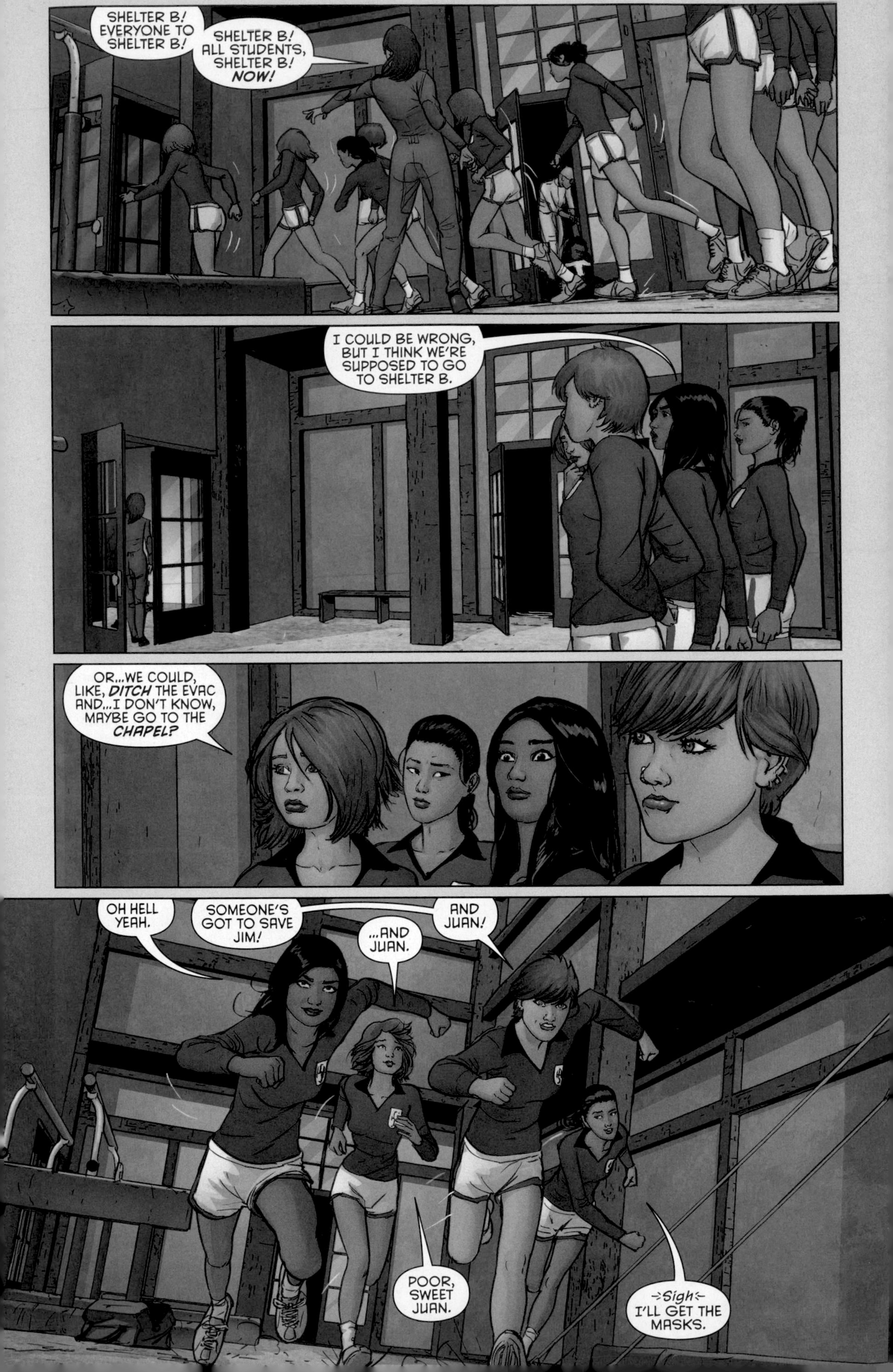
SHELTER B! EVERYONE TO SHELTER B!
SHELTER B! ALL STUDENTS, SHELTER B! NOW!
I COULD BE WRONG, BUT I THINK WE'RE SUPPOSED TO GO TO SHELTER B.
OR...WE COULD, LIKE, DITCH THE EVAC AND...I DON'T KNOW, MAYBE GO TO THE CHAPEL?
OH HELL YEAH.
SOMEONE'S GOT TO SAVE JIM!
...AND JUAN.
AND JUAN!
POOR, SWEET JUAN.
Sigh
I'LL GET THE MASKS.

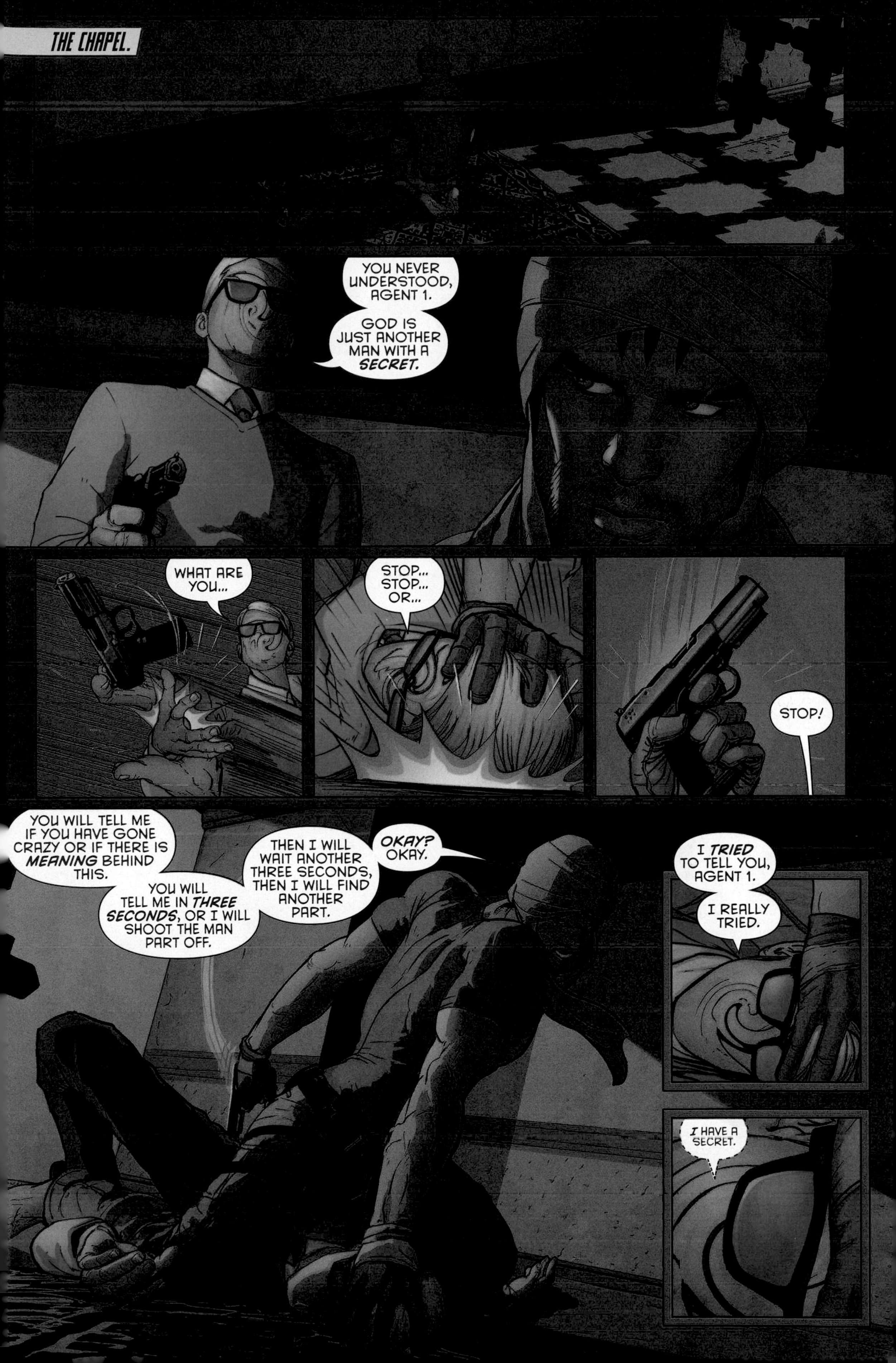
THE CHAPEL.
YOU NEVER UNDERSTOOD, AGENT 1.
GOD IS JUST ANOTHER MAN WITH A SECRET.
WHAT ARE YOU...
STOP... STOP... OR...
STOP!
YOU WILL TELL ME IF YOU HAVE GONE CRAZY OR IF THERE IS MEANING BEHIND THIS.
YOU WILL TELL ME IN THREE SECONDS, OR I WILL SHOOT THE MAN PART OFF.
THEN I WILL WAIT ANOTHER THREE SECONDS, THEN I WILL FIND ANOTHER PART.
OKAY? OKAY.
I TRIED TO TELL YOU, AGENT 1.
I REALLY TRIED.
I HAVE A SECRET.

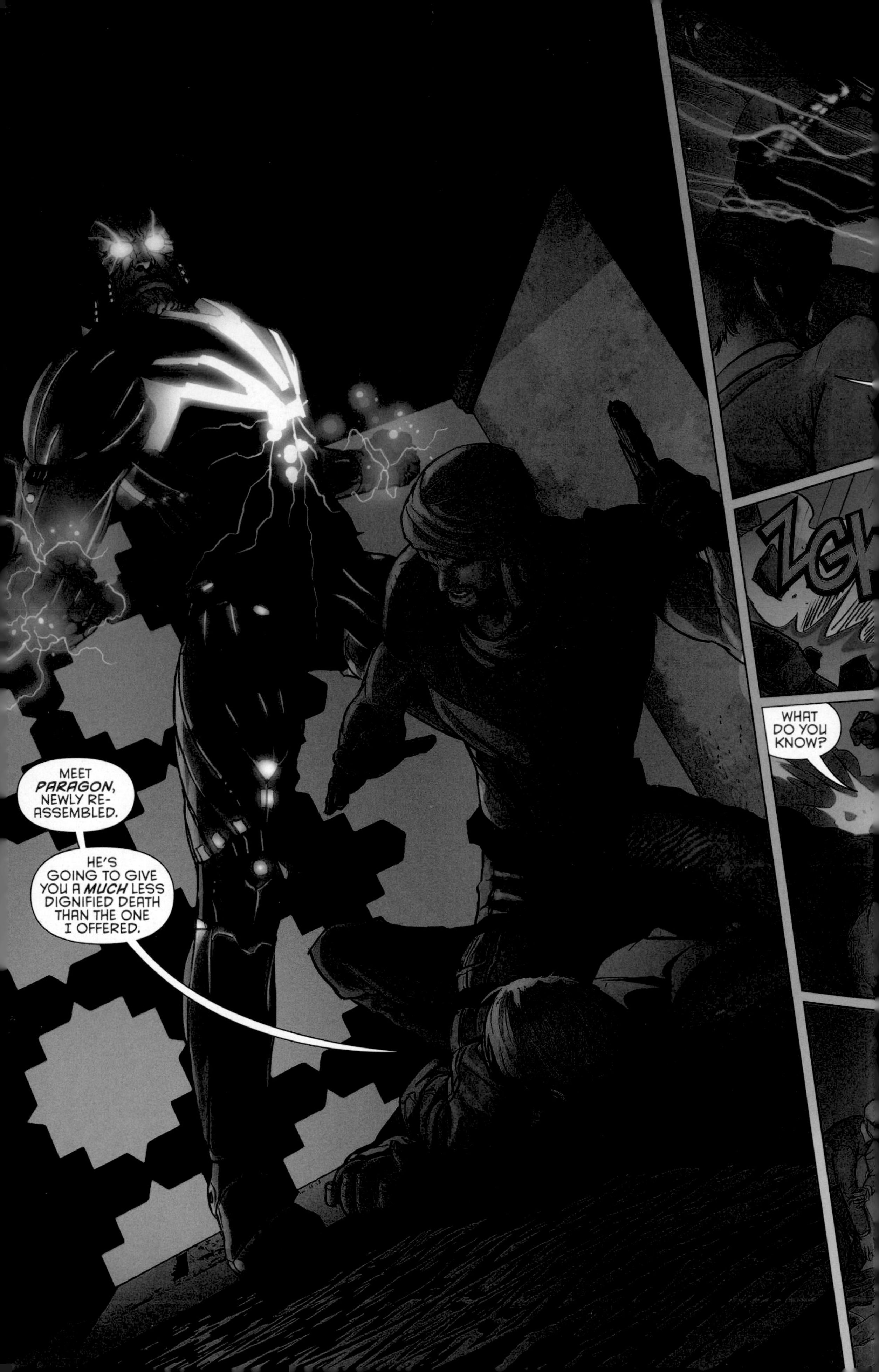
MEET *PARAGON*, NEWLY RE-ASSEMBLED.
HE'S GOING TO GIVE YOU A *MUCH* LESS DIGNIFIED DEATH THAN THE ONE I OFFERED.
WHAT DO YOU KNOW?

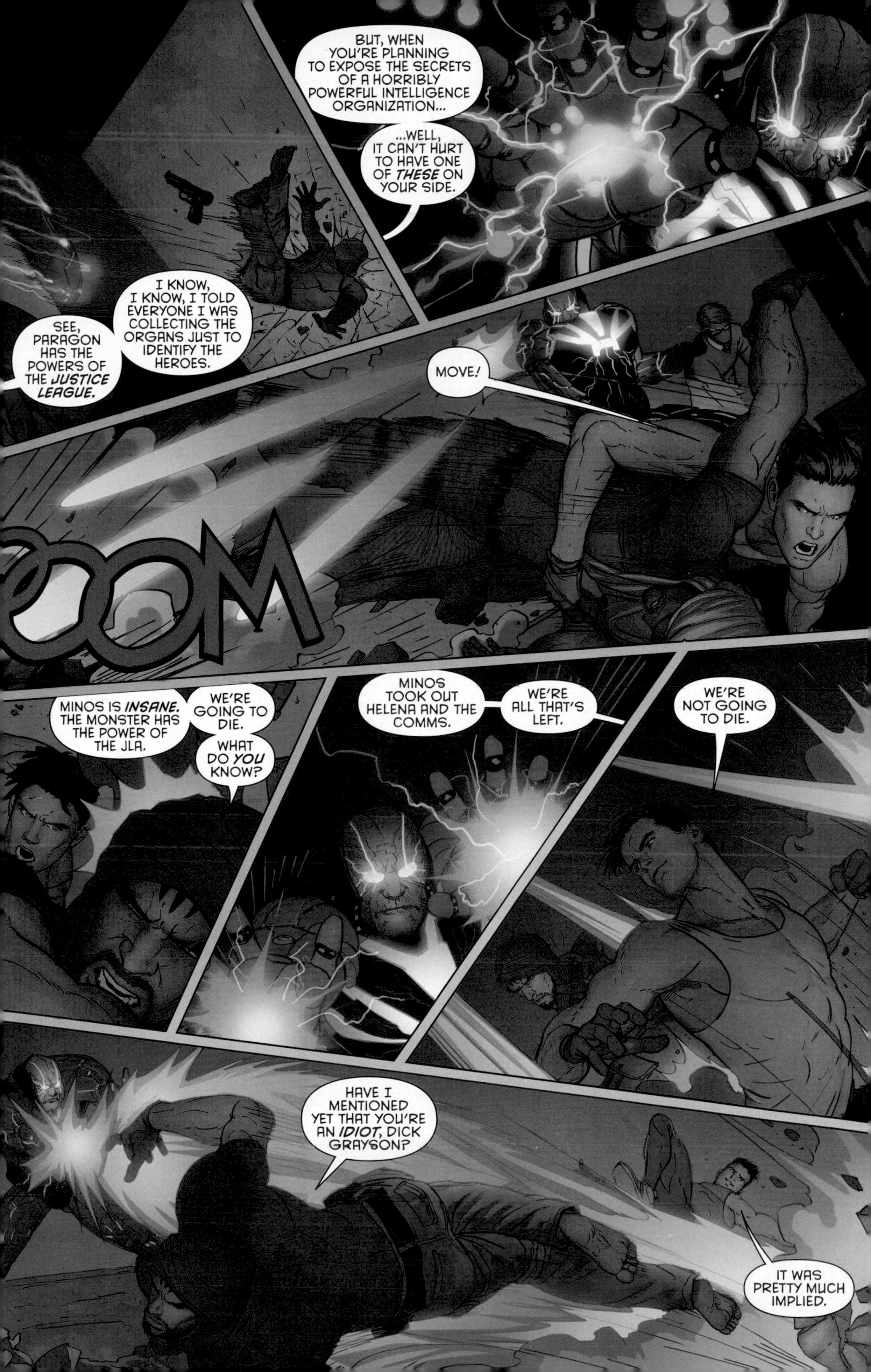
BUT, WHEN YOU'RE PLANNING TO EXPOSE THE SECRETS OF A HORRIBLY POWERFUL INTELLIGENCE ORGANIZATION...
...WELL, IT CAN'T HURT TO HAVE ONE OF *THESE* ON YOUR SIDE.
I KNOW, I KNOW, I TOLD EVERYONE I WAS COLLECTING THE ORGANS JUST TO IDENTIFY THE HEROES.
SEE, PARAGON HAS THE POWERS OF THE *JUSTICE LEAGUE.*
MOVE!
OOM
MINOS IS *INSANE.* THE MONSTER HAS THE POWER OF THE JLA.
WE'RE GOING TO DIE.
WHAT DO *YOU* KNOW?
MINOS TOOK OUT HELENA AND THE COMMS.
WE'RE ALL THAT'S LEFT.
WE'RE NOT GOING TO DIE.
HAVE I MENTIONED YET THAT YOU'RE AN *IDIOT,* DICK GRAYSON?
IT WAS PRETTY MUCH IMPLIED.

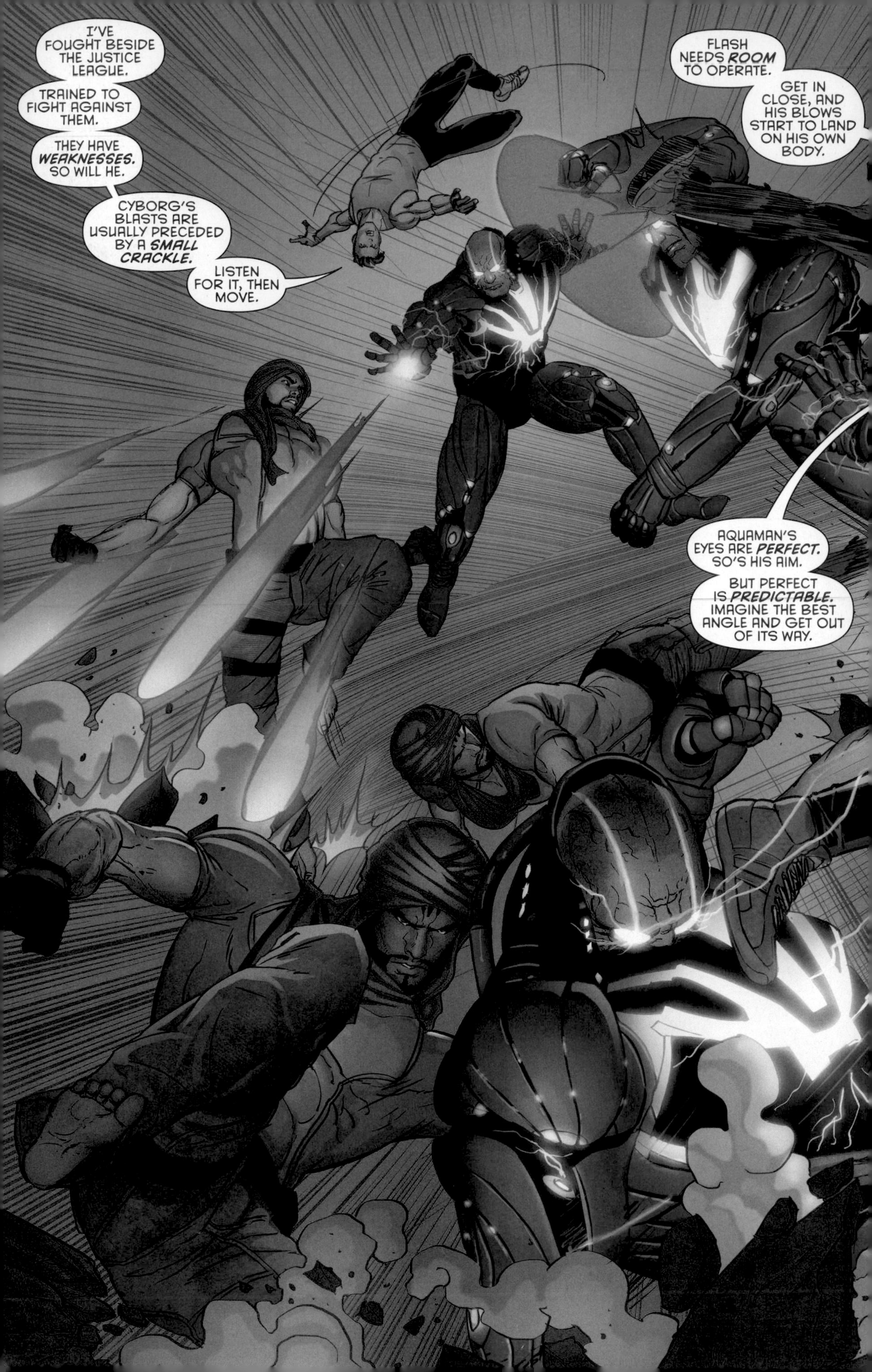
I'VE FOUGHT BESIDE THE JUSTICE LEAGUE.
TRAINED TO FIGHT AGAINST THEM.
THEY HAVE *WEAKNESSES.* SO WILL HE.
CYBORG'S BLASTS ARE USUALLY PRECEDED BY A *SMALL CRACKLE.*
LISTEN FOR IT, THEN MOVE.
FLASH NEEDS *ROOM* TO OPERATE.
GET IN CLOSE, AND HIS BLOWS START TO LAND ON HIS OWN BODY.
AQUAMAN'S EYES ARE *PERFECT.* SO'S HIS AIM.
BUT PERFECT IS *PREDICTABLE.* IMAGINE THE BEST ANGLE AND GET OUT OF ITS WAY.

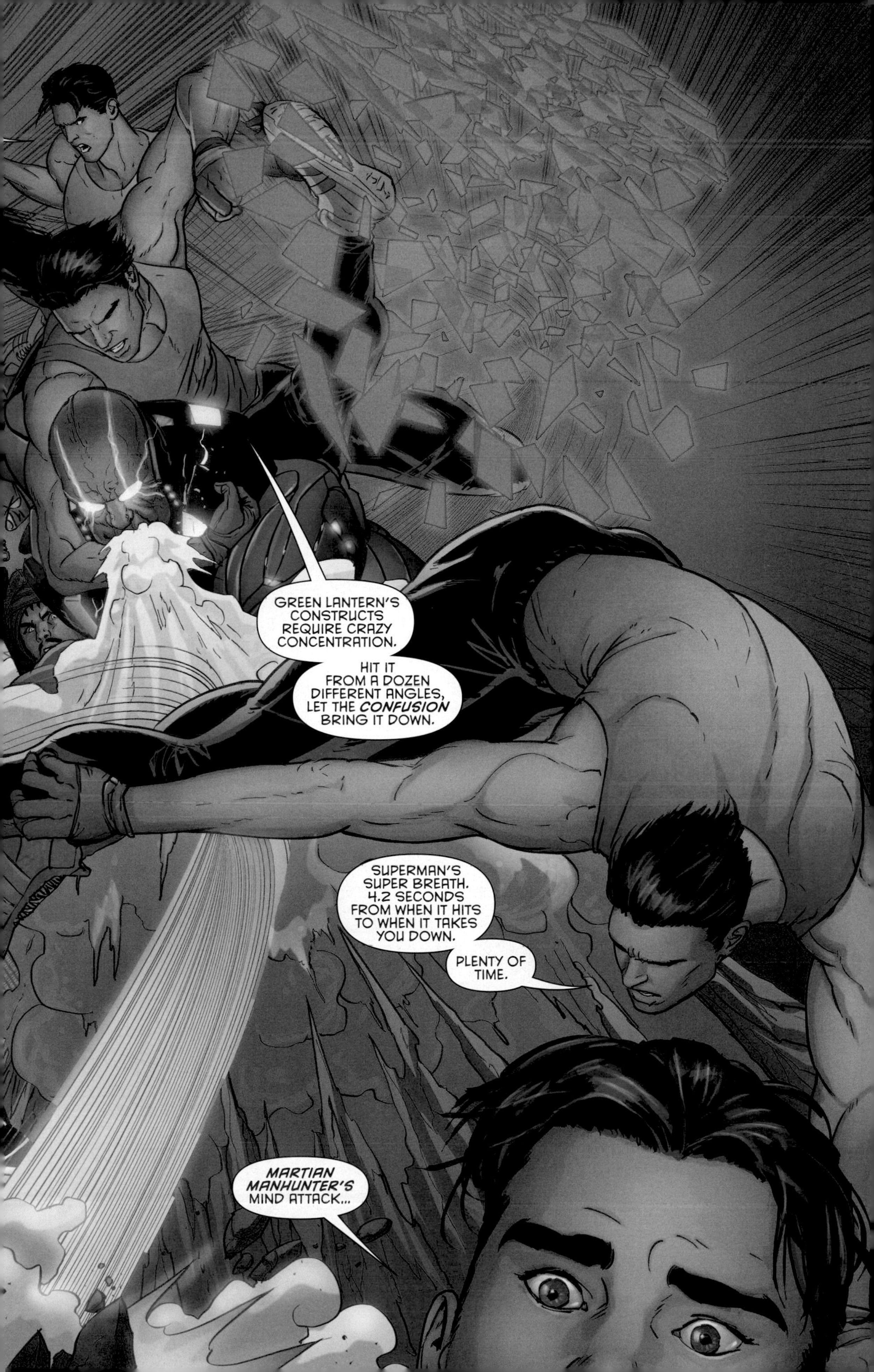
GREEN LANTERN'S CONSTRUCTS REQUIRE CRAZY CONCENTRATION.
HIT IT FROM A DOZEN DIFFERENT ANGLES, LET THE *CONFUSION* BRING IT DOWN.
SUPERMAN'S SUPER BREATH. 4.2 SECONDS FROM WHEN IT HITS TO WHEN IT TAKES YOU DOWN.
PLENTY OF TIME.
MARTIAN MANHUNTER'S MIND ATTACK...

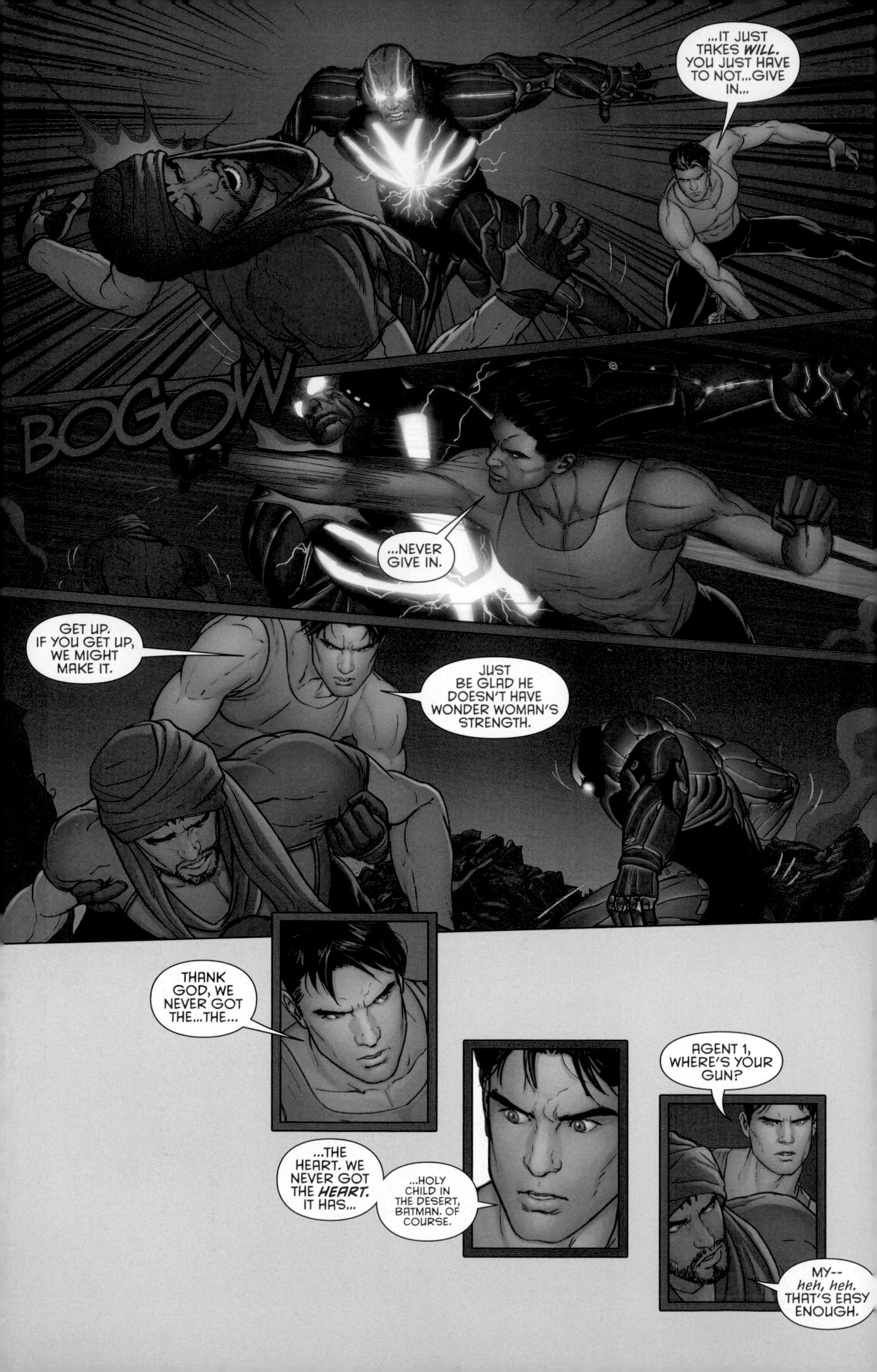
...IT JUST TAKES *WILL.* YOU JUST HAVE TO NOT...GIVE IN...
BOGOW
...NEVER GIVE IN.
GET UP. IF YOU GET UP, WE MIGHT MAKE IT.
JUST BE GLAD HE DOESN'T HAVE WONDER WOMAN'S STRENGTH.
THANK GOD, WE NEVER GOT THE...THE...
...THE HEART. WE NEVER GOT THE *HEART.* IT HAS...
...HOLY CHILD IN THE DESERT, BATMAN. OF COURSE.
AGENT 1, WHERE'S YOUR GUN?
MY-- *heh, heh.* THAT'S EASY ENOUGH.

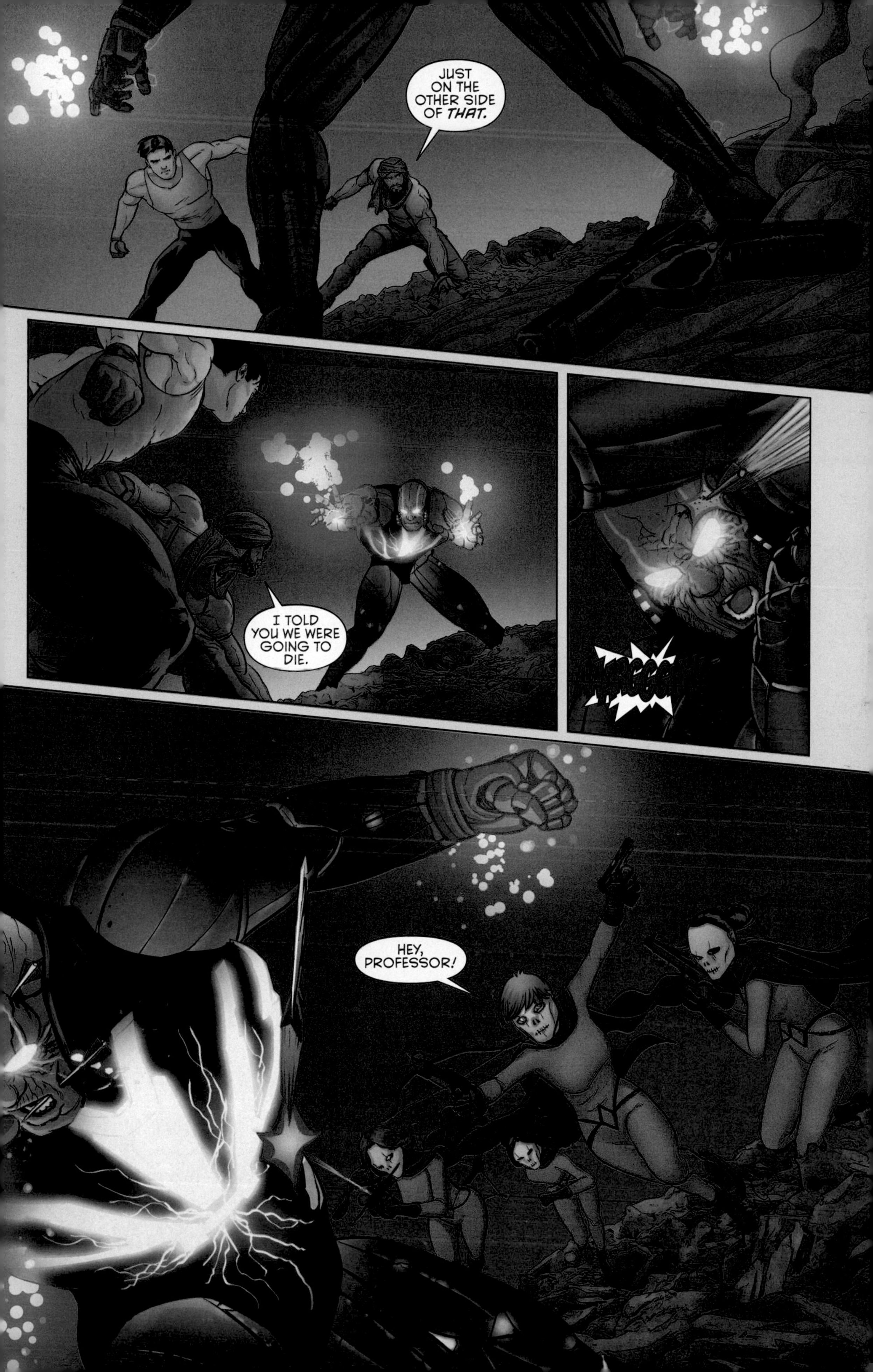
JUST ON THE OTHER SIDE OF *THAT.*
I TOLD YOU WE WERE GOING TO DIE.
HEY, PROFESSOR!

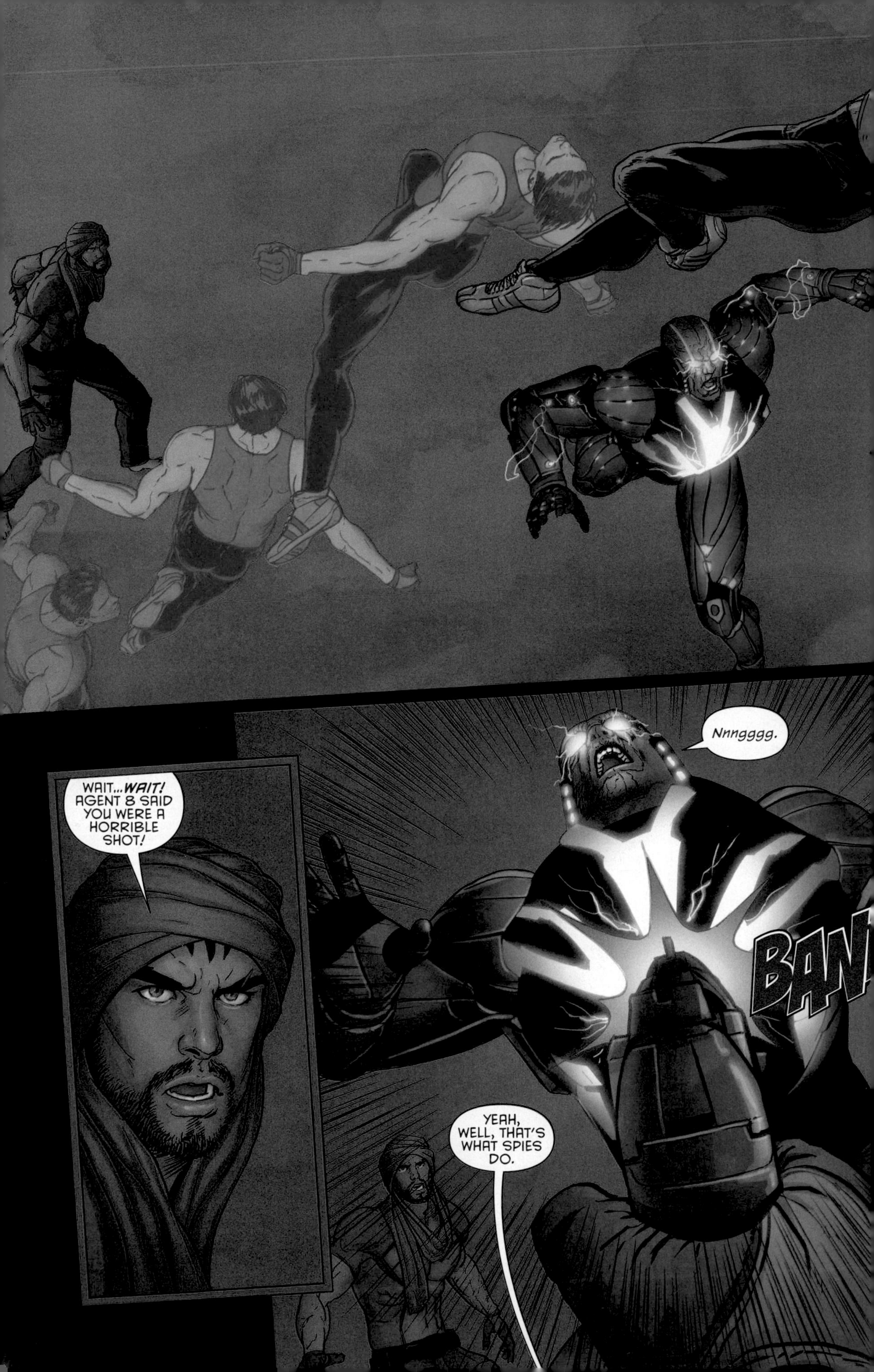
WAIT...WAIT! AGENT 8 SAID YOU WERE A HORRIBLE SHOT!
Nnngggg.
BAN
YEAH, WELL, THAT'S WHAT SPIES DO.

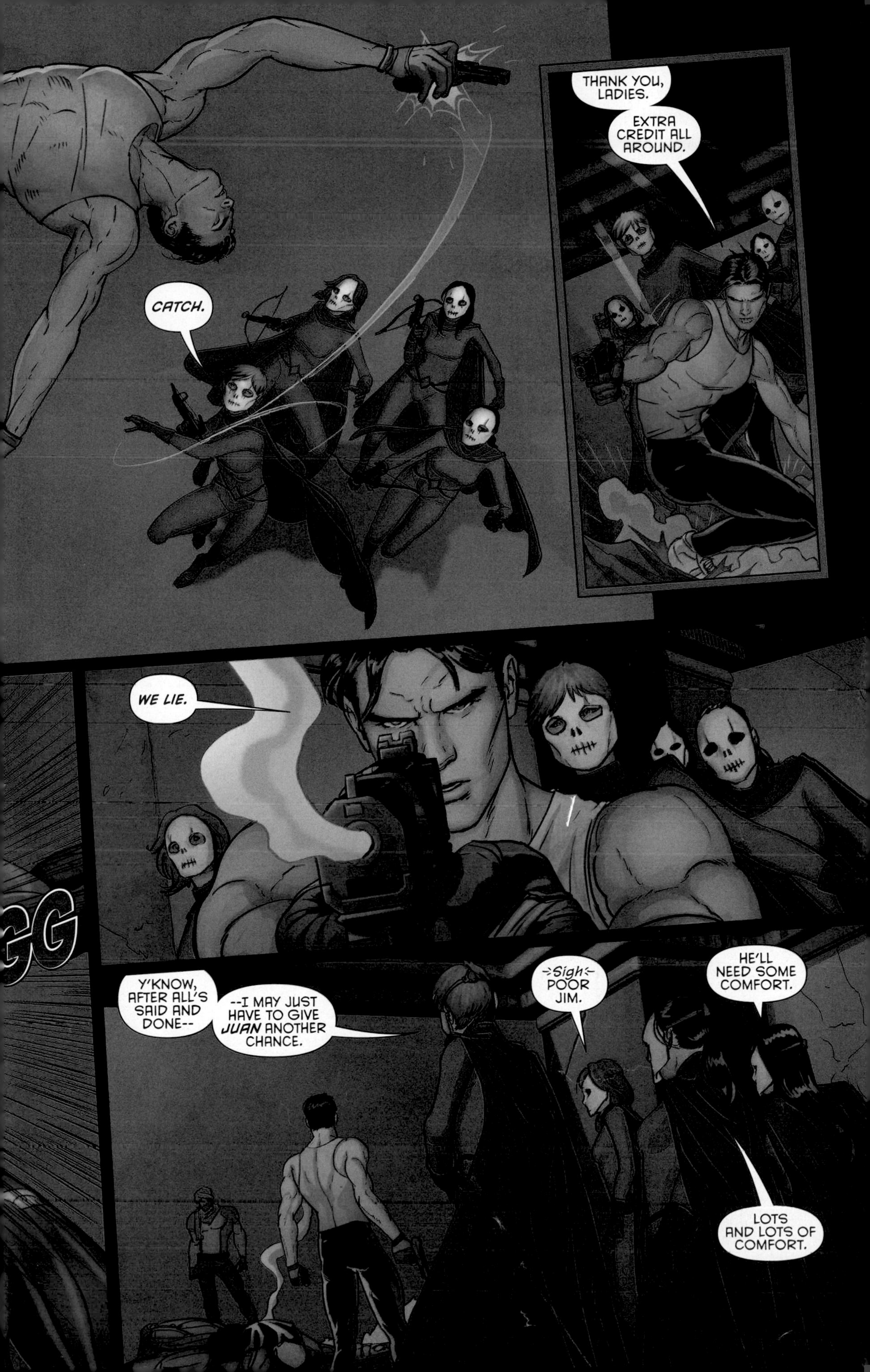
CATCH.
THANK YOU, LADIES.
EXTRA CREDIT ALL AROUND.
WE LIE.
GG
Y'KNOW, AFTER ALL'S SAID AND DONE--
--I MAY JUST HAVE TO GIVE JUAN ANOTHER CHANCE.
-Sigh- POOR JIM.
HE'LL NEED SOME COMFORT.
LOTS AND LOTS OF COMFORT.

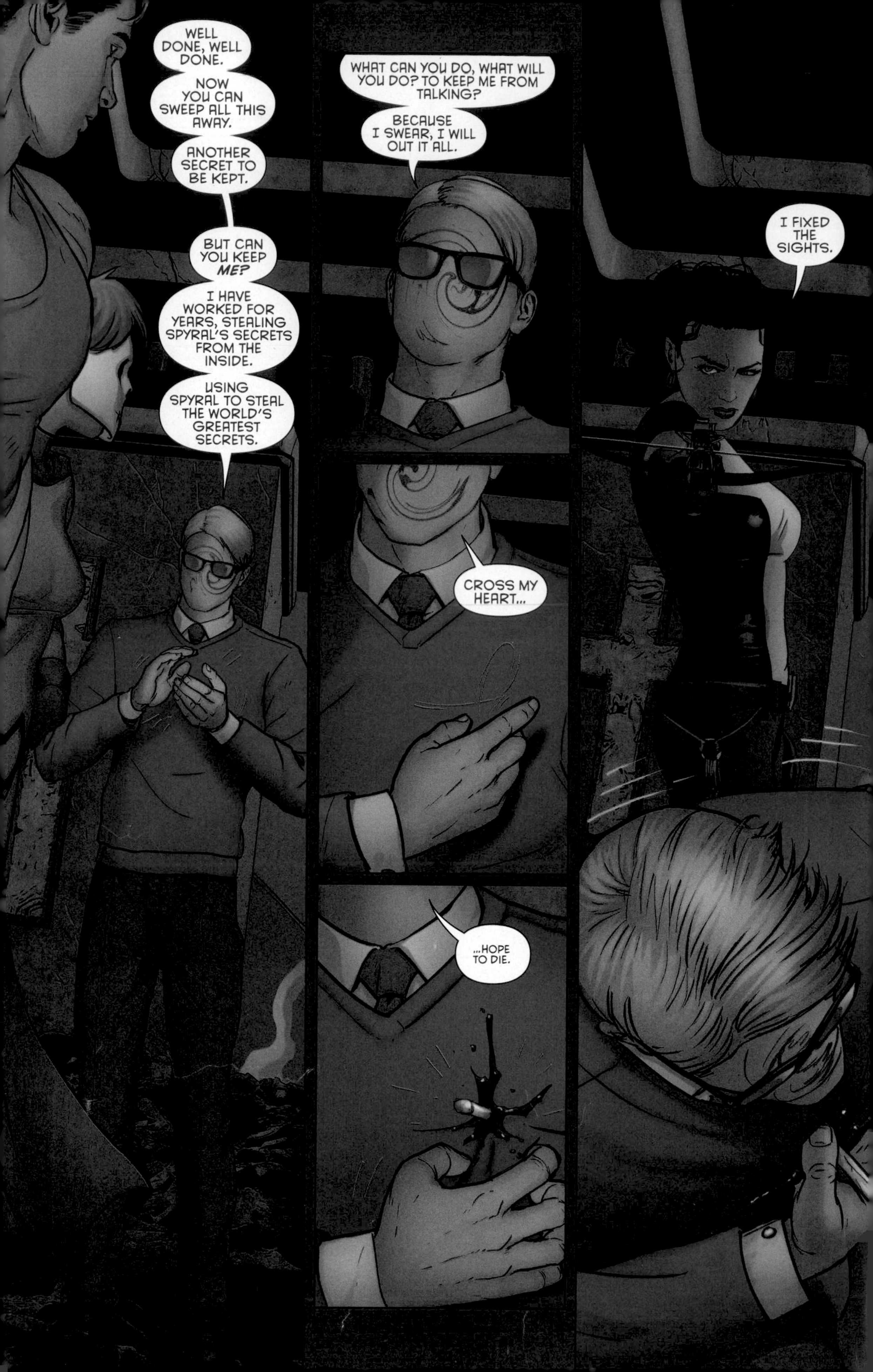
WELL DONE, WELL DONE.
NOW YOU CAN SWEEP ALL THIS AWAY.
ANOTHER SECRET TO BE KEPT.
BUT CAN YOU KEEP *ME?*
I HAVE WORKED FOR YEARS, STEALING SPYRAL'S SECRETS FROM THE INSIDE.
USING SPYRAL TO STEAL THE WORLD'S GREATEST SECRETS.
WHAT CAN YOU DO, WHAT WILL YOU DO? TO KEEP ME FROM TALKING?
BECAUSE I SWEAR, I WILL OUT IT ALL.
CROSS MY HEART...
...HOPE TO DIE.
I FIXED THE SIGHTS.

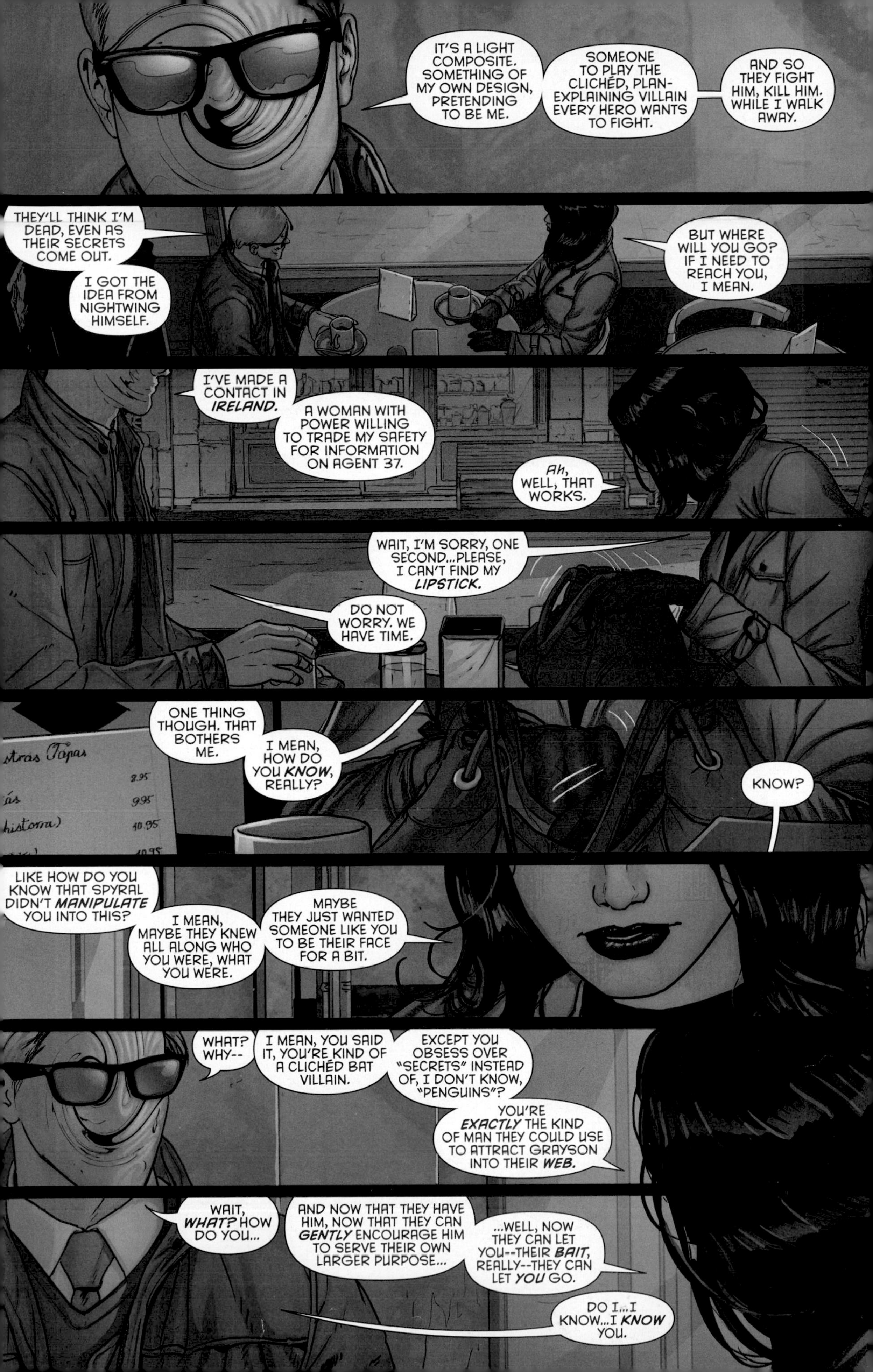
IT'S A LIGHT COMPOSITE. SOMETHING OF MY OWN DESIGN, PRETENDING TO BE ME.
SOMEONE TO PLAY THE CLICHÉD, PLAN-EXPLAINING VILLAIN EVERY HERO WANTS TO FIGHT.
AND SO THEY FIGHT HIM, KILL HIM. WHILE I WALK AWAY.
THEY'LL THINK I'M DEAD, EVEN AS THEIR SECRETS COME OUT.
I GOT THE IDEA FROM NIGHTWING HIMSELF.
BUT WHERE WILL YOU GO? IF I NEED TO REACH YOU, I MEAN.
I'VE MADE A CONTACT IN IRELAND.
A WOMAN WITH POWER WILLING TO TRADE MY SAFETY FOR INFORMATION ON AGENT 37.
Ah, WELL, THAT WORKS.
WAIT, I'M SORRY, ONE SECOND...PLEASE, I CAN'T FIND MY LIPSTICK.
DO NOT WORRY. WE HAVE TIME.
ONE THING THOUGH. THAT BOTHERS ME.
I MEAN, HOW DO YOU KNOW, REALLY?
KNOW?
LIKE HOW DO YOU KNOW THAT SPYRAL DIDN'T MANIPULATE YOU INTO THIS?
I MEAN, MAYBE THEY KNEW ALL ALONG WHO YOU WERE, WHAT YOU WERE.
MAYBE THEY JUST WANTED SOMEONE LIKE YOU TO BE THEIR FACE FOR A BIT.
WHAT? WHY--
I MEAN, YOU SAID IT, YOU'RE KIND OF A CLICHÉD BAT VILLAIN.
EXCEPT YOU OBSESS OVER "SECRETS" INSTEAD OF, I DON'T KNOW, "PENGUINS"?
YOU'RE EXACTLY THE KIND OF MAN THEY COULD USE TO ATTRACT GRAYSON INTO THEIR WEB.
WAIT, WHAT? HOW DO YOU...
AND NOW THAT THEY HAVE HIM, NOW THAT THEY CAN GENTLY ENCOURAGE HIM TO SERVE THEIR OWN LARGER PURPOSE...
...WELL, NOW THEY CAN LET YOU--THEIR BAIT, REALLY--THEY CAN LET YOU GO.
DO I...I KNOW...I KNOW YOU.

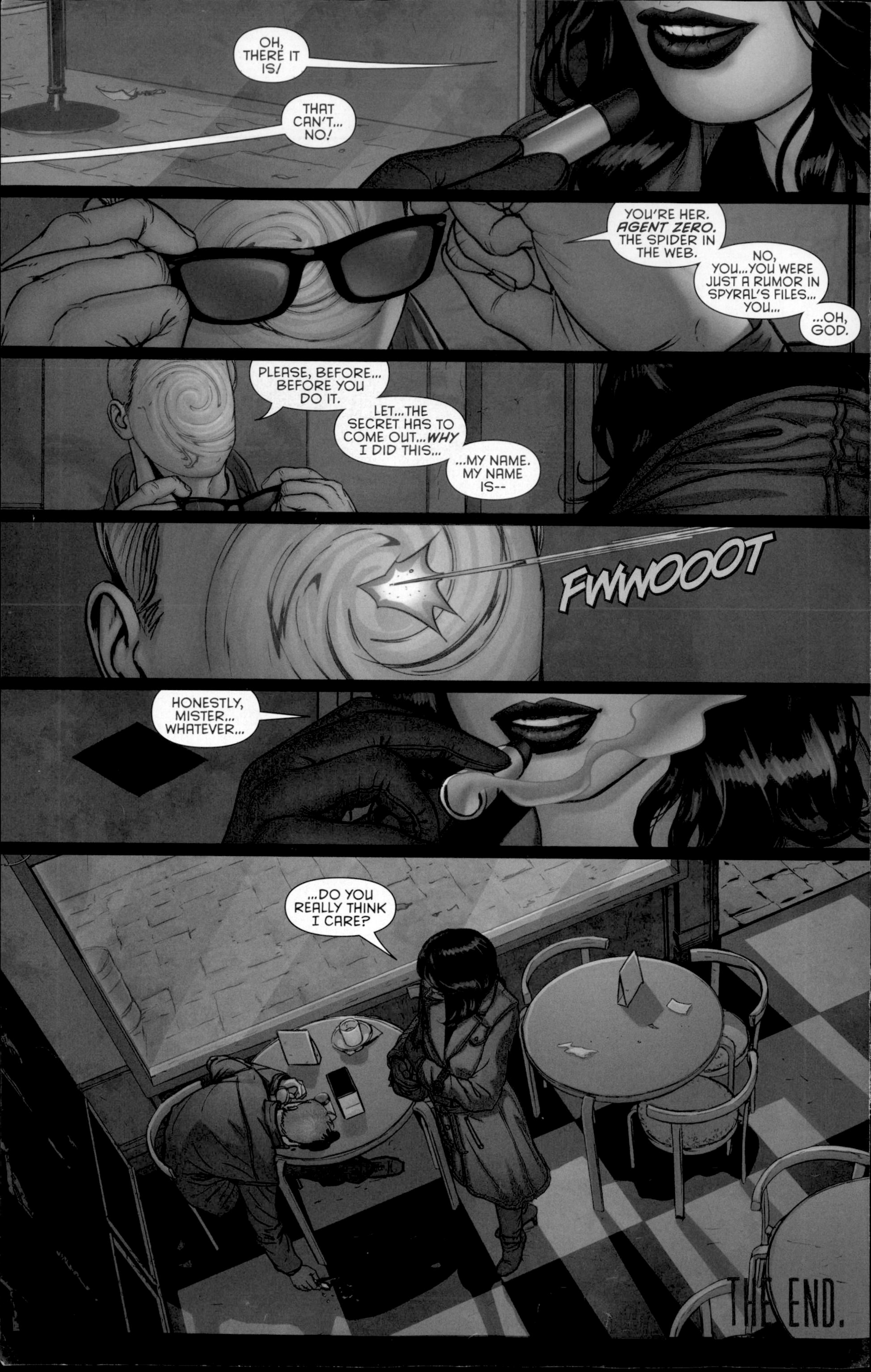
OH, THERE IT IS!
THAT CAN'T... NO!
YOU'RE HER. AGENT ZERO. THE SPIDER IN THE WEB.
NO, YOU...YOU WERE JUST A RUMOR IN SPYRAL'S FILES... YOU...
...OH, GOD.
PLEASE, BEFORE... BEFORE YOU DO IT.
LET...THE SECRET HAS TO COME OUT...WHY I DID THIS...
...MY NAME. MY NAME IS--
FWWOOOT
HONESTLY, MISTER... WHATEVER...
...DO YOU REALLY THINK I CARE?
THE END.

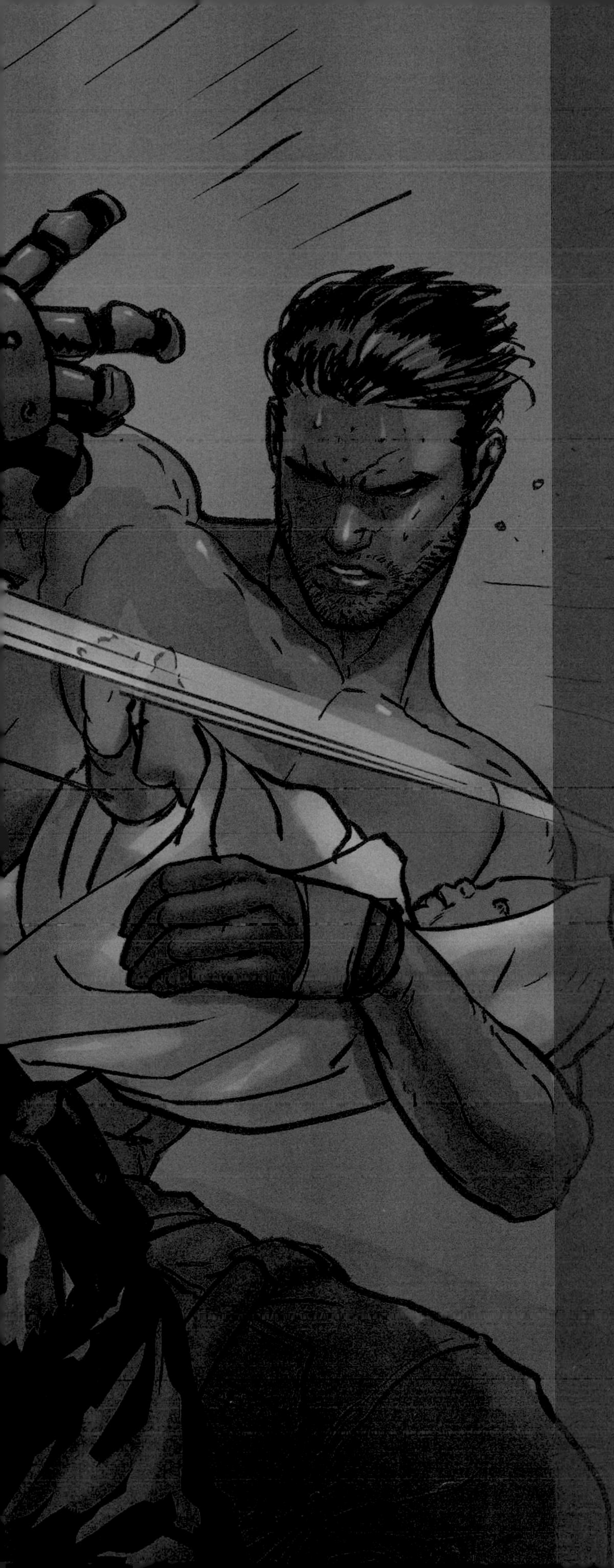

VARIANT COVER GALLERY

GRAYSON #5
VARIANT COVER BY
DARWYN COOKE

GRAYSON #6
FLASH 75TH ANNIVERSARY
COVER BY JOCK

GRAYSON #7
HARLEY QUINN COVER BY
DAN PANOSIAN

GRAYSON #8
ENTER THE DRAGON
MOVIE POSTER VARIANT BY
BILL SIENKIEWICZ

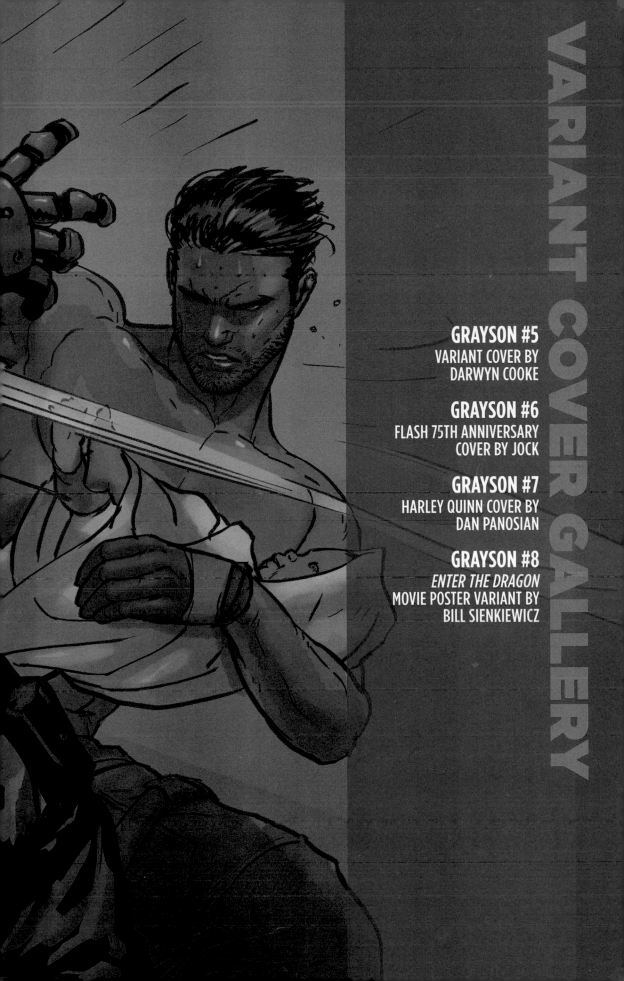

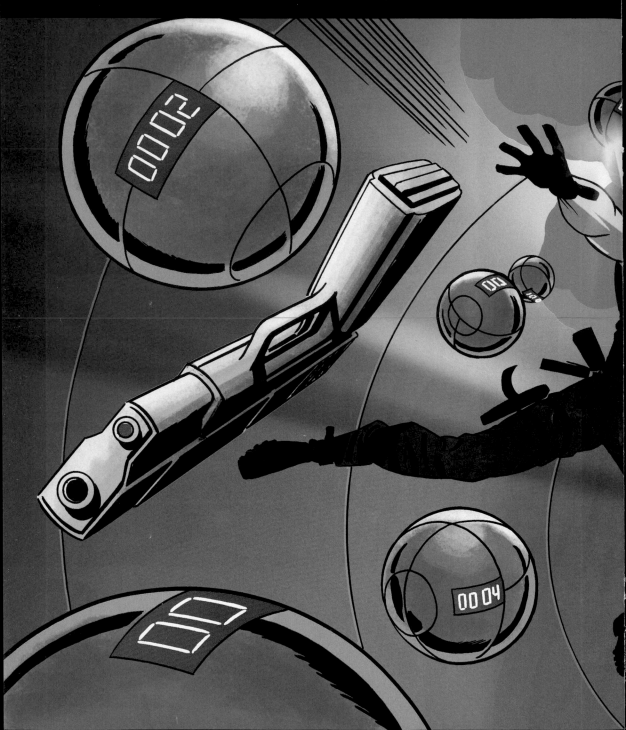

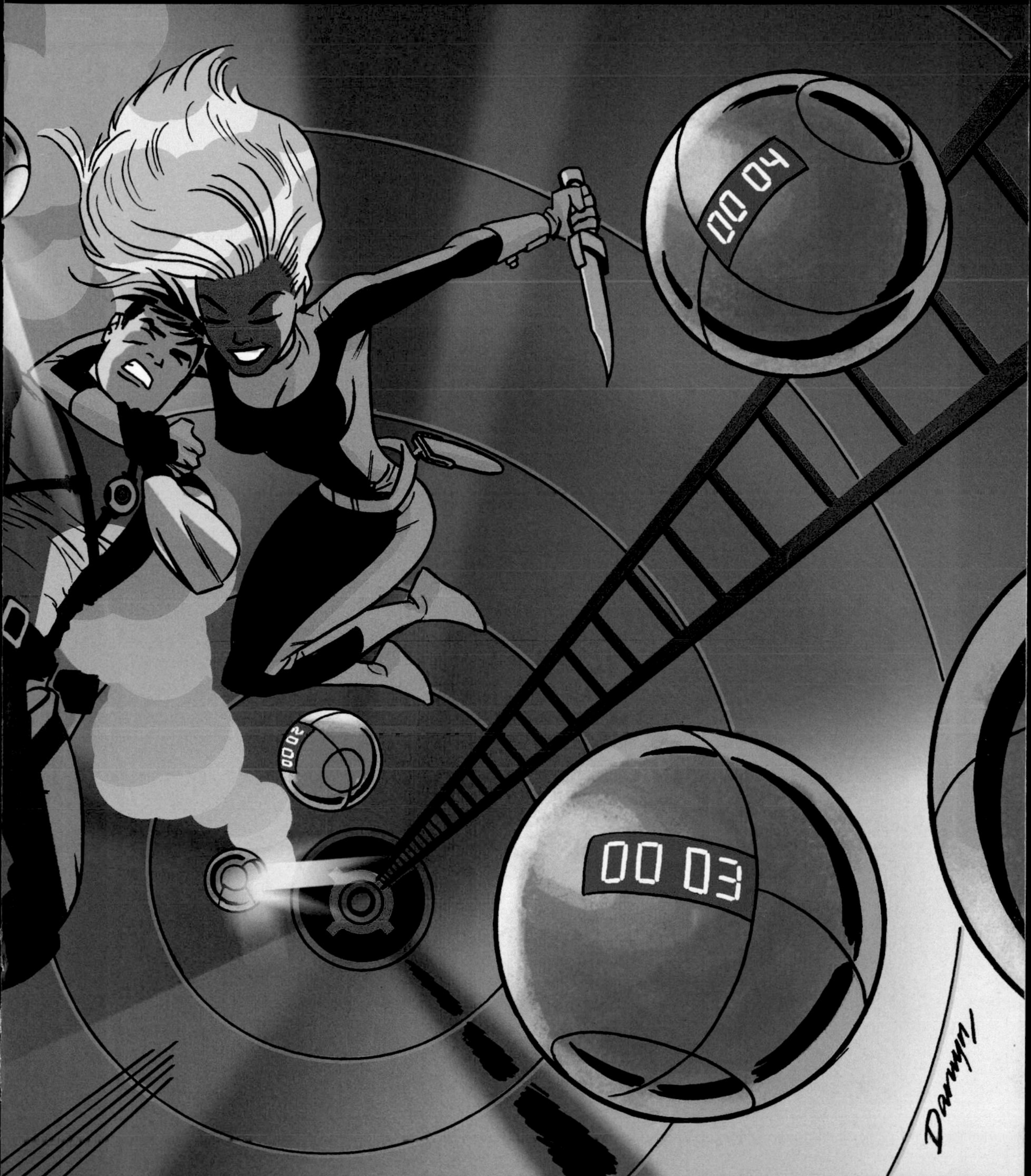
00 04
00 02
00 03
Darwyn

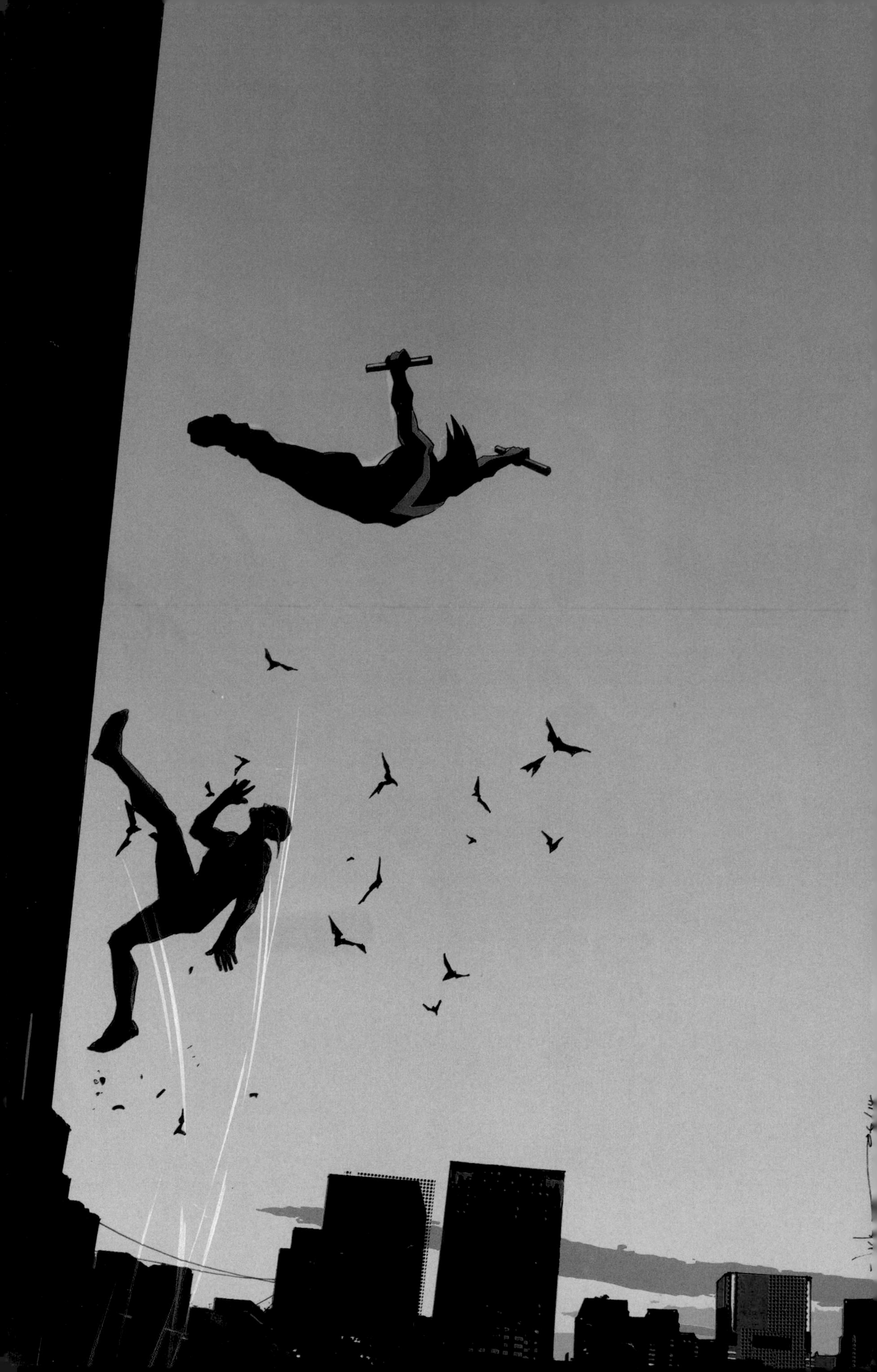

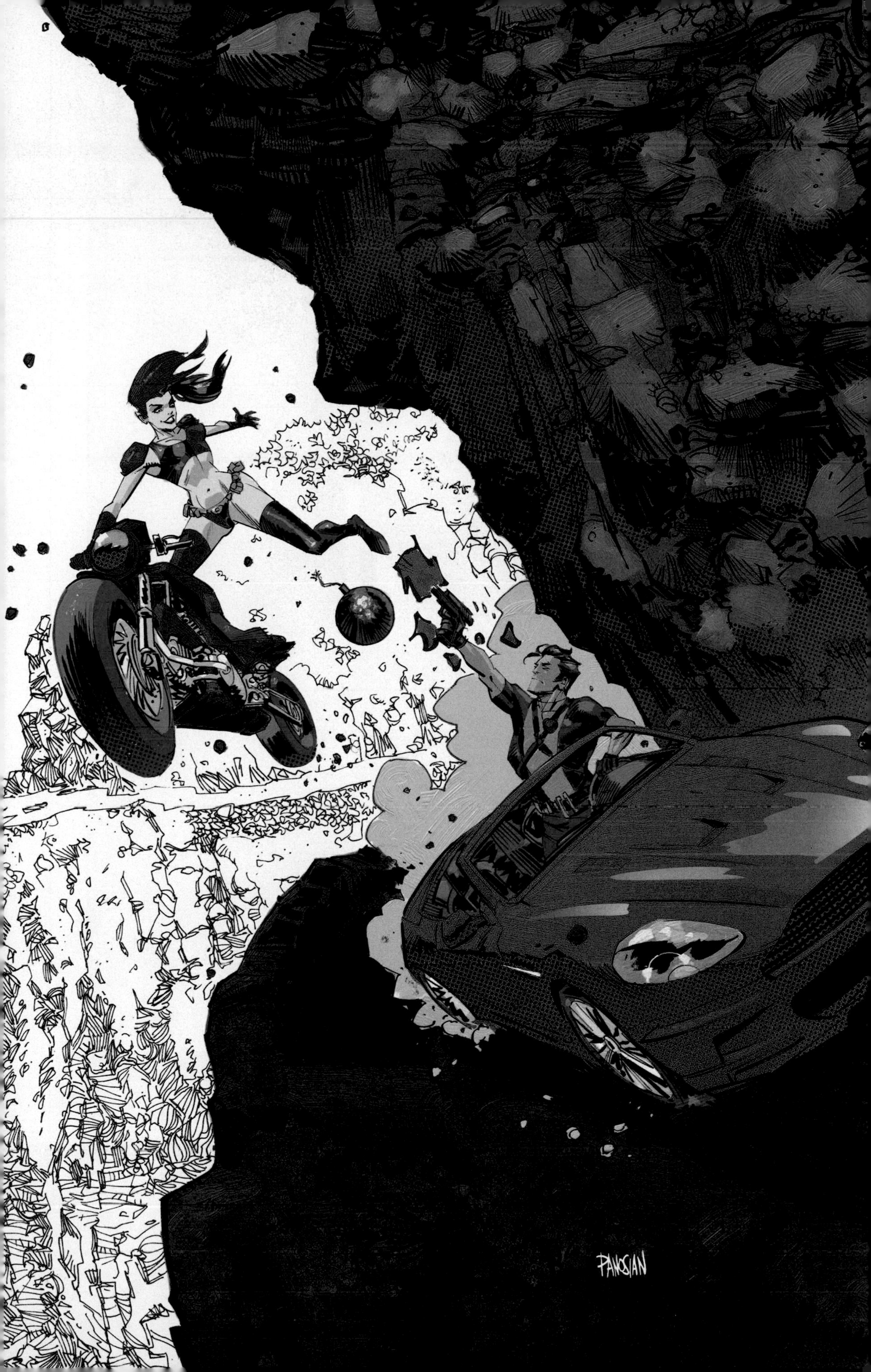
PANOSIAN

Their deadly mission: to crack the code of Spyral!

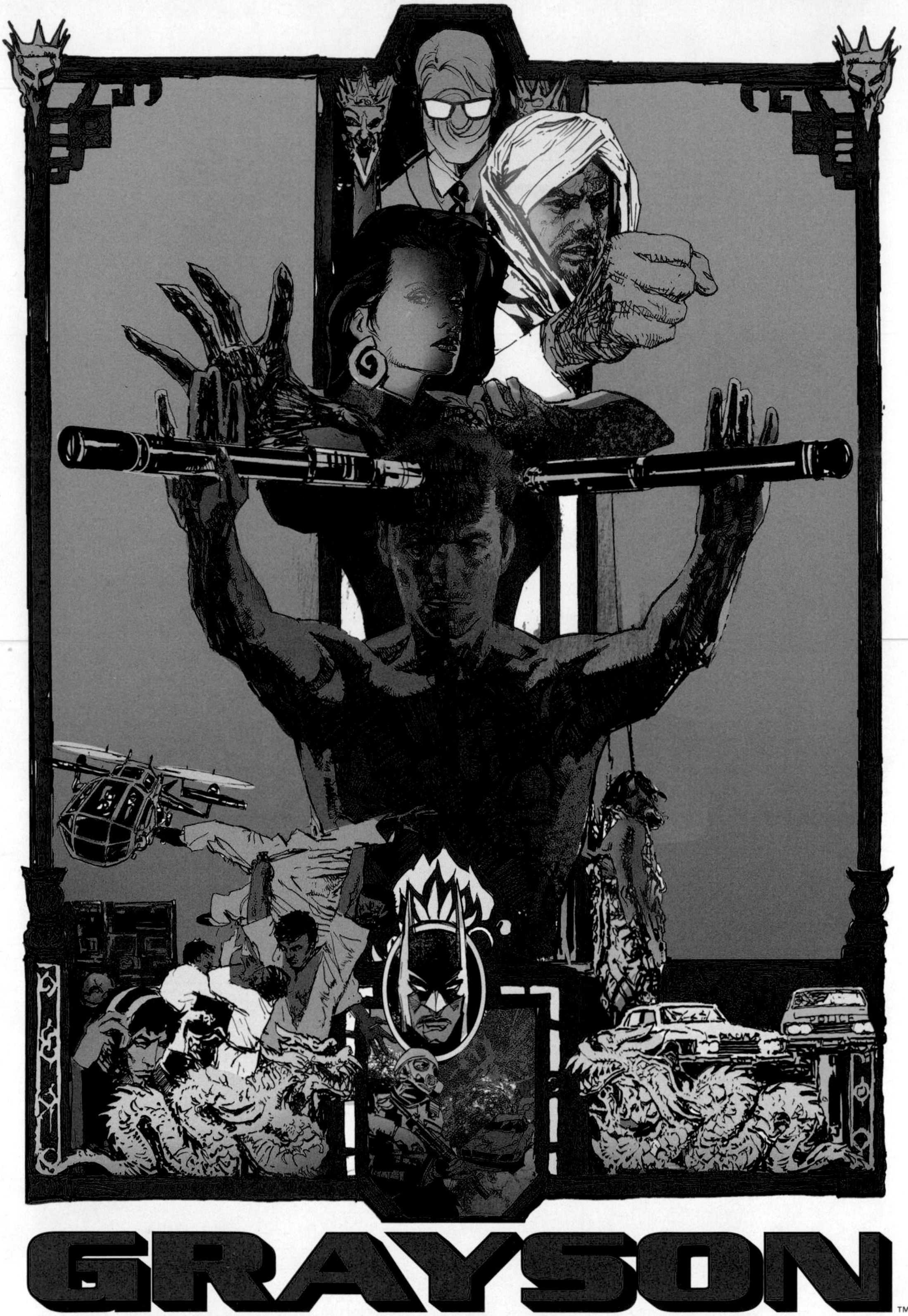
POLICE

GRAYSON™

The ultimate Super Hero/Spy masterpiece. Lavishly published by DC Comics in New York and LA.

GRAYSON ISSUE EIGHT TOM KING WRITER/PLOT TIM SEELEY PLOT MIKEL JANÍN ARTIST JEROMY COX COLORIST CARLOS M. MANGUAL LETTERER
BILL SIENKIEWICZ MOVIE POSTER VARIANT COVER MATT HUMPHREYS ASSISTANT EDITOR MARK DOYLE EDITOR BOB HARRAS SENIOR VP — EDITOR-IN-CHIEF, DC COMICS
RATED T TEEN DAN DIDIO AND JIM LEE CO-PUBLISHERS GEOFF JOHNS CHIEF CREATIVE OFFICER DIANE NELSON PRESIDENT

DC COMICS™

May 2015

GRAYSON #5
COVER SKETCHES BY MIKEL JANÍN

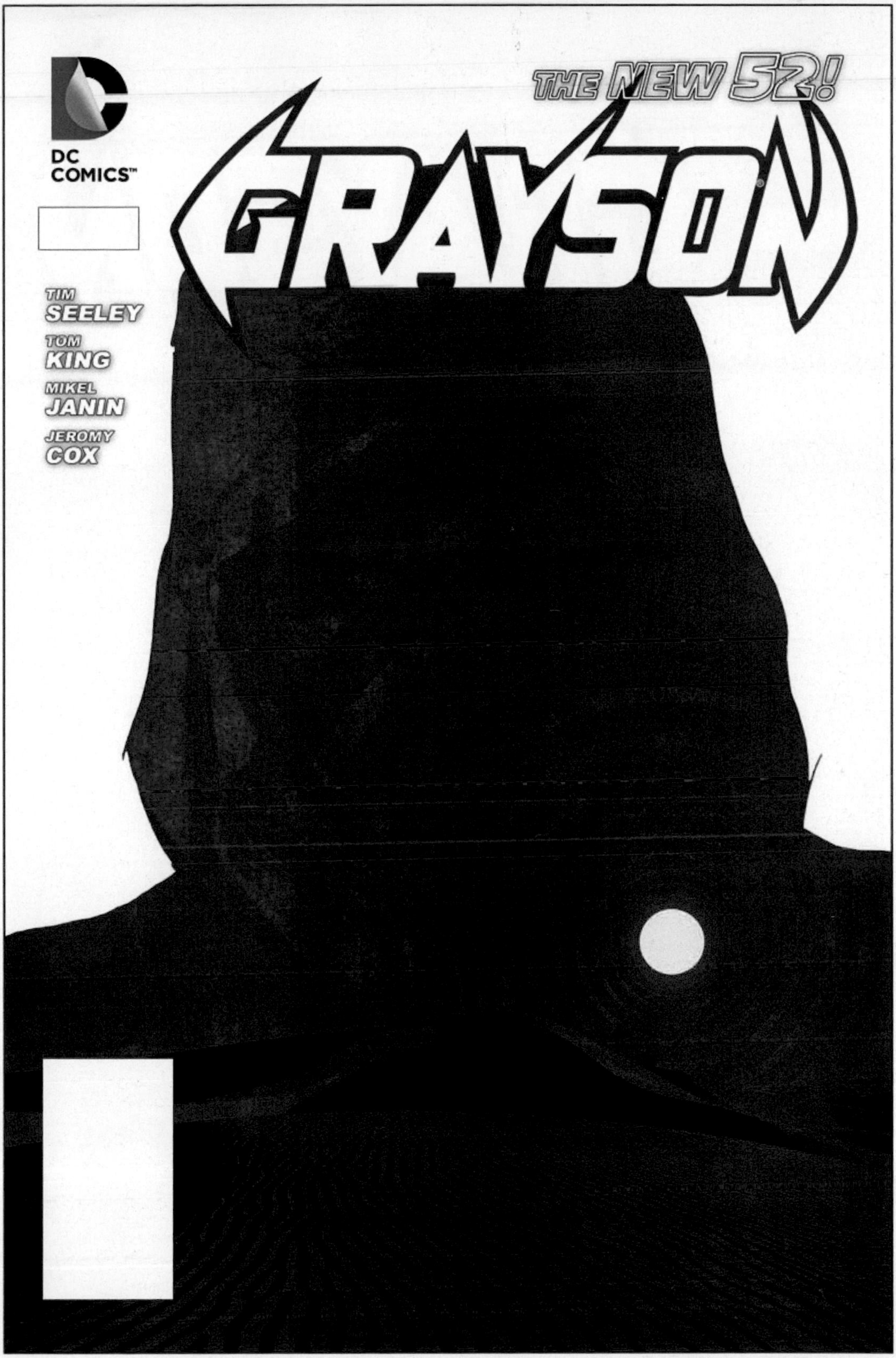
DC COMICS™
THE NEW 52!
GRAYSON
TIM SEELEY
TOM KING
MIKEL JANIN
JEROMY COX

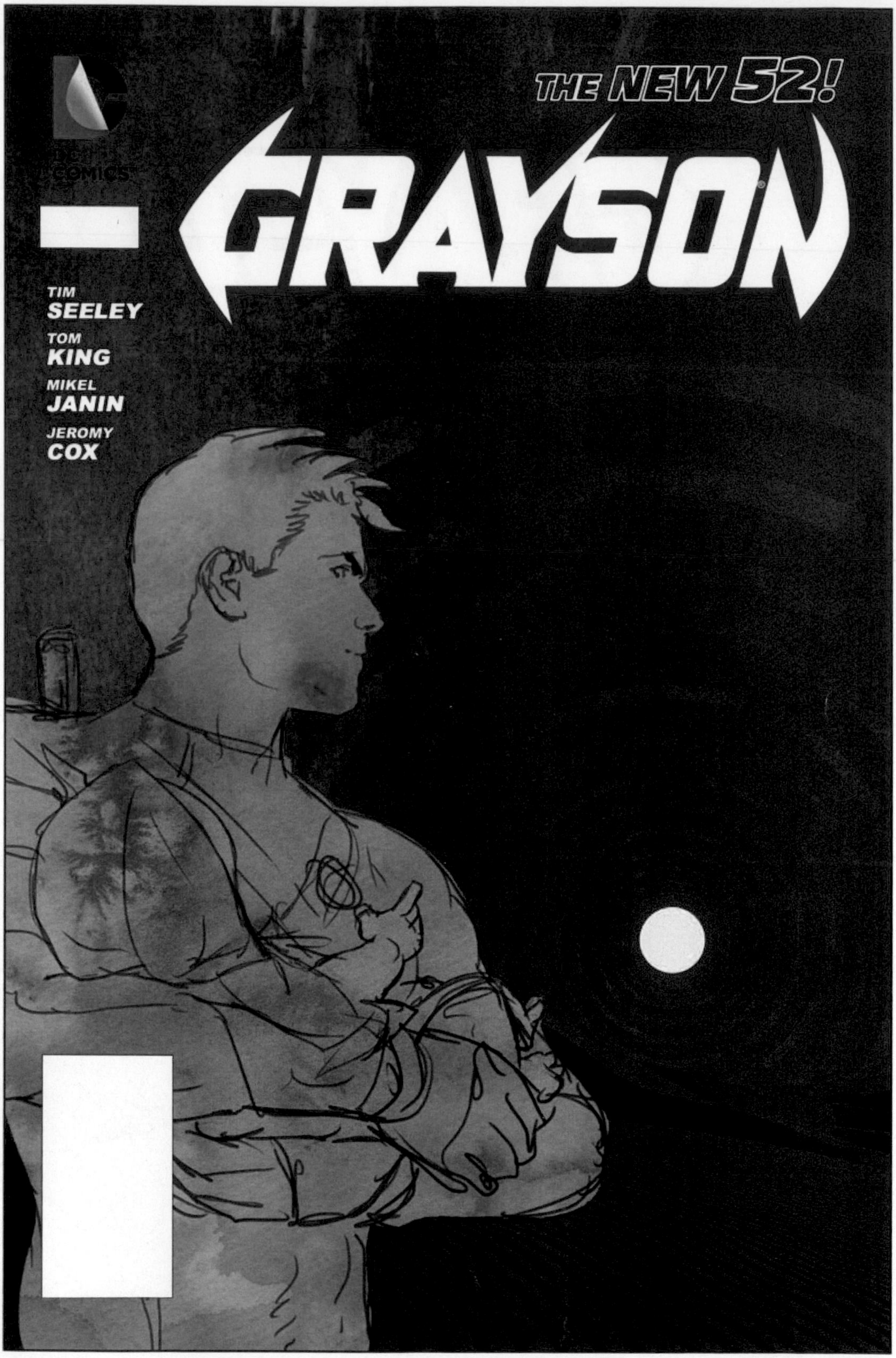
DC COMICS
THE NEW 52!
GRAYSON
TIM SEELEY
TOM KING
MIKEL JANIN
JEROMY COX

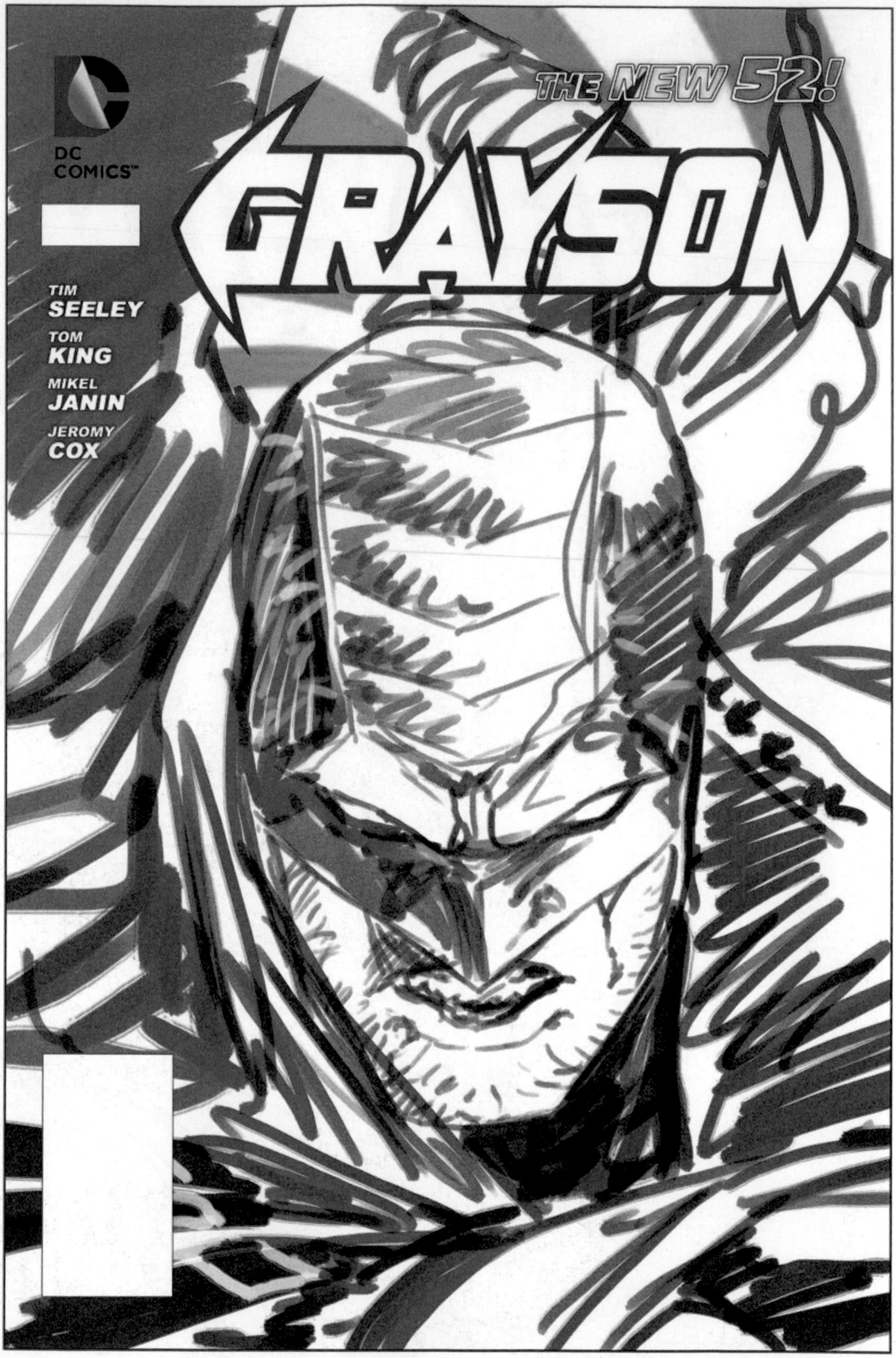
DC COMICS
THE NEW 52!
GRAYSON
TIM SEELEY
TOM KING
MIKEL JANIN
JEROMY COX